Workplace Politics

Workplace Politics

How Politicians and Employers Subvert Elections

TIMOTHY FRYE
ORA JOHN REUTER
DAVID SZAKONYI

OXFORD
UNIVERSITY PRESS

Oxford University Press is a department of the University of Oxford.
It furthers the University's objective of excellence in research, scholarship,
and education by publishing worldwide. Oxford is a registered trade mark of
Oxford University Press in the UK and in certain other countries.

Published in the United States of America by Oxford University Press
198 Madison Avenue, New York, NY 10016, United States of America.

© Oxford University Press 2025

All rights reserved. No part of this publication may be reproduced, stored in a retrieval system, transmitted, used for text and data mining, or used for training artificial intelligence, in any form or by any means, without the prior permission in writing of Oxford University Press, or as expressly permitted by law, by license or under terms agreed with the appropriate reprographics rights organization. Inquiries concerning reproduction outside the scope of the above should be sent to the Rights Department, Oxford University Press, at the address above.

You must not circulate this work in any other form
and you must impose this same condition on any acquirer.

CIP data is on file at the Library of Congress

ISBN 9780197802014

ISBN 9780197802007 (hbk.)

DOI: 10.1093/9780197802045.001.0001

Paperback Printed by Integrated Books International, United States of America

Hardback Printed by Bridgeport National Bindery, Inc., United States of America

Contents

List of Figures	vii
List of Tables	ix
Acknowledgments	xi
1. Introduction	1
2. What Is Workplace Mobilization?	21
3. Is Workplace Mobilization Effective?	79
4. Why Do Employers Mobilize?	101
5. Who Mobilizes?	125
6. Who Gets Mobilized?	145
7. How Do Voters Respond?	171
8. Is Workplace Mobilization Undemocratic?	197
9. Implications and Next Steps	221
Bibliography	229
Index	241

List of Figures

2.1 Level of Comfort with Workplace Mobilization in Turkey, 2015	73
2.2 Perceptions of Workplace Mobilization Cross-Nationally	74
3.1 Clientelism Effectiveness across Brokers	94
3.2 Differences in Means	95
4.1 Procurement Participation after Workplace Mobilizing	117
5.1 Workplace Mobilization by Sector	136
6.1 State Sector Workplace Mobilization across Countries	164
6.2 State Sector Workplace Mobilization across Countries (Restricted)	170
7.1 Workplace Mobilization at Different Levels of Press Freedom	192
7.2 Glasnost Defense Fund Map of Press Openness	196

List of Tables

1.1 Parties versus Employers	10
2.1 Surveys of Employers	27
2.2 Public Opinion Surveys in Russia	28
2.3 Cross-National Public Opinion Surveys	30
2.4 Mobilization in the Workplace (%): Public Opinion Surveys	34
2.5 Mobilization in the Workplace: Employer Surveys in Russia	35
2.6 Prevalence of Various Brokers in Turkey and Argentina	38
2.7 Brokered Electoral Violations Involving Voter Intimidation, Russian 2011 Parliamentary Elections	54
2.8 Brokered Electoral Violations involving Vote Buying, Russian 2011 Parliamentary Elections	55
2.9 List Experiments on Voter Intimidation	58
2.10 Monitoring Schemes Employed in Workplace Mobilization Violation Reports	69
2.11 Survey Question Missingness Rates (%)	77
3.1 Workplace Mobilization and Turnout	87
3.2 Other Brokers and Turnout	88
3.3 Survey Experiment Coverage	91
3.4 Predicted Probabilities by Broker Treatment	97
4.1 Why Don't Employers Like Yours Mobilize?	104
4.2 How Acceptable Is Workplace Mobilization (%)?	105
4.3 Why Do Employers Like Yours Mobilize?	110
4.4 Framing Experiment about Mobilization	112
4.5 Workplace Mobilization and Procurement: Regression Results	119
4.6 Workplace Mobilization and Procurement: Mechanisms	120
5.1 Employer Mobilization, 2011 Survey	139
5.2 Employer Mobilization, 2017 Survey	140
6.1 Workplace Mobilization in *Monogorods*	152
6.2 Single-Company Towns and the Prevalence of Negative/Positive Inducements	154

X LIST OF TABLES

6.3	Labor Market Conditions	157
6.4	Mobilization by Employer Type	162
6.5	State Sector Employment and Workplace Mobilization	163
6.6	Workplace Mobilization in Monogorods (Turnout Buying)	167
6.7	Labor Market Conditions (Restricted Measure)	168
6.8	State Sector Employment and Workplace Mobilization (Restricted Measure)	169
7.1	Perceptions of Workplace Mobilization	176
7.2	Governor Campaigning Framing Experiment	177
7.3	Framing Experiment in the United States	182
7.4	US Survey Experiment Results	184
7.5	Press Freedom and Workplace Mobilization	190

Acknowledgments

In the fall of 2011, we were in Moscow working with colleagues at the Higher School of Economics. A contentious Duma election campaign was unfolding around us and workplace mobilization was playing a major role. The importance of the practice was obvious to us, but we quickly realized that political science had little to say about it. It didn't even have a name. We had no systematic data about its scope in Russia or even the forms that it took.

We began by turning to survey research and posed a few questions to firm managers and employees about their experiences with the practice during that campaign. Our results revealed that workplace mobilization was even more widespread than we had thought: one in four firms were bringing politics to the shop floor. Given its prevalence we turned to understanding its causes: Why did it happen in some firms, but not in others? Was it common outside of Russia? Is it bad for democracy? Thirteen years, five children, two tenures, and one ongoing war later, we present to you our attempt to answer these questions.

Along the way, we accrued many debts. The first words of acknowledgment should go to our decadelong institutional home in Moscow, the International Center for the Study of Institutions and Development (ICSID) housed at the Higher School of Economics. ICSID helped fund the initial surveys that kicked off the project and confirmed our hypotheses about how heavily bosses were involved in elections. For most of this project, ICSID was our home away from home, an academic refuge in an increasingly authoritarian Russia. Many of the project's ideas were initially developed over leisurely "biznes lanchi" with our friends and colleagues at the Center. "Kroshka kartoshka," "Lyudi kak lyudi," "Kitaiskii Lyotchik," and "Prime" provided the food for thought that fueled our initial theories.

At ICSID, special thanks go to the Center's founding codirector, Andrei Yakovlev, whose constant support, wise judgment, and clear moral compass on issues big (the war in Ukraine) and small (navigating the HSE bureaucracy) left an indelible imprint on this project and on all the work of ICSID. We owe Andrei a debt that cannot be repaid. Many others at ICSID provided

xii ACKNOWLEDGMENTS

support and friendship throughout this project, including Noah Buckley, Guzel Garifullina, Eugenia Nazrullaeva, Denis Ivanov, Michael Rochlitz, Anton Kazun, Olga Masyutina, Ekaterina Borisova, and Israel Marques.

More concretely, Tom Remington and Israel Marques very generously shared space on their survey of Russian firms in 2018 for our questions which had little to do with their own research agenda on vocational education. We are immensely grateful for that chance to get another crack at learning how employers view the practice.

When we used to work at ICSID, we were asked (and gladly agreed) to affix the following label to research products that were supported by the center: "This book was prepared within the framework of the HSE University Basic Research Program and funded by the Russian Academic Excellence Project '5–100.'" The statement was and remains accurate, but writing those words is now bittersweet. ICSID was a model for how state investment in basic research can catalyze knowledge creation and build institutional capacity. Many of ICSID's alumni—students, administrators, researchers—are now well established in academia and are pushing the boundaries of social science research on the region. ICSID showed how the government could be a force for good in Russia's long quest to rebuild its human capital. Tragically, it became a casualty of the even more powerful forces destroying Russia from within and trying to destroy Ukraine from without.

Outside of ICSID, we accumulated many other debts in Russia. We offer a huge thank-you to Elena Bashkirova and Tamara Litikova from Baskhirova and Partners, who recruited and conducted the focus groups and many of the semistructured interviews in the book. Tamara is a wizard at conducting focus groups and helped us design a strategy for eliciting the first-person perspectives that really help illuminate how workplace mobilization works. Elena passed away in 2022 but remains a legend in the world of public opinion research in Russia.

The project could not have been completed without the longstanding support and patience shown by Aleksei Grazhdankin, Natalia Zorkaya, and Denis Volkov from the Levada Center. There were multiple occasions where it seemed as if our ambitious survey plans would fall through at the last minute, but Levada never wavered and this book is partly the result. We pay special tribute to Levada's Aleksei Grazhdankin who passed away in 2017.

We were also fortunate in this project to receive generous funding from several sources, including the National Science Foundation (Award Number: 1322732), the University of Wisconsin–Milwaukee's Research Growth

Initiative, the Harriman Institute at Columbia University, and the National Council for East European and Eurasian Research (NCEEER).

Henry Hale and Tim Colton also found space on the 2012 Russian Election Survey (RES) for our probing questions on electoral mobilization. It has been a delight to work with them (and Bryn Rosenfeld and Katya Tertychnaya) on the later iterations of the RES, which proved so useful for tracking the practice over time.

A special thank-you to Tim Colton, Bruce Jackan, and the Harvard Academy for International and Area Studies, which hosted an intense but very useful seminar where many of the book's main ideas were vetted. The academy also provided an unique hideaway for David to buckle down and focus on the final stages of the project.

The Russell Sage Foundation in New York provided a wonderful interdisciplinary setting for Tim to work on this project during a sabbatical leave in 2019–20 as did the Kluge Center at the Library of Congress in the first half of 2023. Thanks to the Carnegie Corporation of New York for funding the latter.

Over the years we've presented this work before many audiences, and their comments shaped and reshaped our ideas. The list of these shadow contributors is long, distinguished, and possibly incomplete: Scott Gehlbach, Kyle Marquardt, Thomas Holbrook, Ivan Ascher, William Bianco, Regina Smyth, Brian Crisp, Daniel Treisman, Jennifer Gandhi, Jordan Gans-Morse, Joshua Tucker, Erik Herron, Paul Secunda, Henry Hale, Alexander Hertel-Fernandez, Marko Klasnja, Holger Kern, Calvin Gardner, Eric Kramon, Noam Lupu, Itumeleng Makgetla, Anton Shirikov, Bill Liddle, Noah Buckley, Graeme Robertson, Sarah Khan, Israel Marques, Gulnaz Sharafutdinova, Bryn Rosenfeld, Guzel Garifullina, Pauline Jones, Jessica Pisano, Alaina Parent, and Samuel Handlin are a few of the scholars whose suggestions you might find in this book.

We also thank seminar and panel audiences at APSA, ISNIE (SOIE), Harvard University, University of Wisconsin–Madison, Higher School of Economics, Georgetown University, Columbia University, ASEEES, Stockholm School of Economics, University of Chicago, Yale University, the PONARS annual meeting, SPSA, and Princeton University.

We give additional thanks to two anonymous reviewers who provided thoughtful and detailed comments that greatly improved the manuscript and to David McBride, our editor at Oxford University Press, for skillfully and speedily shepherding our manuscript to publication.

xiv ACKNOWLEDGMENTS

Some ideas and data in Chapters 2, 3, 5, and 6 have been previously published in *World Politics*, "Political Machines at Work: Voter Mobilization and Electoral Subversion in the Workplace," 66:2, 2014, and "Vote Brokers, Clientelist Appeals; Evidence from Russia and Venezuela," 71:4, 2019, and in the *British Journal of Politics*, "Hitting Them with Carrots: Voter Intimidation and Vote Buying in Russia," 49:3, 2019. We thank Johns Hopkins University Press and Cambridge University Press for permission to use this material.

Finally, we thank our partners, Terri, Kira, and Mary Catherine, especially for approving not one but two book-writing retreats in New York City and Munich, the latter of which included a short but inspirational brainstorming jaunt into the German Alps.

1

Introduction

In late August 2016, workers at *Amuragrocenter*, the largest soybean processing plant in Russia's Far East, were greeted by posters at their plant requiring them to attend a Day of Health on Sunday, September 18. The posters said that the event would be alcohol-free and that attendance was mandatory. The plant's thirty-three hundred workers were encouraged to bring their spouses as well to enjoy kabobs, snacks, and entertainment. They were also told to bring their absentee ballots because the event would kick off with a round of voting for the parliamentary elections scheduled that day. That they would be casting their ballots under the watchful eye of their bosses was not lost on the workers. One employee told a reporter, "They are forcing the workers to vote for one party; they say if you want to work, come vote. People are worried. No one wants to lose their job." There was no need to tell the employees which candidate deserved their vote: the head of the plant, Alexander Vladimirovich Sarapkin, was a candidate from the third electoral district for the Amur regional parliament and was backed by the pro-government United Russia party.

But the story didn't end there. An anonymous worker took a photo of the poster advertising the Day of Health and sent it to Amur.Info, a website specializing in local news. The story was taken down after about forty minutes, but the press took notice. When journalists pressed Sarapkin about the story, he decried the posters as "falsifications posted by yellow journalists" and denied that workers had to bring their absentee ballots to the planned event, which just happened to be scheduled on election day. The local branch of the United Russia party commented that their party "had absolutely nothing to do with the posters" hung at the plant, questioned their authenticity, and called for an investigation to identify the leaker. The local election commission promised to conduct an inquiry, even invoking the possibility of criminal charges.[1]

---

[1] Timofeyeva, Irina, and Liza Miller, "Amurskim izbiratelyam predlozhili otkrepit'sya na zastol'ye s shashlykami," *Kommersant*, August 31, 2018.

Workplace Politics. Timothy Frye, Ora John Reuter, and David Szakonyi, Oxford University Press.
© Oxford University Press (2025). DOI: 10.1093/9780197802045.003.0001

2 WORKPLACE POLITICS

This story highlights several themes that we explore in this book. First, employers are well placed to influence the voting behavior of their workers, and politicians are well placed to pressure employers to get their workers to the polls. Over the past decade, we have collected similar stories of political mobilization in the workplace in dozens of settings: managers of private firms in Turkey forced to join the pro-government party to obtain state contracts, factory workers in the US compelled to attend political rallies or lose pay, public employees in Venezuela forced to donate salary to the pro-government party, mayors threatening businessmen in Burma to support a referendum.[2] To gain more precise data, we also conducted surveys in eight countries—Nigeria, Indonesia, Ukraine, Argentina, Turkey, Venezuela, Russia, and the United States—to ask citizens about their experience with workplace mobilization. Our data show that the practice takes a variety of forms, ranging from get-out-the-vote campaigns to implicit pressure to direct threats of dismissal. Our surveys identify the workplace as a key locus of political activity in many countries. In Russia, which is a primary focus in this book, our data show that mobilization by employers is by far the most common form of electoral clientelism used by the regime. The episode at *Amuragrocenter* is far from unique.

Second, some firms are much more likely than others to engage in workplace mobilization. A central task of this book is to explain this variation in the propensity to mobilize. As a large, state-dependent industrial plant, operating in a slack labor market, *Amuragrocenter* fits the standard profile of a Russian firm that engages in workplace mobilization. Across the diverse settings in our study, we find that factors such as these increase the leverage of politicians over employers and employers over employees and thereby make workplace mobilization more likely.

Third, while workplace mobilization can be effective, it is also highly unpopular among workers and the broader public. Using this technique risks provoking an electoral backlash. From Nigeria to Indonesia to Venezuela, we find that voters strongly oppose workplace mobilization. Even in Russia, a country with a long history of workplace mobilization,

---

[2] For Turkey, see "CHP Vice President Krabiyi: "Subcontractor Workers in AKP Municipaities Were Threatened with Their Jobs," *CHP Bulletin*, September 11, 2020. For the United States, see Colvin, Jill, and Josh Boak, "In Western Pennsylvania Donald Trump Claims Credit for Shell Plant Created under Barack Obama," *Philadelphia Inquirer*, August 13, 2019. For Venezuela, see "Empleados públicos obligados a dar un día de salario para financiar ampana de MADURO," *Dolar Today*, March 16, 2013. For Burma, see "Burmese Authorities Said Using Intimidation to Get 'Yes' Votes," BBC Monitoring Pacific Asia, May 4, 2008.

voters overwhelmingly object to the practice. This highlights a point that is core to our argument: workplace mobilization is not costless for employers and politicians. In addition to being unpopular, the practice is organizationally, financially, and reputationally costly. Thus, we identify a tradeoff that politicians and employers face when contemplating whether to mobilize voters in the workplace. Pressuring workers may increase turnout among the employed, but it also may turn off voters outside the workplace who disapprove of the practice. How politicians, employers, and voters navigate such tradeoffs is at the heart of this book.

Despite its prevalence in diverse settings, workplace mobilization is surprisingly neglected in political science. A host of questions call for examination. How does the practice work? Is it effective? Why do employers mobilize their workers in some settings, but not in others? And what are the implications of this practice for democracy and autocracy? Our main goal in this book to identify the conditions under which employers bring politics to the shop floor at election time as a means to shed light on these questions.

We argue that workplace mobilization is rooted in power relations among politicians, employers, and employees. Politicians tend to use workplace mobilization when they have leverage over employers. Public officials are well placed to pressure employers to get their workers to the polls when employers depend on the state for financing, sales, or their job, or when employers cannot easily move their assets to other jurisdictions. In addition, when employers have more leverage over their employees, workplace mobilization is far more likely. Workers facing slack labor markets are prime candidates for electoral mobilization. However, the decision to mobilize voters in the workplace is also shaped by normative considerations. Employees and voters both view most forms of workplace mobilization as morally problematic, considerably more so than other forms of political campaigning. Politicians risk electoral backlash from voters who view workplace mobilization with distaste, and employers risk a reaction by workers who generally prefer to keep politics out of the workplace. These dangers are heightened when media are free to report on these controversial tactics.

Therefore, we expect that workplace mobilization will be especially likely both in settings where power relations provide leverage over employers and employees (in the state sector, firms that depend on the state, and weak labor markets), as well as in information-poor settings where voters outside

4   WORKPLACE POLITICS

the workplace are less likely to learn about the practice. In sum, we argue that power relations and normative considerations are central to the study of workplace mobilization.

Our work demonstrates that employers are a common and understudied conduit of clientelist exchange and electoral subversion in the contemporary world. Economic development often makes traditional clientelist hierarchies obsolete, but industrialization creates new ones in the workplace. These hierarchies create opportunities for politicians and employers to diminish voter autonomy, undermine electoral integrity, and skew electoral outcomes in favor of entrenched political groups. In this way, our work suggests several new microfoundations for why we so often see economic and political liberalization go hand in hand. Economic liberalization increases the autonomy of employers and employees from the state, raises the costs of subverting elections via voter intimidation in the workplace, and thereby facilitates political liberalization that may be threatening to the incumbent. More generally, these results help explain why countries whose economies are dominated by state ownership, immobile capital, fiscal dependence on the state, and slack labor markets may be especially prone to autocratic rule.

Mediated Vote Mobilization

Whether in democracies or autocracies, politicians need to mobilize voters in order to win elections (Rosenstone and Hansen, 1993). Mobilizing voters requires time, effort, and resources, so politicians seek to mobilize at the lowest possible cost. Some votes can be earned solely via programmatic appeals; many choose to vote purely on the basis of a candidate's political views (Kitschelt, 2000). But most politicians must do more than just passively rely on their programmatic stance to win votes. They must contact voters. These direct appeals—via the media, campaign rallies, or personal contacts—serve not only to highlight the candidate's policy platform but also act as a vehicle for highlighting the candidate's personal attributes and charisma.

However, in modern elections of any size, candidates recognize that these direct appeals are usually insufficient to bring victory. Instead, they usually rely on *intermediaries* to help them mobilize votes. These intermediaries convey the candidate's message and use various other tactics, such as persuasion, reminders, vote buying, harangues, social pressure, and coercion to get voters to the polls. Candidates can, and often do, rely on their own, specially trained campaign employees, but it is often cheaper and more effective to rely on external intermediaries with some preexisting capacity for social influence. These intermediaries—also called brokers—come in many varieties, including party activists, landowners, religious leaders, traditional leaders, social media influencers, and employers.

Relying on such vote brokers comes with many advantages. Some intermediaries can deploy their own financial or organizational resources on behalf of politicians. Others can offer information to candidates, particularly about public opinion and the political attitudes of the voters with whom they are in contact. Brokers who are embedded in local communities can help candidates microtarget appeals or help monitor the clientelist exchange of economic benefits for political support. Sometimes brokers offer not only material resources or information but their personal sway over voters. Intermediaries such as traditional leaders, local bosses, and civil society leaders can mobilize votes by virtue of their social authority. Others, such as landowners, employers, and gang leaders may have economic or physical leverage over voters.

The Limitations of Political Parties

Of all these intermediaries, researchers have devoted by far the most attention to party activists. In democracies and autocracies, candidates rely on parties to help spread their message and get out the vote (Rosenstone and Hansen, 1993; Friedgut, 1979; Stokes, 2005). Indeed, some argue that the raison d'être of parties is to help like-minded candidates mobilize voters in a cost-effective way (Aldrich, 1995). Given this, it is not hard to see why most studies of political mobilization focus on party activists.

But parties are not necessarily the most effective brokers, especially in much of the contemporary world. The classical vision of parties as agents of mass mobilization with a well-developed network of grassroots activists is both anachronistic and geographically limited. In most advanced industrial democracies, levels of party membership and activism have been declining for decades (Scarrow, 2000; Whiteley, 2011). For a variety of reasons—rising levels of education, the expansion of mass media and the internet, increasing campaign professionalization, the erosion of group-based politics, and the

6 WORKPLACE POLITICS

proliferation of special-interest groups—parties in established democracies now lack the activist base they once enjoyed.

Outside long-standing democracies, mass-based parties are even more of an exception. After the Cold War, scholars quickly discovered that new democracies were not developing the stable, institutionalized party systems that characterized some Western democracies. Instead, emerging party systems from Latin America to Eastern Europe to Africa and Southeast Asia were volatile, weakly organized, and held in low regard by voters (Mainwaring and Scully, 1995; Hale, 2005; Hicken, 2009; Kuenzi and Lambright, 2001). These new democracies were emerging just as mass parties were in decline in Western Europe, where ties to traditional organizational allies, such as unions and churches, were fading (Biezen and Poguntke, 2014).

In autocracies, meanwhile, mass-based ruling parties have also become increasingly rare. As early as the 1970s, Linz noted that most modern autocracies were avoiding the mass-mobilizing model of communist regimes (Linz, 2000). Modern autocrats instead promote political apathy. They do not ask their subjects to be ardent supporters, just that they acquiesce to autocratic rule (Guriev and Treisman, 2022). They eschew political organization and drain politics from the public space. While most autocrats in the post–Cold War world do govern with some sort of ruling party (Reuter, 2017), these are typically elite organizations with a weak mass basis.[3] Modern autocracies rely on many of the same new technologies and campaign strategies that have obviated much of the need for party-based mobilization in democracies.

In sum, parties often lack the ability to be effective instruments of grassroots mobilization. Of course, when preexisting party organizations are lacking, politicians can, and often do, build such parties from scratch. But building strong grassroots parties is difficult and time-consuming. It is rarely possible to create effective party organizations in time for a single election cycle. Party organization is also costly. Aside from the material costs, building a party can limit a leader or politician's freedom of maneuver as activists and cadres may seek to influence the leadership (Kitschelt, 2000; Reuter, 2017). Thus, politicians often turn to other intermediaries.[4]

---

[3] There are, of course, exceptions. China, Venezuela, and, until recently, Malaysia stand out as contemporary regimes with relatively high levels of mass party organization.

[4] Indeed, politicians may eschew investment in parties precisely because there are pre-existing party substitutes which can perform the task of vote mobilization for them (Hale, 2005; Smyth, 2006).

Political Mobilization in the Workplace

While party activists have received the most attention from scholars, many other intermediaries have been identified in the literature. Landowners (Scott, 1972), traditional leaders (Koter, 2013; Lemarchand, 1972; De Kadt and Larreguy, 2018), strongmen and local bosses (Sidel, 1999), interest-group leaders (Alexander, 2002), celebrities (Austin et al., 2008), gangs and warlords (Anderson, 2002), religious leaders (Koter, 2022), state employees (Oliveros, 2016), union bosses (Larreguy, Marshall, and Querubin, 2016), civil society leaders (Holland and Palmer-Rubin, 2015), and employers (Frye, Reuter, and Szakonyi, 2014) have all been studied as vote brokers in different settings. This book focuses on one broker in particular: employers.

Relative to party activists and these other brokers, we know far less about how employers function as vote brokers. This is unfortunate given that employers are one of the most commonly used vote brokers. The practice of employers—for example, bosses, overseers, directors, management — attempting to influence the political behavior of their employees during election campaigns has a long history and has been documented in a number of historical settings, including nineteenth- and twentieth-century America (Argersinger, 1985; Gaventa, 1982), communist Europe (Remington, 1984), Imperial Germany (Mares, 2015), and postwar Chile (Baland and Robinson, 2007). In the contemporary world, recent work has described the practice in settings as diverse as Ukraine (Allina-Pisano, 2010), the United States (Hertel-Fernandez, 2018), Argentina (Oliveros, 2021), and Hungary and Romania (Mares, Muntean, and Petrova, 2016; Mares and Young, 2019). Beyond description, however, far fewer works have analyzed the reasons that politicians rely on employers to mobilize votes.[5]

Comparing Party Mobilization and Employer Mobilization

Employers merit attention as vote brokers not just because workplace mobilization is common but also because employers interact with voters in far different ways than do other brokers. These differences have crucial implications for how we analyze workplace mobilization. On the one hand,

---

[5] As we discuss later, there are, of course, important exceptions to this lack of study, including Mares (2015) and Hertel-Fernandez (2018).

8 WORKPLACE POLITICS

employers and party activists both often appeal to voters' sense of civic duty, ideology, or affinity with the candidate, and both may rely on their personal authority to persuade voters. These types of purely persuasive appeals are less costly than the transactional politics of clientelism, but, in many instances, they may also be less effective at turning out votes.[6]

For this reason, parties and employers often pair their persuasive techniques with some form of specific inducements that are disbursed to voters in exchange for their vote (Hicken, 2011). These can be positive inducements, as in the case of vote buying or turnout buying, or they can be negative inducements that involve the use or threat of sanction for not complying.

As we discuss in Chapter 2, while both types of brokers use positive and negative inducements to get voters to the polls, employers are better placed to use negative inducements than are party activists. Employers can and do use carrots, such as promises of promotion and increases in salary, but sticks are far more common. Employers can threaten to fire workers, either implicitly or explicitly, or they may dock pay or prevent workers from advancing in their career. As this book shows, the power asymmetries of the employer-employee relationship make negative inducements especially credible and effective in the workplace.

In contrast, party activists tend to rely on positive inducements when they turn to clientelism. A vast literature examines how party activists use vote buying to encourage turnout (Stokes, 2005; Schaffer, 2007). In some settings where parties have close ties to government officials, party activists may threaten to cut off government services for those who do not vote accordingly (Mares and Young, 2019), but this is less common than the pervasive use of sanctions that occurs during workplace mobilization. Thus, this book places more emphasis on negative inducements than does much of the recent literature on clientelism.[7]

In general, we observe that employers tend to have more influence over targeted voters in their employ than do party activists. Threats of job dismissal, cuts in pay, or demotions often carry more weight than the small gifts typically involved in vote buying by party-based intermediaries. In most settings, party activists simply lack the powerful carrots and sticks available

---

[6] Note, however, that employees may perceive as implicitly coercive employers engaging in such acts of persuasion. We return to this issue in Chapter 2.

[7] Gans-Morse, Mazzuca, and Nichter (2014) make this very point in their work on "portfolios of strategies."

to employers. As we explore, leverage is a significant comparative advantage that employers have vis-à-vis many other brokers.

Another key difference between parties and employers is that parties exist solely to serve a political function, whereas politics is, in normal circumstances, not the focus of most employers. Employers' primary objective is to generate profits or otherwise advance organizational goals. For this reason and others that we discuss in the coming chapters, employers are frequently reluctant to engage in political mobilization. In many instances, they themselves must be persuaded, induced, and cajoled by politicians. This observation forms the basis for much of our theory of workplace mobilization that we develop in the pages to come.

The misplacement of politics in the workplace also affects how voters view the practice. There is nothing out of the ordinary about party activists asking for your vote. The same is not true of workplace mobilization. The insertion of politics into the workplace strikes many voters as an unseemly distraction. Voters are, of course, aware of the clear power dynamic that exists between themselves and their employer, and this makes workplace mobilization feel all the more inappropriate. And since, as we show, there is a logical nexus between the use of negative inducements and mobilization by employers, voters have even more reason to take a dim view of the practice. It should come as no surprise then that most respondents in our surveys view workplace mobilization as morally problematic.

Thus, workplace mobilization comes with the risk of turning off voters, including those who are not being mobilized. This marks a contrast with party activists, whose election-related activities do not provoke similar ire. As we explore, the outsized possibility that workplace mobilization may provoke voter backlash is an important constraint on its usage.

Finally, employers and party activists also differ in their scope. The reach of employers is necessarily limited to voters who are employed. Workplace mobilization is not relevant to large swaths of the population, including pensioners, students, the unemployed, or the nonemployed. By contrast, party activists can, in theory, reach just about any voter, no matter their employment status. This has implications for how we evaluate the effectiveness and relevance of workplace mobilization.

Table 1.1 summarizes some of the key differences between these two types of mobilization. As we shall see, these differences have important consequences for how one approaches theorizing about workplace political mobilization.

10 WORKPLACE POLITICS

Table 1.1 Parties versus Employers

	Political Parties	Employers
Leverage	Usually low	Usually high
Type of Inducements	Usually positive (e.g., vote buying)	Usually negative (real or implied threats of wage cuts, dismissal)
Reach	Universal	Limited to employed voters
Normative Perceptions	Generally viewed as morally acceptable	Generally viewed as morally problematic

Why Workplace Mobilization?

The differences between employers and parties constitute a starting point for investigating one of the central questions in this book: Why do employers mobilize their workers to vote? In some sense, the answer is obvious. It works. Workplace mobilization can help get voters to the polls. Employers often have extensive economic and social leverage over their employees, who are structurally dependent on them for their well-being. Employers are attractive intermediaries for politicians because they sit atop preexisting hierarchies and have leverage over significant parts of the voting population. These hierarchies need not be constructed or maintained by the politician. They need only be activated around elections and used to the politicians' advantage.

In Chapter 3, we explore the effectiveness of workplace mobilization vis-à-vis other types of brokered mobilization. Many studies of clientelism have identified the prevalence of different mobilization tactics and the type of voters likely to be targeted, but far fewer studies have analyzed the relative effectiveness of different brokers (Stokes, Dunning, and Nazareno, 2013).[8] To this end, we marshal observational and experimental data from a range of settings, including Argentina, Indonesia, Nigeria, Russia, Turkey, Ukraine, and Venezuela, to test which brokers are more capable of turning out the vote. Our surveys show that being mobilized in the workplace is correlated with a considerably greater likelihood of going to the polls. More in-depth analysis in Russia and Venezuela indicates that the correlation between employer mobilization and turnout is

---

[8] However, see Hertel-Fernandez (2018) and Mares and Young (2019).

actually stronger than the association between turnout and mobilization by other brokers, including party activists. Because voters are not randomly mobilized by brokers, we supplement these observational analyses with framing experiments in Russia and Venezuela. We find that voters respond much more strongly to turnout appeals from employers than from party activists and other types of brokers. This chapter presents one of the first studies that compares the effectiveness of different brokers, demonstrating that the effectiveness of clientelism hinges crucially on the identity of the broker.[9]

This finding raises a puzzle. If workplace mobilization is so effective, then why is it not even more widespread? The simple answer is that workplace mobilization is far from costless. For politicians, workplace mobilization often requires that substantial benefits be delivered to employers, and it risks sparking a backlash from voters who disapprove. For employers, workplace mobilization is organizationally and financially costly, and risks damaging worker morale. These costs place limitations on the practice, limitations that ultimately help us understand why workplace mobilization occurs in certain countries, firms, and historical settings, but not in others.

Since workplace mobilization imposes significant costs on employers, we argue that they must be motivated to do so. After all, a key difference between employers and party activists is that the former are not under the direct command of politicians. Whereas party activists are simply employees of the politician or party that is mobilizing votes, employers are not.[10] This heightens the potential for agency loss. Employers may refuse to obey demands by politicians to mobilize their workers or they may shirk their duties by devoting little real effort to the task. This approach to analyzing vote mobilization by employers aligns with recent work that treats brokers as imperfect agents who must be inspired to mobilize on politicians' behalf (Stokes, Dunning, and Nazareno, 2013; Camp, 2017; Novaes, 2018; Brierley and Nathan, 2022; Ravanilla, Haim, and Hicken, 2022).[11]

---

[9] See also Mares and Young (2019) and Hertel-Fernandez (2018).

[10] Of course, this may not be as true of public sector employers or state enterprise directors in weakly institutionalized states. We return to this important distinction throughout the book.

[11] As we discuss in Chapter 4, employers do, of course, sometimes choose to mobilize on their own accord, without any expected inducements from politicians. This special case is common in the United States and can happen, for example, when employers have strong ideological preferences. But in most of the settings that we study, politicians cannot rely solely on voluntary mobilization by employers to provide the votes that they require, especially since mobilization is costly.

In Chapter 4, we present rich data from Russia to illuminate the fundamentals of this exchange relationship. Two surveys of firm managers demonstrate that employers perceive workplace mobilization as burdensome and costly. In addition, we draw on conversations with workers, press accounts, leaked internal documents, and firm surveys to show that politicians mobilize in response to incentives from the Russian state. We also use original data on public procurement to demonstrate that Russian firms that mobilize are more likely to win and retain state contracts than those that do not mobilize. Workplace mobilization often begins when politicians give economic benefits to employers who, in turn, pressure their workers to vote.

We then build on this insight in more detail by laying out conditions that are most conducive to workplace mobilization. In Chapter 5, we develop a theory of workplace mobilization that is rooted in a standard principal-agent logic, whereby employers serve as the mobilizational agents of politicians and politicians use a mix of positive and negative inducements in order to incentivize mobilization. In this way, our theory conceives of employers "selling" the support of their workers to the politician. Where existing theories of workplace mobilization focus mostly on power relations between employers and their workers (Mares, 2015; Hertel-Fernandez, 2018), our theory differs by also examining power relations between politicians and employers.

Under our simple framework, several factors emerge as important for understanding variation in workplace mobilization. First, when politicians have more leverage over firms, they can force employers to internalize the costs of workplace mobilization, thus reducing the cost of workplace mobilization for the politician. The dependence of firms on the state is the main factor that affects politicians' leverage in most settings. To make the case, we present data from two surveys of Russian firm managers to show that workplace mobilization is considerably more common in state-owned firms and in firms that depend on state contracts.

Second, the specificity of firm assets matters. Some firms are vulnerable to state pressure because they cannot easily change their production lines or move to a different jurisdiction in order to avoid such pressure (Bates, 2014; Williamson, 1983). We show that firms with such immobile assets—for example, steel plants, oil companies, mining concerns—are more likely to mobilize their workers politically. In most settings, incumbents have much more leverage than the opposition, since they are better positioned to use the state apparatus to pressure firms and thus can mobilize at lower cost.

Indeed, the fact that incumbents are better positioned to carry out workplace mobilization is one of the reasons that we view the practice as anathema to pluralist politics.

In Chapter 6, we turn to relations between employers and their workers, again drawing on the concept of leverage as a determining factor. When employers have more leverage over their employees, they find it easier to mobilize them. This reduces the cost of mobilization for not only the employer but also the politician, who can induce employers to mobilize at a lower price. A key driver of leverage is state employment: we find that workplace mobilization is far more common in the public sector. In almost every country we study, teachers, healthcare workers, state enterprise employees, police officers, and other government workers are far more likely to be mobilized at work. Managers in the public sector are more vulnerable to pressure from incumbent politicians, and public sector workers are more vulnerable to pressure from their employers than are their counterparts in the private sector. Political patronage is often important to their career advancement (Oliveros, 2021), and they often have skills that are difficult to transport to the private sector.

An additional source of employer leverage is the condition of the labor market (Mares and Zhu, 2015; Hertel-Fernandez, 2018). In settings where workers have difficulty finding satisfactory alternative employment—such as in slack labor markets or single-company towns—job loss can be catastrophic. This makes workers more responsive to the will of employers. In Chapter 6, we show that workers in Russia who reported greater job insecurity and believed that it would be more difficult to find alternative employment are more likely to report being mobilized by their employer. We also find that workplace mobilization is much more common in Russia's 333 single-company towns (*monogoroda*), which collectively house over 10 percent of the country's population. Legacies of Soviet economic planning, *monogoroda* have one or two large enterprises accounting for the vast majority of economic output and employment. Such concentration means workers in these towns have few opportunities for employment outside the main enterprises, giving the dominant employer great leverage over their employees.

Having explored relations between politicians and employers and between employers and employees, in Chapter 7 we look beyond these dyadic relationships and bring the broader voting public into our analysis. Because workplace mobilization is widely seen as morally problematic, politicians and employers need to consider the potential for electoral backlash when deploying this strategy. Politicians may be dissuaded from relying on workplace mobilization if they believe that it will cost them more votes than it generates. Thus, following Weitz-Shapiro (2014), our theory integrates the externalities of clientelist practices into a theory about their prevalence. Using survey experiments from Russia and the United States, we show that voters punish candidates who advocate for coercive forms of workplace mobilization.

The relevance of such attitudes, we argue, hinges on the likelihood that workplace mobilization will have public resonance. If information about electoral intimidation remains confined only to the shop floor where coercion occurs, then politicians and employers would face few reputational costs for mobilizing in the workplace. On the other hand, if broader publics are likely to learn about intimidation, then reputational costs become a pertinent consideration for politicians. We argue that freedom of the press is one major determinant of whether voters can find out about workplace mobilization. Greater press freedom may deter politicians from turning to employers to mobilize due to the threat of electoral blowback among voters who disapprove of the practice. Using data from Russia, we demonstrate that indeed coercive forms of workplace mobilization are less likely in regions with greater media freedom. This chapter shows how institutions like a free press reduce the incentives for politicians to engage in the most morally problematic forms of workplace mobilization.

Chapter 8 considers the normative implications of workplace mobilization for democracy. It is easy to condemn as undemocratic the most coercive forms of workplace mobilization. Employers who order their workers to vote under threat of dismissal undermine voters' ability to express their views without fear of retribution—a key tenet of democratic theory. However, workplace mobilization can also take forms that are more morally ambiguous. For example, noncoercive, nonpartisan get-out-the-vote campaigns may increase turnout, which is usually seen as a desirable democratic goal. We argue that workplace mobilization is compatible with democracy when it recognizes voter autonomy and does not systematically bias outcomes in favor of one group. However, these conditions are difficult to meet in practice. To illustrate this argument, we draw from our sample of seven countries, as well as from the United States, a country with a long history of workplace mobilization and where courts, regulators, and legal scholars have wrestled with the democratic implications of the practice. Today, the most heavy-handed forms of workplace mobilization are rare in the United States, even as less coercive forms are still legal and common. Based on surveys conducted in 2020 and 2021 in the United States, and a review of secondary literature, we argue that even in this "best-case" scenario for workplace mobilization, it is difficult to argue that most forms of workplace mobilization are compatible with democratic principles. Chapter 9 concludes by drawing together our findings and discussing new avenues for research on the topic.

Workplace Mobilization and the Study of Politics

The study of workplace mobilization is situated at the intersection of several major literatures in the social sciences. One of the main goals of this volume is to demonstrate how a better understanding of this practice can help advance research in these key areas. An examination of workplace mobilization should lead scholars to reassess some long-standing themes in the study of politics.

Electoral Subversion

Our research first helps shed light on electoral subversion. Voter autonomy—the freedom to vote one's preferences without fear of retribution or expectation of individual reward—is a central component of democracy. Elections translate individual preferences into democratic outcomes most efficiently when citizens exercise autonomy in politics. When politicians and employers put pressure on employees, they undercut this core ideal of democracy. From ballot-box stuffing to intimidation to vote buying, scholars have produced a rich literature on electoral subversion (Lehoucq, 2003; Hicken, 2011). To these techniques, we add workplace mobilization as a widespread but understudied type of electoral subversion. Indeed, relative to other techniques, politicians and employers may find workplace mobilization especially attractive because it often occurs well beyond the prying eyes of election observers and, in some forms, can leave few footprints. Understanding how and why politicians and employers subvert elections via workplace mobilization should interest scholars of electoral manipulation.

Democracy and Autocracy

The study of workplace mobilization also has consequences for the study of regime type. Our work accords with a long scholarly tradition that views labor repression as a politically advantageous strategy (Marx and Engels, 1967; Moore, 1993; Gerschenkron, 1962). Specifically, our work accords with those who view the economic dependence of workers on the state as inimical to democracy (Dahl, 1998; McMann, 2006; Mares, 2015; Gervasoni, 2018; Rosenfeld, 2020). But in contrast to much of the literature on the economic foundations of democracy, we highlight how the dependence of employers on the state is an important factor that facilitates electoral subversion and thereby undermines democracy. When incumbents can pressure employers to help them win votes, accountability suffers and voters lose their ability to remove unpopular or poorly performing leaders from office. Authoritarian regimes that can rely on workplace mobilization to dominate elections may be able to hold onto power longer.

Our work thus highlights an understudied way that authoritarian regimes can generate electoral support. In many electoral autocracies, regime leaders try hard to generate voter turnout in order to create an impression of legitimacy (Simpser 2013; Magaloni 2006). Mobilizing workers in state-dependent sectors is one way to generate such turnout. Finally, existing literature on the political uses of labor repression rarely considers the electoral costs of the practice (Dean, 2022). Forms of labor repression such as workplace mobilization are unpopular and may turn off voters who do not experience mobilization themselves. We highlight this as a significant constraint that shapes the decision of politicians to use workplace mobilization.

Our research also provides new insight on the microfoundations of arguments about the economic bases of transitions from autocratic rule. Boix (2003) and Acemoglu and Robinson (2006), for instance, identify asset specificity as a key obstacle to democratization, but our argument and data suggest a different mechanism by which asset specificity may influence democratic transitions. Firms in sectors dominated by specific assets that are not easy to move or convert to other product lines may subvert democracy not just because they fear redistribution via high taxation under democracy as these scholars argue, but also because they are vulnerable to pressure from the autocrat.

INTRODUCTION 17

Finally, our work also has implications for questions about institution-building, such as party development. The traditional long-run solution to the problem of mobilizing electoral support has been to build strong grass-roots party organizations. But building such organizations is costly (Slater, 2010; Levitsky et al., 2016), and politicians have weaker incentives to pay those costs when there are other ways of mobilizing votes (Hale, 2005). Our work highlights one such alternative: employer-based clientelist networks can obviate the need for party-based organization and clientelism. This can help explain the otherwise puzzling lack of both strong grassroots organization and party-based clientelism in Putin's Russia. Since the Kremlin can mobilize so many votes at relatively low cost in the workplace, regime leaders have less reason to pay the costs of building grassroots infrastructure for the ruling party.

Political Economy and Development

Our theory suggests that the prevalence of workplace mobilization will track with stages of economic development. In subsistence economies where few individuals have employment outside the home, opportunities for employer-based clientelism are scarce. As economies develop and the formal sector emerges, however, so do the conditions for workplace mobilization. In late-developing twentieth-century economies, the early and middle stages of economic modernization are frequently characterized by state domination of industry and concentration in asset-specific sectors (e.g., extraction and manufacturing) that are vulnerable to state interference (e.g., Gerschenkron 1962). In these settings, workplace mobilization is likely to flourish. Further economic development, however, typically leads to economic diversification and the development of a robust service sector. Our theory predicts that workplace mobilization should decline at these levels of development. This is one of the reasons why workplace mobilization is more common in middle-income countries than in either the developed world or the world's poorest countries.

While the focus of this book is mostly on the *political* implications of workplace mobilization, our study also has important implications for the politics of economic reform and business-state relations. For one thing, we highlight an underappreciated way that businesspeople can secure

18 WORKPLACE POLITICS

influence with politicians. The traditional view is that business uses its economic resources to provide money, information, and votes (Grossman and Helpman, 2001; Hillman, Keim, and Schuler, 2004). However, far less attention has been paid to how and why businesses can provide this third category of contribution—votes—to politicians in exchange for political benefits. This volume demonstrates how business can gain access to benefits and protections from the state by directly turning out its employees to vote.

Our work also suggests that workplace mobilization may provide a disincentive to conduct economic reform if politicians rely on workplace mobilization for electoral support. Workplace mobilization is more effective when incumbents have leverage over business. Reforms such as privatization, deregulation, and combating corruption all reduce the leverage of the state over business and thus make it harder for politicians to generate votes in the workplace by pressuring employers (Shleifer and Vishny, 1994).

Clientelism

We conceive of workplace mobilization as a variety of clientelism, but employers are often overlooked in this literature. We hope that this volume helps catalyze a research agenda on workplace mobilization within the clientelism literature. More generally, our study highlights how the type of broker used in clientelist exchange can matter greatly for the effectiveness of clientelism. Under some conditions employers can be more effective than other types of clientelist brokers, which, on its own, suggests that these brokers deserve more attention from scholars of clientelism. The comparative study of brokers is still in its infancy (Mares and Young, 2016), and we hope that this study helps advance that agenda.

Another contribution of our study to the clientelism literature is to highlight the important differences between negative and positive inducements. The recent literature on clientelism has increasingly noted important analytic distinctions between these two strategies (Mares and Young, 2019; Frye, Reuter, and Szakonyi, 2018; Gonzalez-Ocantos et al., 2020), but the question of why brokers rely on one strategy over another is still underexplored. Our account suggests that the type of inducement used will depend in part on the type of broker. Employers excel at using negative inducements, so in an environment such as Russia, where employers are the primary clientelist broker, then negative inducements will likely predominate.

INTRODUCTION 19

The externalities of clientelism depend heavily on the type of inducement. More coercive forms of clientelism draw more ire from voters and are more likely to cause backlash in the broader electorate. This is an important limitation on workplace mobilization.

Our study also has implications for the study of clientelism in the twenty-first century. Influential accounts of clientelism have argued that vote-buying tends to decline with economic modernization and industrialization (Stokes, Dunning, and Nazareno, 2013; Kitschelt, 2000; Weitz-Shapiro, 2014), as voters become wealthier and less dependent on largesse from traditional patrons. But our work shows that industrial modernization does not necessarily mean an end to clientelism. Although modernization may undermine traditional hierarchies, the expansion of the formal sector creates new ones in the workplace. In an era when traditional opinion leaders—for example, religious leaders, editorial writers, unions, community leaders—are losing influence over voters, employers remain as an opinion leader with significant leverage and therefore influence over voters.

Russian Politics

Finally, our findings also have important implications for the study of politics in Russia. Much of the richest data in this book is drawn from Russia, where workplace mobilization is common and has become a crucial feature of electoral politics in the Putin era. Workplace mobilization helps Russia's leaders win elections and prevent democratic change. The practice is sufficiently widespread that it has a major impact on election outcomes. Our surveys find that upward of one-quarter of all Russian employees experience workplace mobilization in the run-up to elections, most of it is organized by the pro-government United Russia party. Workplace mobilization allows the Kremlin to comfortably win elections without always having to resort to massive ballot box fraud. By skewing electoral outcomes in favor of the regime, workplace mobilization has contributed to the consolidation of autocracy under Vladimir Putin. As the government continues to expand its foothold in the economy, we should expect even greater dependence of employers on the state and increasing reliance on workplace mobilization in future elections.

Our work also helps resolve a long-standing puzzle in the study of Russian elections: Why is vote buying so rare? Vote buying is common in many autocratic countries that share Russia's level of development. Our study shows that electoral clientelism does exist in Russia, but the primary locus of this clientelism is the workplace and it occurs under the specter of coercion. Workplace mobilization, which our data show to be more effective than vote buying, appears to be the preferred mode of clientelist exchange in Russia. As the primary vote broker relied upon by Russian politicians, employers exploit their leverage over workers to disburse negative inducements.

In the chapters that follow, we describe the explorations of workplace mobilization that have led to these conclusions. Throughout the work, we note that workplace mobilization can take a variety of forms, from nonpartisan get-out-the-vote campaigns to highly coercive appeals involving threats and intimidation. In the next chapter, we unpack the concept of workplace mobilization in more detail and probe its subtleties. Most importantly, we present evidence from a range of countries that demonstrates that workplace mobilization is far more prevalent than is commonly understood, often coercive, and generally reviled by the mass public.

2

What Is Workplace Mobilization?

We define workplace mobilization as attempts by employers to influence the political behavior of their employees during election campaigns.[1] The most common type of workplace mobilization is the encouragement of employees to turn out to vote. But aside from mobilizing voters on election day, bosses may also try to influence their employees' choice of party or candidate, or change their opinions on a particular policy. In some countries, employers try to get their employees to participate directly in election campaigns, inducing them to donate money, attend rallies, or campaign on behalf of candidates.

As we will see, employers often use negative inducements to achieve these goals. At the extreme, bosses may threaten termination, salary cuts, or a loss of benefits if workers do not vote or do not vote "correctly." More commonly, they may direct, exhort, or ask their employees to vote without making such threats explicit. Still, employees may believe there will be negative consequences for disobeying these requests, even if the consequences are not fully articulated. Employers also use positive inducements to mobilize, such as raises, bonuses, one-time gifts, or even time off as rewards for obeying political directives, but these are less common. Since workplace mobilization involves the exchange of selective inducements (negative or positive) for political support, it can be construed as a type of clientelism (see Frye, Reuter, and Szakonyi, 2018; Hicken and Nathan, 2020).[2]

---

[1] Our study of workplace mobilization does not encompass all types of political activity in the workplace. We focus on the mobilization of employees by management. Thus, we do not study the ways that workers try to exert political influence on each other or the ways that workers talk about politics in the workplace (Mutz and Mondak, 2006). We also do not study how unions or trade associations politicize the workplace. Both are widespread and substantively important phenomena, but nonetheless fall outside the scope of our analysis.

[2] As Hicken (2011) notes, there is no universally accepted definition of clientelism, but many definitions have four key features: (1) dyadic relations between patron and client, (2) a hierarchy between the two, (3) support that is contingent on the inducement, and (4) iteration. The political mobilization of voters by their employers fulfills all of these criteria.

Workplace Politics. Timothy Frye, Ora John Reuter, and David Szakonyi, Oxford University Press.
© Oxford University Press (2025). DOI: 10.1093/9780197802045.003.0002

22 WORKPLACE POLITICS

This chapter uses data from countries around the world, and in particular Russia, to highlight the different forms of workplace mobilization. Our analysis of surveys and primary source materials highlights three fundamental facts about the practice. First, workplace mobilization is prevalent, occurring frequently during elections in all eight countries we examine. Second, it is often coercive and can involve significant pressure being applied on workers. Finally, it is deeply unpopular with voters who mostly see the practice as morally problematic. The latter two characteristics—coercion and moral disapproval—have important implications for how our theory of workplace mobilization unfolds. But first we begin with a brief review of relevant literature on the topic.

Workplace Mobilization around the World

References to political mobilization by employers can be found in scholarly work in many world regions and historical eras. Indeed, historical accounts suggest that employers began engaging in electoral mobilization almost as soon as suffrage was extended. Intimidation of workers was so widespread in late-nineteenth-century America that labor leaders began to see electoral reform as necessary to improve labor conditions (see Argersinger, 1985; Barnes, 1947). Mares (2015) shows how politicians and employers used threats of job loss in Imperial Germany to get their employees to the polls, all while defending explores their actions publicly. In another study of Imperial Germany, Ziblatt (2009) how landlords used their leverage over tenants to subvert the democratic process. Indeed, the role of politically repressive landlords plays a central role in many classic works of political economy and democratization (Gerschenkron, 1962).

Such practices continued into the twentieth century. Communist systems, for example, were an epicenter of workplace mobilization, as worker agitation was sewn into the very fabric of the Bolshevik Revolution (Remington, 1984). After seizing control of Russia's factories, the Bolsheviks immediately turned enterprises into loci of regime propaganda. Party agitators were permanently embedded in factories. Working in tandem with directors, these activists cajoled and supplicated voters at election time (Friedgut, 1979). This helped ensure the 99 percent turnout that marked communist-style elections. In China and Vietnam, employers have long played a key role in turning out the vote (Wang and Sun, 2017; Schuler, 2021).

Outside the communist world, such practices have also been common over the past century. Baland and Robinson (2008) examine how landlords in Chile pressured their employees to vote in the 1950s, but lost leverage after the introduction of the secret ballot in 1958. In subsequent years, rural laborers decreased their support for parties backed by their employers relying on anonymity provided by the secret ballot.

In the United States, the most famous depiction of employer intimidation for political purposes is John Gaventa's (1982) account of Appalachian coal mining towns in West Virginia. In the absence of any alternatives to coal mining, Gaventa argues that employers exercised their authority over miners not only by setting terms of employment and dictating the political agenda, but also by controlling information and building a form of solidarity with workers by which their acquiescence to domination was seen as normal.

More recent studies document workplace mobilization in the contemporary world as well. Mares, Muntean, and Petrova (2016) explore the frequency with which state officials and employers use positive and negative inducements to increase turnout in Bulgaria and Romania. They show that state officials and employers are both commonly used to mobilize voters and that employer coercion of their employees during elections is especially likely in small localities dominated by a few employers. Oliveros (2021) documents how state employees without tenure in Argentina are mobilized not only to vote on behalf of the incumbent mayor, but also to mobilize voters for their political patrons. Mares and Young (2019, 123) demonstrate how mayors in rural Hungary illegally employed welfare recipients on their farms and then used threats of dismissal to secure their votes on election day. Allina-Pisano (2010) and Darden (2008) have described patterns of workplace mobilization in Ukraine, while McMann (2006) has identified economic coercion by employers as one of the key factors that undermines democracy in Russia and Kyrgyzstan. Pisano (2022) documents in great detail how a range of actors, including employers, state bureaucrats, teachers, collective farm managers, and civic organizations in towns big and small, pressured citizens in Ukraine to support a referendum to amend the constitution in April 2000.

Hertel-Fernandez (2016) provides the most extensive contemporary treatment of the topic in his study of workplace mobilization in the United States. He examines various forms of workplace mobilization, from employers emailing employees with advice on how to vote to running voter

24 WORKPLACE POLITICS

education campaigns and holding political rallies. He finds that nearly one in four workers have experienced some form of political activity in their workplace and that workplace mobilization frequently targets those concerned about their job security. He documents not only how businesses mobilize their employees for political action, but also how business associations such as the Business Industry Political Action Committee (BIPAC) have developed sophisticated targeting strategies designed to change workers' views on political issues and to encourage them to act on those views.

As subsequent chapters make clear, our work differs from much existing scholarship on workplace mobilization in a variety of ways. While much, but far from all of the literature focuses on a historical setting, we examine workplace mobilization in the contemporary period. Given changes in technology, norms, and education levels, the dynamics of workplace mobilization in the contemporary period may differ from past practices.

In addition, our study examines this practice across a range of countries and settings. Existing work tends to focus on a single country. This is understandable given the difficulty of studying a practice that is often illicit. To get the facts of the case right requires time and effort, and to this end we do a deep study of workplace mobilization in a single country that we know well, Russia. But, in contrast to previous work, we also explore the extent and dynamics of workplace mobilization in seven other diverse contexts. By asking a standard set of survey questions about workplace mobilization in a broad range of countries, we can begin to identify how the case of Russia does and does not resemble other cases. This helps to put our main findings about Russia in a comparative context, while also allowing us to explore the practice in new settings.

We also devote far more attention to relations between politicians and employers than does existing scholarship. The handful of prominent works on workplace mobilization cited earlier focus on how employers pressure employees to go to the polls. We do too. But we also examine relations between politicians and employers. As we shall see, employers and politicians often have different motives when it comes to politics. Politicians seek to maximize votes, and employers seek to maximize profits. And because many employers view workplace mobilization as costly, politicians must motivate employers to mobilize their workers. In many settings, this step is crucial to workplace mobilization, but is not well understood.

Finally, we pay more attention to the moral dimension of workplace mobilization than does most existing scholarship. Employers, employees, and the mass public tend to view workplace mobilization as morally problematic—more so than other forms of political mobilization. Party-based brokers can rally the faithful without expecting much backlash from other voters, but politicians seeking to mobilize workers must take this possibility into account. Indeed, we identify a tradeoff that politicians and employers face when contemplating workplace mobilization. Pressuring workers to get to the polls may increase turnout among the employed, but it may also turn off voters outside the workplace who disapprove of the practice.

In sum, there is still much that we do not know about workplace mobilization. Empirically, we lack the in-depth data that would allow us to understand the forms that workplace mobilization takes and the conditions that make it more likely to occur. With this in mind, we have conducted postelection surveys on workplace mobilization in Russia and a range of countries over the past decade.

Our Data

Surveys of Employers in Russia

To study workplace mobilization in depth, we require various types of evidence: from fine-grained information provided by employees and employers themselves to administrative data that help us unpack relations between employers and politicians. Each type of evidence is helpful for answering different aspects of our research question. In the next section, we discuss our strategy for employing the diverse data sources that we have collected.

As scholars of Russian politics, we have used our contextual knowledge to gather a diverse set of data from Russia that would be hard to assemble for multiple countries. Workplace mobilization is common in Russia, and the vast majority of Russians are familiar with it. This makes it easier to compile systematic data on details about workplace mobilization. Russia is also a useful case because it has a well-developed survey infrastructure, capable of producing high-quality survey data—including surveys of employers—a rarity outside developed democracies.

26 WORKPLACE POLITICS

Moreover, Russia is a good case for making general claims about workplace mobilization in "electoral authoritarian regimes." Elections in Russia during the period of our study, 2011 to 2021, would certainly be familiar to students of other such regimes. Russian authorities allowed elections, parties, and political protest, but tilted the playing field to drastically reduce the chances of the opposition taking power. In the 2011 parliamentary elections, the pro-Kremlin United Russia party won just 49 percent of the vote, and large protests ensued to oppose vote fraud and corruption. Five years later, United Russia won 55 percent of the vote with Kremlin-friendly opposition parties receiving the other 45 percent of the vote. In presidential elections in 2018, the Kremlin barred one of Putin's main challengers, Alexey Navalny, from running, which sparked significant protests from his supporters. Competitive but unfair elections are a hallmark of this type of regime. By the end of the decade, Vladimir Putin had managed to sideline all of his political opponents and drain elections of any remaining unpredictability, but for much of the period of our study, Russia can be seen as a competitive authoritarian regime. As such, the experience of workplace mobilization in Russia may provide lessons for politics in other such autocracies.

Our most important data source comes from surveys of employers themselves. Our primary aim in later chapters is to understand the reasons why employers engage in political mobilization, so asking employers themselves is important. This approach allows us to explore how employer characteristics shape workplace mobilization, and one clear advantage of focusing our empirical attention on Russia is the relative ease of accessing and conversing openly with the top leadership of Russian companies. Several of Russia's leading survey firms specialize in conducting these surveys, and such interviews are familiar to Russian CEOs and their management teams. Managers are uniquely positioned to answer questions on the costs and benefits of workplace mobilization as well as the frequency of its use. These data provide firsthand reports of the use of workplace mobilization.

To this end, we added to the surveys of firm managers in Russia a module of questions about workplace mobilization. The first was conducted by the VTSIOM polling organization in November and December 2011. We drew a sample of 922 small, medium-size, and large firms in fifteen regional capitals.[3] Interviews were conducted face-to-face with a member of the firm's

---

[3] Voronezh, Ekaterinburg, Kemerovo, Kursk, Moscow, Nizhnii Novgorod, Novgorod, Omsk, Rostov, Smolensk, Tula, Ulyanovsk, Ufa, Irkutsk, and Khabarovsk.

Table 2.1 Surveys of Employers

Country	Year	N	Type of Election
Russia	2011	922	National
Russia	2017	690	National

top management: either the chief executive officer, chief financial officer, or chief legal officer. The sample captured political activity around the time of the parliamentary elections of December 4, 2011.

The second survey was conducted from August to October 2017 by Bashkirova and Partners and was commissioned by the International Center for the Study of Institutions and Development at the Higher School of Economics in Moscow, as part of a study on vocational education in Russia. In collaboration with the principal investigators, we included a battery of questions about workplace mobilization.[4] The survey sampled 690 medium-size (100 to 249 employees) and large (over 250 employees) firms in twelve regional capitals. The regions were chosen based on the high marks they received from the Russian Agency for Strategic Initiatives for supporting vocational education.[5] The end sample is not representative of all firms operating in Russia, but is representative of medium-size and large firms operating in the chosen sectors in each region. All interviews were conducted face-to-face.

Individual-Level Surveys in Russia

In addition to firm surveys, we also conducted five nationally representative, face-to-face surveys of Russian voters following national elections, as described in Table 2.2. These surveys help us to understand workplace mobilization from the workers' perspective and to study how individual characteristics of workers influence the likelihood of workplace mobilization. In two of these surveys (2011 and 2018), we added questions to existing omnibus polls carried out by the Levada Center, Russia's oldest and most

---

[4] For more information on survey aims and methodology, see Remington and Marques 2020. We are grateful to Thomas Remington and Israel Marques for making room for our module on their survey.

[5] The firms operated in Chelyabinsk, Krasnoyarsk, Kursk, Novosibirsk, Perm, Samara, Sverdlovsk, Tambov, Ulyanovsk, Vladimir, Vologda, and Voronezh. Because our colleagues' goal was to interview firms capable of and interested in investing in these types of employee training, the number of sectors covered was limited to manufacturing firms (including resource extraction, transportation, and construction). Thus, most service sector firms are excluded.

28 WORKPLACE POLITICS

Table 2.2 Public Opinion Surveys in Russia

Country	Year	N	Type of Survey	Type of Election
Russia	2011	1,600	Nationally representative	State Duma
Russia	2014	4,273	Multistage sampling design with oversample of workers	Regional: Gubernatorial and Legislative
Russia	2016	2,361	Nationally representative	State Duma
Russia	2018	1,612	Nationally representative	Presidential
Russia	2021	3,245	Nationally representative	State Duma

reputable polling firm. In 2016 and 2021, we added a battery of questions to the long-running Russian Election Study (also conducted by the Levada Center during these years).[6] And in 2014, we fielded our own, standalone survey solely on the topic of workplace mobilization in regional elections. That survey included oversamples both of employed individuals as well as workers vulnerable to workplace mobilization, such as those living in single-company towns and working in heavy industry.

Cross-National Public Opinion Surveys

To understand the scope of workplace mobilization in other settings, we also conducted seven nationally representative public opinion surveys in Argentina, Indonesia, Nigeria, Turkey, Venezuela, Ukraine, and the United States. By drawing on over fourteen thousand survey responses across these countries, we provide a more comprehensive picture of the phenomenon than has been offered to date. Each survey battery contained a series of questions about citizens' experience with workplace mobilization, as well as questions about their attitudes toward the practice. Our objective with these surveys is not to make generalizations across countries; resource constraints did not allow for conducting surveys in a large sample of countries. Instead,

---

[6] In 2016, we also included an oversample of respondents living in single-company towns, which are common sites of workplace mobilization.

we use these data to illustrate the commonalities of workplace mobilization across different settings.

We used the following criteria to select the seven countries. First, we considered countries that held meaningful, semicompetitive national elections from 2014 to 2018, our primary period for data collection. Conducting such an array of studies is expensive, and we were fortunate to receive grants from a variety of sources, in particular the US National Science Foundation. We focused our efforts on identifying the scope of the practice across different settings. From the list of countries holding elections during this time period, we selected countries that varied on key political and economic variables, such as regime type, strength of the party system, economic development, and economic structure.

In addition, we conducted surveys in the United States, even though it is much wealthier and has a longer history of democratic rule, freer media, and a more diversified economy than the other countries we study. As we shall see in the last two chapters, the US case is especially useful for studying the normative dimensions of workplace mobilization. It also allows us to compare workplace mobilization in countries with varying levels of institutional strength.

Because surveys were our primary tool for collecting data on the incidence of workplace mobilization, we needed to identify reputable firms working in each country that could implement a nationally representative poll and accept money from foreign scholars. For each country holding an election, we solicited recommendations from country experts and contacted at least two survey firms with our questionnaire. In most cases, our solicitations were successful and we were able to contract out our questions and validate the data. However, because of concerns about data quality, we opted not to analyze a survey we conducted in Algeria in 2014.[7] Fear of administrative interference led us to cancel a survey we had planned around 2015 elections in Uzbekistan. In Venezuela and Argentina, we commissioned standalone surveys, while in the other countries we placed our questions on omnibus surveys. The Argentina survey was conducted by phone rather than face-to-face and is less representative of the general population than our other surveys. The share of the employed population in our survey is similar to official data, but the share of self-employed respondents is slightly higher

---

[7] Analysis of responses indicated that the survey was contaminated by fabricated duplicate interviews.

30 WORKPLACE POLITICS

Table 2.3 Cross-National Public Opinion Surveys

Country	Year	N	Election Type	Survey Firm	Format
Ukraine	2012	2,048	National	KMIS	Face-to-Face
Indonesia	2014	2,649	National	CSIS	Face-to-Face
Nigeria	2015	5,049	National	TNS	Face-to-Face
Turkey	2015	1,508	National	Frekans Research	Face-to-Face
Venezuela	2016	1,400	National	Consultores 21	Face-to-Face
Argentina	2018	1,198	National	Poliarquia	Telephone

than official statistics suggest.[8] The full list of countries can be found in Table 2.3.

Cross-national surveys of employees not only help us understand the prevalence of workplace mobilization in a diverse set of countries; they are also well suited to help understand the extent of coercion employed in workplace mobilization. Employers may be unreliable guides about how workers perceive workplace mobilization, so it is important to ask workers directly about their experience with it.

Focus Groups in Russia

These public opinion surveys provide systematic and comparable data across multiple countries. But closed-ended survey questions cannot capture the fine texture of workplace mobilization. Interviews are well suited for gaining insight into the nuanced ways that employees experience workplace mobilization. This evidence is especially important given the varied and subtle ways that employers may influence the political behavior of their employees. Capturing the feel of workplace mobilization is best done using a more qualitative approach.

To gain such insight, we commissioned four focus groups and ten in-depth interviews with Russian voters who had experienced workplace mobilization. The interviews were conducted in October 2017 by Bashkirova and Partners, one of Russia's leading public opinion research firms.

---

[8] For robustness, we used three different types of survey weights and estimated the share of workers mobilized by their employers in Argentina. We find little difference from estimates using unweighted data. For consistency and simplicity, we report the unweighted data in this table and in other analysis in the book.

All respondents were recruited first via a screener survey to identify individuals who had experienced workplace mobilization. On the basis of this screener survey, the survey firm reached out to those who had experienced workplace mobilization and received informed consent. These focus groups were done anonymously, and no information about specific places of work was shared. We have audio recordings of all focus group sessions, which allow for direct validation of responses.

As research sites, we selected three cities in Chelyabinsk Oblast. The capital, Chelyabinsk, is Russia's seventh-largest city (with 1.1 million people) and is one of the country's leading industrial centers. Miass, sixty miles away from Chelyabinsk, is a city of 150,000 and the home of UralAZ, one of Russia's largest truck producers. Satka, with 45,000 people, is less urban than the other interview sites, but is a major magnesite mining center. Workplace mobilization is known to be widespread in all three cities. In order to identify respondents who had experienced workplace mobilization, we first designed a short, regionally representative screener survey and selected respondents from that survey who reported having substantial experience with political mobilization in the workplace in a recent election. Bashkirova and Partners then organized focus groups of eight to ten respondents in each of the cities and also carried out two to four in-depth interviews in each city. These focus groups provide richly detailed accounts of workplace mobilization that are essential to our argument and could not have been obtained otherwise.

Other Data Sources

We also mined other primary source materials to learn how Russian citizens experience workplace mobilization, such as the crowdsourced *Karta Narusheniye* (KN, translated as "map of violations") database, which Russia's leading election monitoring group, Golos, has run since 2011 to collect firsthand information on electoral manipulation. To construct this database, Golos created a web-based platform that allows citizens and activists to report electoral violations. The reports are then cleaned and categorized by the nongovernmental organization (NGO) and posted online. For the 2011 elections, we scraped all seventy-eight hundred of the violation reports and coded all of the reports that involved workplace mobilization. The KN data also contain a treasure trove of leaked documents, emails, text messages, faxes, and telegrams about workplace mobilization. Over the course of our research, we examined hundreds of these documents from the 2011, 2016, 2018, and 2021 elections.

32 WORKPLACE POLITICS

Crowdsourced data like these are unlikely to capture all violations, and opposition activists have greater incentives to report violations than do pro-regime activists. Nonetheless, these data offer a wealth of insight into the specific practices associated with workplace mobilization. Some of the most useful documents in this database are leaked internal documents that reveal how local governments mobilize employers and how employers organize the process of workplace mobilization. These data allow us to compare the frequency of political appeals inside and outside the workplace and to capture the relative frequency of different types of electoral subversion.

In addition, we tasked research assistants to comb several large, electronic Russian-language media databases for mentions of workplace mobilization in the press from 1991 to the present. We draw on all of these accounts at multiple points in our analysis. Taken together, this quantitative and qualitative data collection generates a rich catalogue of the various forms of workplace mobilization prevalent in Russia, while also giving us a window into the practice in other settings. These data also allow us to examine workplace mobilization form various points of view. This is important, as employers, employees, and citizens each experience workplace mobilization from different perspectives. Moreover, by combining surveys, administrative data, crowdsourced accounts, and press reports, we hope to offset some of the biases inherent in these different forms of evidence.

Workplace Mobilization in Comparative Perspective

In the following sections, we draw on our diverse data sources to describe the prevalence and characteristics of workplace mobilization. We begin by drawing on our public opinion surveys, which asked respondents about their experience with a wide range of political activities in the workplace. For example, in each survey in our study, we asked a version of the following question:

Now, we would like to ask you about your experience with politics and political activities in your place of work during the recent election campaign. During these elections did you ever notice [Mark all that apply]:

1. Your supervisor or management discussing politics or elections with employees

2. Your supervisor or manager expressing his opinions to you about politics
3. Your supervisor or manager publicly endorsed a candidate
4. The distribution of campaign materials in the workplace
5. Your employer offered transportation for employees to the polling place
6. Your supervisor or manager encouraging you to attend a political event/rally
7. Your supervisor or manager encouraging you to vote
8. Your supervisor of manager asked you to vote for a particular candidate or party

Our question formulations asked about many possible forms of workplace mobilization for several reasons. First, our familiarity with anecdotes about workplace mobilization in Russia led us to believe that respondents might perceive and characterize a given mobilizational act in different ways. Therefore, in order to pick up all instances of workplace mobilization we designed a battery that would include various forms. Second, we wanted to measure both the more coercive, clientelistic forms of workplace mobilization, as well as forms that might be more benign. As we discuss later (and much more deeply in Chapter 8), tactics of workplace mobilization vary in the extent to which they are coercive. But even the most benign forms have the potential to be coercive, given the power differentials between employers and employees. And, as we discuss, workers differ in how they perceive the intent of workplace mobilization. Our goal in the surveys was to capture all types of workplace mobilization. Finally, when designing our surveys we presumed that the form of workplace mobilization might differ across settings, so we designed our instrument to capture multiple forms of the practice. Table 2.4 provides an overview of our survey findings across seven countries. The penultimate rows of the table show the share of employees in each country that experienced any particular form of workplace mobilization.

The results show that employees encounter workplace mobilization in a wide range of settings. In Venezuela, 51 percent of employed respondents experienced at least one form of voter mobilization in the workplace, and about a third did in Argentina, Russia, Nigeria, and Turkey. Techniques vary significantly, but some patterns are evident. Employers discussing the election or sharing political opinions are usually more common than more direct forms of mobilization such as asking employees to attend a rally or providing them with transportation to the polls—although in Russia and Venezuela,

Table 2.4 Mobilization in the Workplace (%): Public Opinion Surveys

	Argentina	Indonesia	Nigeria	Russia	Turkey	Ukraine	Venezuela
Employed	24	45	21	49	51	38	55
Employer:							
(1) Discussed Election	19	18	38	19	25		21
(2) Shared Political Opinions	30				26		38
(3) Endorsed a Candidate		15	20			12	
(4) Distributed Materials	8	10	13	10	6	18	13
(5) Provided Transport	0	4	10	4	4		10
(6) Encouraged to Attend Rally	4	7	14	4	4	14	12
(7) Asked to Vote	10		31	25	9	9	42
(8) Asked to Vote for Specific Party/Candidate	6			5	6	4	22
Any Employer Mobilization	37	27	46	34	32	26	51
Employer Mobilization (only rows 3–8)	17	21	30	29	13	22	44
Sample Size	1,198	2,649	5,049	1,612	1,508	2,048	1,400
Survey Year	2017	2014	2015	2018	2015	2012	2015

This table shows the percentage of employed respondents (excluding self-employed) reporting having experienced the above forms of political mobilization in the workforce. The Venezuela survey contained a nationally representative sample of one thousand adults, and an additional stratified sample of four hundred employed individuals. Endorsement is from a separate question battery in the Nigeria survey. The employment rate among our Argentina survey respondents is significantly lower than the rate reported in official statistics. This is because our survey was a telephone survey and the sample was skewed toward women, older, and self-employed respondents. However, when using probability weights, our estimates of workplace mobilization among the employed population differ little from those reported here among the unweighted sample. All other surveys were nationally representative face-to-face surveys.

Table 2.5 Mobilization in the Workplace: Employer Surveys in Russia

Activity	2011	2017
Employer:		
(1) Endorsed a Party or Candidate	7	7
(2) Held Rally	6	14
(3) Distributed Materials	5	15
(4) Held a "Meeting" with Voters	6	24
(5) Asked Employees to Join a Political Party	1	1
(6) Asked Employees to Attend a Rally		1
(7) Asked Employees to Vote		10
(8) Asked Employees to Vote for Specific Party/Candidate	4	4
(9) Offered Material Support to a Party or Candidate	1	2
(10) Provided Transport		4
Comparable Employer Mobilization	22	33
Any Employer Mobilization	22	39
Sample Size	922	690

This table presents the percentage of employers who answered yes for each activity we asked about on the 2011 and 2017 firm surveys conducted in Russia. Comparable Employer Mobilization totals the percentage of employers engaging in workplace mobilization using only questions that were asked on both surveys. Any Employer Mobilizations totals across all the questions that were asked in each survey.

directly asking employees to vote is the most common type of mobilization. In Ukraine, Turkey, and Argentina, about 10 percent of employees reported that their employer asked them to vote.

Table 2.5 shows results from two surveys of firm managers in Russia that we conducted in 2011 and 2017. They paint a similar picture. In 2011, 22 percent of employers reported that they conducted some sort of political activity in the workplace. In the 2016 elections (the 2017 survey referenced the 2016 State Duma elections), 39 percent of large and medium-size enterprises reported that they engaged in some form of workplace mobilization.

36 WORKPLACE POLITICS

In 2017, almost 10 percent of firm managers reported that they had asked their employees to vote.

Across countries, employees are more likely to ask employees to vote than to vote for a particular candidate or party. When an employer exhorts employees to turn out, it is often tacitly understood that they should vote for a certain party. This is especially true in settings where the political preferences of management are common knowledge, or in some autocratic settings, like Russia, where the vast majority of workplace mobilization occurs at the behest of the pro-government party even as it often struggles to get a majority of votes. Roman, one of our focus group respondents in Zlatoust, put it this way:

> Everybody knows who you are supposed to vote for. [The director] doesn't need to create unnecessary problems for himself. To concretely say to someone, "Go vote for this guy"—You'd have to be a complete idiot to do that. Of course, not every person will complain, but a few will. So, nowadays, it is enough to simply tell people to go vote and it is understood who for.[9]

Sergei in the same focus group agreed and offered a similar sentiment:

> In the municipal enterprises there is pressure. We had early voting [recently] and they handed out these invitations, multicolored ones. The candidate wasn't specified, but they asked us to vote for "our" candidate. Well, "for our candidate"—that's enough said. If all the directors are United Russia, who are we going to vote for? Without even specifying, it is understood who we should vote for.[10]

Why is asking employees to turn out so much more common than asking them to vote for a specific candidate or party? Part of it surely has to do with our earlier discussion: exhorting voters to vote for a specific candidate is unnecessary in many contexts. And as we discuss later, voters are more disapproving of employer attempts to influence vote choice than of attempts to induce turnout. Moreover, since almost all contemporary elections use a secret ballot, it is much easier for employers to monitor and verify turnout than it is to monitor and verify vote choice (Gans-Morse, Mazzuca,

[9] Focus Group Response Roman, Focus Group, Bashkirova & Partners, Zlatoust, Russia. October 4, 2017.
[10] Focus Group Response Sergei, Focus Group, Bashkirova & Partners, Zlatoust, Russia. October 4, 2017.

and Nichter, 2014). This makes it easier to enforce employee compliance with turnout mobilization. Given that turnout mobilization is so much more common than attempts to influence vote choice, we more often analyze the former throughout the book.

Taken as a whole, these cross-national statistics give the lie to some pre-conceived notions about workplace mobilization. For one, the practice is not a historical anachronism. It persists on a large scale in a variety of contemporary settings. Nor is it limited only to autocratic settings or to poor countries or, for that matter, industrialized economies. And as the findings in Africa, Asia, and Latin America testify, the practice is not just a remnant of Soviet-style economic systems.

Workplace Mobilization in Context

We can put workplace mobilization into some context by comparing how frequently it is used in relation to mobilization by other vote brokers. Although party development has stalled around the world, many countries still have relatively strong grassroots parties that can mobilize large numbers of voters. In other settings, traditional brokers such as chiefs or religious leaders hold considerable political sway. One might expect workplace mobilization to play a less prominent role when other established brokers are active.

In several of our surveys—in Argentina, Turkey, Russia, and Venezuela—we placed questions that would allow us to compare the prevalence of mobilization by different types of brokers. Because Argentina and Turkey are two countries with developed grassroots parties, one might expect workplace mobilization to be used less often. In each country, we asked respondents an identical battery of questions about their experiences with mobilization in the formal sector by employers and party activists. The findings shown in Table 2.6 are somewhat surprising. In both Argentina and Turkey, the share of employed voters mobilized by their employers was *higher* than the share of voters in the total population who reported being mobilized by parties.

Similar results can be gleaned from Russia and Venezuela. While we lack a full battery of mobilization questions in those countries, we asked specific questions about whether respondents received specific turnout appeals from employers and party activists. In Venezuela, 41 percent of employed voters reported that their employer asked them to vote; 25 percent of voters

38 WORKPLACE POLITICS

Table 2.6 Prevalence of Various Brokers in Turkey and Argentina

Mobilized by:	Argentina	Turkey
Party Activist	35	24
Religious Leader		3
Civic Association Leader		6
Employer (as share of employed)	37	32
Employer (as share of total population)	11	16

This table shows mobilization rates (%) from the Argentina (2017) and Turkey (2015) public opinion surveys. Cell entries show share of voters who reported that the respective broker did one of the following: (1) discussed the elections with them, (2) asked them to vote, (3) asked them to vote for a certain candidate, (4) tried to pressure them to vote/vote a certain way, or (5) tried to buy their vote, (6) encouraged them to attend a rally, or (7) offered them transportation to the polls.

reported being mobilized by a party activist. In the 2016 State Duma elections in Russia, our survey showed that 17 percent of employed voters were asked by their employer to vote, while 12 percent of all voters reported that a party activist asked them to vote. These findings are striking given that party activists are usually considered the main broker that politicians use to get out the vote. Employers engaged their workers politically at high rates even when parties were active in society.

The findings from Turkey and Venezuela also show that employers are more common than other types of brokers as well. In Turkey, mobilization by employers was several times more likely than mobilization by religious leaders and civic association leaders. In Venezuela, 31 percent of respondents reported that a neighborhood leader asked them to vote and the same percent reported that the leader of a community council asked them to vote.

Of course, a significant limitation of employer-based mobilization is that it can only reach those who are working. Unemployed and self-employed individuals cannot be mobilized via this method. Party activists and other brokers, by contrast, can reach these voters. This constraint on workplace mobilization bites hardest in countries with large informal sectors or where most are non-employed. Thus, in Argentina, where only 43 percent of our sample was employed, 35 percent of those voters reported workplace mobilization, but that figure was 11 percent in the total population. Still, even with this constraint, the share of the total population mobilized by employers can be substantial. In Turkey, 16 percent of the total sample experienced workplace mobilization, far ahead of the population rate of mobilization by religious and civic association leaders and not too far behind the rate of total mobilization by party activists. In most of our surveys party activists are the most common vote broker among the general population. But employers are also prominent brokers. Indeed, among employed voters, employers often mobilize workers at higher rates than do party-based brokers.

Means and Methods of Workplace Mobilization

We have seen that workplace mobilization is common, but what does it look like in practice? In some instances, political mobilization in the workplace can be relatively mundane. Many of our respondents reported that they encountered campaign materials—flyers, posters, banners, magnets, and the like—in the workplace. Our focus group participants did not seem particularly fazed by this practice. In Russia, many large factories are festooned with such agitation.

Our interest lies primarily in more intensive forms of mobilization. Rallies, campaign events, meetings, and other workplace gatherings enable employers to reach their workers en masse. In Russia, candidates often go to workplaces to campaign. In our 2017 survey of firm managers in large and medium-size Russian firms, 15 percent of managers reported that they had allowed a party or candidate to distribute campaign materials in the workplace, and 14 percent reported that they had allowed a candidate to hold a rally. Managers frequently ask, suggest, or order their employees to attend such events. Maksim, one of our focus group participants in Chelyabinsk, describes a typical scene:

> Well, you are sitting at work, without a choice. And they [management] announce that in the evening a wonderful guy will come from some such party (we won't say which one) and he will deliver his pitch. Then, closer to lunch, he came, gave his speech, told us about his election platform, something about how "Russia is getting up from its knees" and so on and so

forth, as they usually do. Afterward, we could ask questions, and then he left some fliers, calendars, magnets, and other very useful things.[11]

As the American legal scholar Paul Secunda points out, such meetings are morally problematic because, as in the scenario described by Maksim, workers are a "captive audience" for politicians (Secunda, 2010). They cannot excuse themselves from such meetings without bearing a cost. Even if employers are not sharing their opinions, workers are deprived of the "freedom not to listen" (Hartley, 2010). In Russia, directors often order their employees to attend such meetings during the workday.

Managers also capitalize on these captive audiences to endorse candidates or advance their political views. During the 2012 elections in the United States, such practices drew significant media attention as Mitt Romney encouraged employers to "make it very clear to your employees what you believe is in the best interest of your enterprise and therefore their job and their future in the upcoming election."[12] In the 2016 election, supervisors at a U-Haul facility in the area of Phoenix, Arizona, were told to bring their workers to attend a rally in support of a Republican candidate for Congress. The company provided free food and drinks at the event. While the company argued that it was not engaged in partisan politics and that participation in the rally was voluntary, some workers felt otherwise. One reported that the company favored Republicans and gave bonuses after the 2016 election, reminding workers that they did so "because of all the good work Trump was doing for American business."[13]

In Russia and other countries, many firm managers are themselves candidates (Szakonyi, 2020). Several of our interview respondents reported that their bosses had asked for their vote, often intimating that this was required. Because the directors of large industrial enterprises are particularly likely to enter politics, the practice is most common in factories—but employers asking their employees for their vote is not limited to those settings. Svetlana, a confectioner working at a shopping mall in Chelyabinsk, tells the following story:

They announced to us that the guy who owns the mall was running in the election. . . . So one day they chased us all out on the street for [his] campaign rally. We all stood there, freezing. . . . And then on election day, the shift that was working was allowed to leave early so that they could go vote.

[11] Focus Group Response Maksim, Focus Group, Bashkirova. & Partners, Chelyabinsk, Russia. October 3, 2017.
[12] See "Hot Election 2012 Trend: Bosses Advising Employees How to Vote," Slate.com, October 27, 2012.
[13] Fang, Lee, and David Dayen, "How Companies Pressure Workers to Vote for Corporate Interests over Their Own," *The Intercept*, November 6, 2018.

And the [mall] director told everyone: "We are letting you all off so that you go vote for our candidate."[14]

As Svetlana's story suggests, managers not only try to influence their employees, but also ask them to get involved with campaigns themselves. Our surveys indicate that the most common form of this practice is asking employees to participate in campaign rallies. As Table 2.4 indicates, one in ten Russian employees reported that their employer asked them to go to a political rally before the 2018 elections. Plates 2.1–2.4 show examples of these "captive audience" meetings in Russia, while Plates 2.5–2.7 show examples of employers publicly endorsing United Russia to their employees. In Nigeria, 14 percent of employees reported that their employer asked them to attend a campaign rally outside work; in Ukraine 15 percent reported the same.

Sometimes employees are enlisted to engage in much more intensive forms of campaigning, such as handing out fliers or agitating door-to-door. In our 2014 Russia survey, 4 percent of employees reported that their employer had asked them to campaign on behalf of a candidate or party. During the 2015 elections in Turkey, the AKP forced thousands of

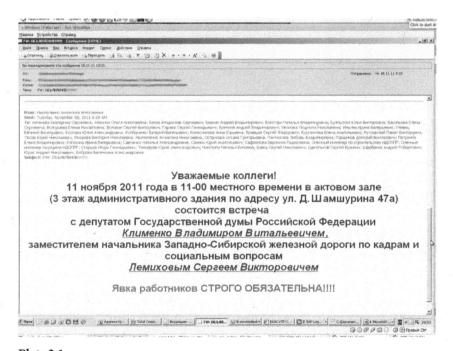

Plate 2.1

[14] Interview with Svetlana, In-depth Interview, Bashkirova & Partners, Chelyabinsk, Russia. October 2, 2017.

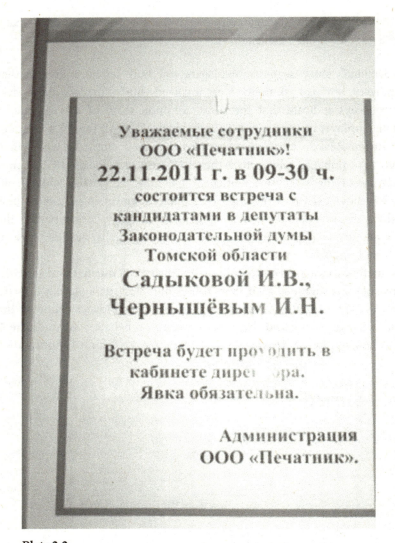

Plate 2.2

municipal employees in Ankara to use their personal cars (under implicit threat of dismissal) to help the ruling party campaign door-to-door. Word of this practice spilled into the headlines when hundreds of these workers were left disgruntled by the cancellation of their short-term work contracts after the election.[15] During the 2015 Venezuelan parliamentary elections, the ruling United Socialist Party of Venezuela (PSUV) required public sector

[15] Cepni, Ozan, "ASKi'de isci kiyimi," *Cumhuriyet*, April 22, 2016.

> Для руководителей подразделений.
>
> Уважаемые коллеги!
>
> 29 ноября предприятие принимает участие в митинге, посвященном предстоящим выборам.
> Целесообразность и смысл – не обсуждаются. *Выезд в 15.00 от Треста*.
>
> От каждого подразделения (в зависимости от количества работающих) необходимо выделить 1 (2) представителя. Фамилию сообщить Ю.А. Бурсиной (по разнарядке).
>
> Для: СУ-1, СУ-3, СУ-4/8, СУ-7, УМ, УПТК, Гл. энерг., АХО, бух., ПЭО, Юр.отдел, ПТО, БМТС, СБ, ОКС, ОПОЖ, ОТ и ТБ, сис.админ, мед.пункт.
>
> Спасибо. С уважением.
> Е.В. Швыркалова
> 28.11.2011

Plate 2.3

employers to involve workers in turnout mobilization. Called the 1X10 Campaign, each party activist and public sector employee was required to mobilize an additional ten voters.[16]

In another such message, shown in Plate 2.8, the deputy head engineer of MosGaz, Moscow's municipal gas provider, sent an assignment to all department heads asking them to help their employees get absentee ballots in order to vote at a specific precinct. The document concludes with an underlined sentence in bold: **Every supervisor carries personal responsibility for every employee that does not vote.** Plates 2.9 through 2.11 shows other examples of top managers in Russia directing supervisors to get out the vote.

Employers often supplement direct appeals with actions meant to encourage voting. As Table 2.4 shows, one common way is to transport voters to the polls. As we discuss later, such efforts make it easier for employers to monitor the compliance of voters with requests to go to the polls. In extreme cases, they may also be used to aid ballot-stuffing or multiple-voting schemes, often called *karusels* in Russia.

In Russia, another common technique is to make election day (which is always a Sunday) a working day and require workers to either vote at polling places in the workplace or to take an absentee ballot and vote at a precinct nearby.

---

[16] "Obligan a personal de empresas de la CVG and Pdvsa cumplir con el 1x10," *El Nacional* Venezuela, November 27, 2015.

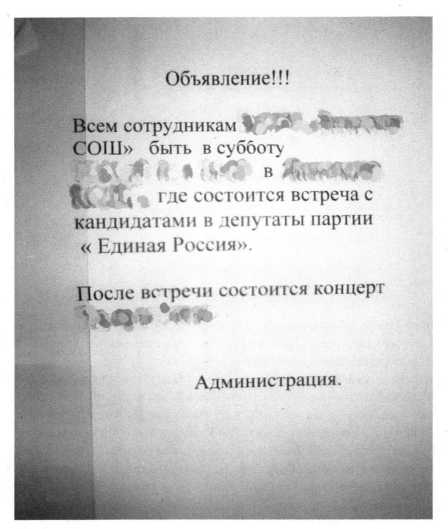

Plate 2.4

Such practices are not limited to Russia. In the US Democratic primary caucus in Nevada in 2016, Hillary Clinton faced a challenge from a rising Bernie Sanders. Former president Bill Clinton was tasked with asking several casino owners to extend paid hours for workers, provide box lunches, and give workers more time off so that they could take part in Democratic Party caucuses. It is hard to know the effect of these efforts, but candidate Clinton swept all six caucuses held at casinos.[17]

[17] Karni, Anne, "Wiki Hack Reveals Bill Clinton's Role in Campaign," *Politico*, October 12, 2016.

WHAT IS WORKPLACE MOBILIZATION? 45

Plate 2.5

In the remainder of the book, we embrace a broad conception of workplace mobilization that includes clearly coercive forms, like threatening workers with dismissal, with arguably more benign forms, like holding rallies in the workplace. This is important given the subtle and diverse ways that employers can mobilize their workers. At the same time, we recognize the challenge of identifying specific forms of workplace mobilization as coercive. This is difficult because we find that workers can perceive even seemingly innocuous interactions as coercive. For example, an email calling for turnout might be seen as coercive in autocracies and when labor markets

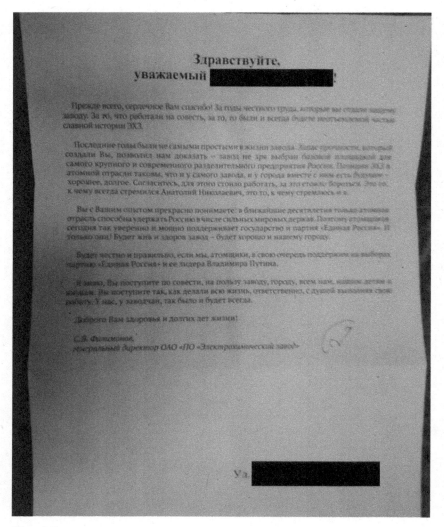

Plate 2.6

are loose. This might be why we see the seemingly more benign forms of workplace mobilization in democracies, but also why they may still be troubling.

In our empirical work we often divide workplace mobilization into forms that would be coercive under any conditions and those that might be

БЛАНК

сбора подписей в поддержку всероссийской политической Партии «Единая Россия» 2011 г.

«Дорогие земляки! Все мы видим, как изменился Воронеж, когда к руководству пришла новая сила. Сила ответственная и работающая на перспективу – политическая Партия «Единая Россия». Коренные изменения к лучшему произошли во всех сферах нашей жизни. Я прошу вас поддержать «Единую Россию» на выборах в Государственную Думу 4 декабря 2011 года. Мы готовы работать для того, чтобы будущее нашего города, наших семей и наших детей было светлым!»

А. В. Гордеев, губернатор Воронежской области, член Бюро Высшего совета Партии «Единая Россия»

№ п/п	Фамилия Имя Отчество	Адрес регистрации	Телефон	Год рождения	Подпись
1					
2					
3					
4					
5					
6					
7					
8					

Plate 2.7

more context specific. Each of these measures has strengths and weaknesses. The former is clearer but likely misses many instances of coerced mobilization, while the latter is noiser but likely captures the more subtle forms of workplace mobilization, particularly those found in democratic settings.

Sticks over Carrots: Workplace Mobilization and Voter Coercion

There is little doubt that direct appeals to vote are a common and important form of workplace mobilization. But how exactly do employers induce their employees to vote, or to vote a certain way? In subsequent chapters we attempt to quantify the effectiveness of workplace mobilization and discuss how employers get their workers to do their bidding. Here we simply give an overview of the main types of inducements that employers offer and the reasons for these types of inducements.

Акционерное общество "МОСГАЗ"
Управление аварийно-восстановительных работ
105120, Россия, Москва, Мрузовский пер., 11. Тел.: (495) 621-51-57, ф. (495)917-79-64

02 февраля 2018г.   № 4/18

ПРОТОКОЛ

совещания у заместителя главного инженера АО «МОСГАЗ» - начальника Управления Романова И.В.

ПРИСУТСТВОВАЛИ: Игонин И.Г., Днепровский Д.А., Ефимов М.М., Амелин В.С., Вершута Р.З., Шевченко Е.К., Калмыкова Е.С., Юдина Л.С., Коноплева Н.А., Иванова Е.А., Козорез А.П., Сафонов А.Н., Бляблин В.М., Левин П.В., Конрад И.О.

1. **Начальникам подразделений.**

1.1. Довести до своих подчиненных, у которых постоянная регистрация не в г. Москве, процедуру голосования на выборах Президента Росси в г. Москве. Необходимо заблаговременно обратиться в МФЦ, подать заявление с указанием места и избирательного участка, где планируете опустить бюллетень. Подробная информация расположена на стенде в Управлении. <u>Каждый руководитель несет персональную ответственность за каждого не проголосовавшего.</u> Поручение от 01.02.2018г.

2. **Игонину И.Г.**

2.1. Провести разбирательство по двум фактам неправильного выполнения работ. Поручение от 02.02.2018г.

Заместитель главного инженера АО «МОСГАЗ» -
Начальник Управления   И.В. Романов

Протокол вела
Инюшева Н.С., доб. 23-71

Plate 2.8

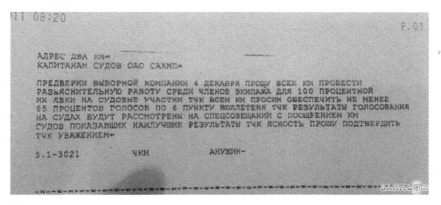

Plate 2.9

Employers use both carrots and sticks, but the latter are much more common. The most common positive inducements include time off from work or a bonus in exchange for voting. Less frequently, employers may engage in vote buying by offering one-time informal cash payments or small enticements such as vodka, gift cards, food, or lottery tickets.

However, we find that sticks are more the norm. Negative inducements are attractive because they can impose significant costs on voters. Employers have a comparative advantage over other brokers on this score, because the inherently hierarchical nature of the employer-employee relationship makes it relatively easy for employers to credibly threaten consequential sanctions in the event of noncompliance. The implicit or explicit threat of job loss, salary reduction, or demotion can make noncompliance potentially very costly. Relative to the typically small payments associated with vote buying, these forms of negative inducement can provide a far more consequential incentive.

Moreover, the physical costs associated with using negative inducements are often lower than for positive inducements.[18] Ordering employees to vote or issuing threats does not require politicians or their agents to provide a material benefit to the voter as does a positive inducement. In addition, economies of scale associated with intimidation lower its cost vis-à-vis vote buying. If implicit oral intimidation is all that is necessary, then voters can be gathered in a single place and addressed (that is, threatened) simultaneously. By contrast, vote buying generally requires transacting face-to-face with each voter to ensure they receive the good or service and acknowledge the exchange being offered. Thus, employers are much more

---

[18] As in Robinson and Torvik (2009) and Mares, Muntean, and Petrova (2016). For a review of the economics of coercion, see Acemoglu and Wolitzky (2011).

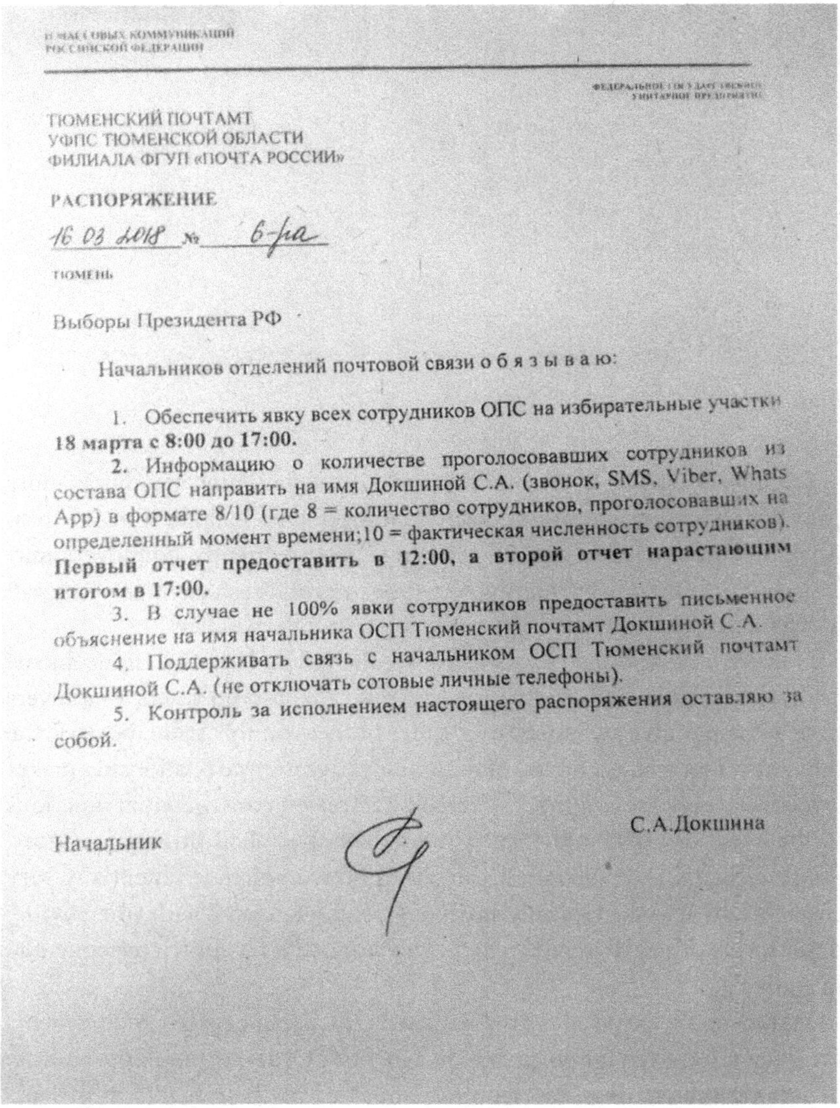

50 WORKPLACE POLITICS

б массовых коммуникаций
российской федерации

ФЕДЕРАЛЬНОЕ ГОСУДАРСТВЕННОЕ
УНИТАРНОЕ ПРЕДПРИЯТИЕ

ТЮМЕНСКИЙ ПОЧТАМТ
УФПС ТЮМЕНСКОЙ ОБЛАСТИ
ФИЛИАЛА ФГУП «ПОЧТА РОССИИ»

РАСПОРЯЖЕНИЕ

16 03 2018 № 6-ра

ТЮМЕНЬ

Выборы Президента РФ

Начальников отделений почтовой связи о б я з ы в а ю:

1. Обеспечить явку всех сотрудников ОПС на избирательные участки 18 марта с 8:00 до 17:00.
2. Информацию о количестве проголосовавших сотрудников из состава ОПС направить на имя Докшиной С.А. (звонок, SMS, Viber, Whats App) в формате 8/10 (где 8 = количество сотрудников, проголосовавших на определенный момент времени;10 = фактическая численность сотрудников). **Первый отчет предоставить в 12:00, а второй отчет нарастающим итогом в 17:00.**
3. В случае не 100% явки сотрудников предоставить письменное объяснение на имя начальника ОСП Тюменский почтамт Докшиной С.А.
4. Поддерживать связь с начальником ОСП Тюменский почтамт Докшиной С.А. (не отключать сотовые личные телефоны).
5. Контроль за исполнением настоящего распоряжения оставляю за собой.

Начальник   С.А.Докшина

Plate 2.10

likely to rely on real or implied negative inducements than they are to offer positive inducements.[19]

---

[19] Of course, voter intimidation also comes with significant costs. In particular, most voters find it morally objectionable. We return to this issue in Chapter 7.

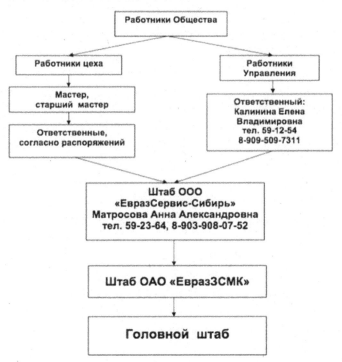

Plate 2.11

Plate 2.11 *Continued*

Available data indicate that employers use such negative inducements in countries around the world. In Venezuela, researchers have found that those who signed a leaked anti-Chávez petition in 2004 (the Maisanta list) suffered earnings and job loss as a result (Hsieh et al., 2011). Years later, state employees were told they would be sacked if they did not vote in a 2017 election for

WHAT IS WORKPLACE MOBILIZATION? 53

a new superbody legislative assembly.[20] Sometimes employers make continued employment contingent on electoral outcomes, subtly (or not so subtly) implying that workers' jobs depend on their vote. For example, in the run-up to the 2009 parliamentary elections in Montenegro, many private companies known to be affiliated with the Socialist Party told workers that the only way they could keep their jobs would be if the party won the election and changed labor regulations. Press reports suggest that these communications were paired with strong suggestions about how to vote.[21]

At other times, pressure follows turnover in office, as the new incumbents pressure public sector workers to toe the new party line. For example, in 2011, the new ruling party in Panama, Democratic Change, started a campaign to goad government officials and their family members into registering as party members—or else lose their jobs.[22]

Our data from Russia illustrate the outsized role that negative inducements play in that country. In Table 2.7, we code and analyze the 2,328 "brokered" violations from the aforementioned *Karta Narusheniya* dataset for 2011. These are violations in which a vote broker targets individual voters or groups of voters and infringes on their electoral rights. Violations in our dataset that involve brokered mobilization include voter intimidation, vote buying, attempts to violate the secret ballot, and the organization of repeat-voting schemes.[23] As the table shows, the workplace is by far the most common site of brokered violations in Russia: 56 percent of all such violations occur at work. By contrast, party activists—the vote broker most frequently discussed in the literature on vote buying—are implicated in just over 10 percent of violations (9.24 percent by ruling party agitators and 1.56 percent by opposition party agitators). Even more starkly, the table shows that most reports of electoral intimidation occur in the workplace (83 percent) and most employer-brokered violations (82 percent) involved the use of intimidation. As Table 2.8 shows, party activists by contrast were far more likely to use positive inducements like vote buying (84 percent). In addition, Employer is the only broker category to show a positive and statistically significant bivariate association with voter intimidation

---

[20] "Venezuela's Maduro Orders State Workers to Vote for Assembly," *Voice of America News*, July 7, 2017.

[21] "Montenegrin Daily Warns about Pressure on Employees to Vote for Ruling Coalition," *BBC Monitoring*, February 16, 2009.

[22] "Government Workers Forced to Change Parties or Save Jobs - Deputy." *Newsroom Panama*, November 20, 2011.

[23] As in Robinson and Torvik (2009) and Mares, Muntean, and Petrova (2016). For a review of the economics of coercion, see Acemoglu and Wolinsky (2011).

Table 2.7 Brokered Electoral Violations Involving Voter Intimidation, Russian 2011 Parliamentary Elections

Broker	Number of Violations	% of all Violations	Number with voter intimidation	% with voter intimidation	Share of all voter intimidation by broker
Employer	1307	56.46	1087	83.17	81.98
Party Activists:					
United Russia	214	9.24	14	6.54	1.06
Opposition	36	1.56	0	0.00	0.00
Public Sector:					
University	269	11.62	160	59.48	12.07
School (nonworkplace)	173	7.47	28	16.28	2.11
Government Official	122	5.27	37	30.33	2.79
Hospital (nonworkplace)	62	2.68	17	27.42	1.28
Other Actors:					
Electoral Official	21	0.91	9	42.86	0.68
Candidate Representative	95	4.10	1	1.05	0.08
Other Individual	29	1.25	8	27.59	0.6

Share columns may not sum to 100 because multiple brokers may be involved in a single violation report. The Other category includes social organizations, priests, police officers, election observers, and government employees (*budzhetniki*) aside from those in hospitals and schools.

Table 2.8 Brokered Electoral Violations involving Vote Buying, Russian 2011 Parliamentary Elections

Broker	Number of Violations	% of all Violations	Number with vote buying	% with vote buying	Share of all vote buying by broker
Employer	1307	56.46	148	11.32	23.72
Party Activists:					
United Russia	214	9.24	180	84.11	28.85
Opposition	36	1.56	35	97.22	5.61
Public Sector:					
University	269	11.62	84	31.23	13.46
School (nonworkplace)	173	7.47	7	4.05	1.12
Government Official	1 22	5.27	78	39.34	7.69
Hospital (nonworkplace)	62	2.68	10	16.13	1.6
Other Actors:					
Electoral Official	21	0.91	11	52.38	1.76
Candidate Representative	29	1.25	11	37.93	1.76
Other Individual	95	4.1	54	56.84	8.65

Share columns may not sum to 100 because multiple brokers may be involved in a single violation report. The Other category includes social organizations, priests, police officers, election observers, and government employees (*budzhetniki*) aside from those in hospitals and schools.

56 WORKPLACE POLITICS

using a chi-squared test, while Government Official, Candidate Representative, Opposition Agitator, Electoral Official, and UR Party Activist show a positive and statistically significant bivariate association with vote buying.

Surveys paint a similar picture. In Russia, Turkey, and Venezuela we carried out a list experiment that asked respondents the following:[24]

> Please tell me how many of the following things happened to you in the past three months. Don't tell me which ones happened. Just tell me HOW MANY of these happened to you during this time.

> 1. You saw election posters/campaign materials
> 2. You met a candidate for parliament
> 3. You saw a news story about politics[25]

> **4a. Someone gave you the impression that there would be negative consequences for you if you did not vote or did not vote a certain way [treatment 1]**

> **4b. You received a material gift or reward in exchange for your vote [treatment 2]**

The sample was divided randomly into three parts: a control group that was presented with the three innocuous items, a treatment group that was presented with the three innocuous items in addition to a sensitive vote-buying item, and a treatment group that was presented with the three innocuous items in addition to a sensitive intimidation item. Table 2.9 shows the results. In Russia, the results indicate that approximately 8 percent of all respondents reported that someone gave them the impression that there would be negative consequences for them if they did not turn out to vote.

---

[24] As discussed later, we often rely on indirect question methods when studying the more sensitive forms of workplace mobilization, such as direct threats or vote buying. List experiments are a common technique used by social scientists to elicit truthful answers to potentially sensitive questions. The technique works as follows. First, respondents are randomly assigned to one of two groups, treatment and control. Respondents in both groups are asked to count the number of items in an identical list that are correct. Key to the experiment is that a sensitive item is added to the list of items that members in the treatment group (but not the control group) see. The data are analyzed by comparing the average number of responses between the treatment and control groups (those who did and did not see the sensitive item); the difference between the two represents the level of the sensitive behavior within the population. Privacy is enhanced because respondents are asked only to count the number of items in the list that are "correct," and not to identify which individual items on the list are "correct." We used such question formats here because respondents may be hesitant to admit that they engaged in vote buying or were intimidated.

[25] In Russia, the control group list was four items and slightly different. They were (1) saw a campaign poster, (2) attended a meeting with a presidential candidate, (3) the electoral campaign annoyed you, (4) you saw a campaign ad on TV or heard one on the radio.

In Venezuela, that figure was 17 percent. By contrast, the percentage of respondents who reported being part of a vote-buying transaction was not statistically distinguishable from zero in either country.

To explore whether voter intimidation should be more likely in the workplace, we divide our survey sample into employed and nonemployed subsamples. The nonemployed group includes individuals who are unemployed and looking for work, as well as the structurally unemployed (for example, pensioners, students, stay-at-home parents). We then compare the mean number of responses across the list experiment's treatment and control groups in each subgroup (employed and nonemployed). The results in Table 2.9 indicate that 17 percent of employed respondents in Russia experienced intimidation before the elections. Nonemployed respondents, by contrast, experienced almost no statistically detectable coercion. Since employers are responsible for 82 percent of voter intimidation cases in Russia (according to the Golos data), we believe that most of those who reported intimidation were intimidated by their employers.[26]

In Turkey, 21 percent of employed voters reported that someone implicitly or explicitly threatened them to vote, but, unfortunately, this question was only administered to employed voters, so we cannot compare this figure to the full sample. In Venezuela, 17 percent of all respondents reported feeling intimidated, but for employed respondents that figure was 22 percent. Thus, in both Russia and Venezuela, intimidation appears more common among employed voters than it is among nonemployed voters.

And consistent with the Russian election violation reports, vote buying was much less common among employed voters than was intimidation. In Russia and Turkey, the share of employed voters who received vote-buying offers was not statistically distinguishable from zero. In Venezuela, a sizable share of employed voters received vote-buying offers, but the share who experienced intimidation was considerably higher.

How do employers use negative inducements? What kind of coercion do they employ? The KN data paint a rich picture.[27] We coded the types of coercion that were mentioned in the 1,087 cases of workplace mobilization that involved intimidation. In over 50 percent of cases, the enforcement

[26] Threats of physical violence were extremely rare (reported in only 0.5 percent of cases).

[27] Violations in the *Karta Narusheniya* dataset that are not "brokered" include problems with voter lists, mass clientelism, counting irregularities, obstruction of election monitors, campaigning before the official start of the campaign, misuse of state resources, ballot stuffing, and illegal postering (e.g., in the polling place). We also exclude violations that describe pressure on businesses to mobilize their workers, as well as violations that were difficult to classify according to violation type, broker, or both.

Table 2.9 List Experiments on Voter Intimidation

	Control Group	Vote-Buying Treatment		Coercion Treatment	
	Mean	Mean	Difference from Control	Mean	Difference from Control
Turkey:					
Only Employed	2.01	2.06	0.05	2.22	0.21**
Venezuela:					
Full Sample	2.26	2.28	0.03	2.43	0.17***
Employed	2.25	2.40	0.14*	2.47	0.22***
Russia:					
Full Sample	2.05	2.05	−0.005	2.13	0.08*
Employed	2.09	2.06	−0.03	2.25	0.16***

***p<0.01, **p<0.05, *p<0.1 This table shows mean outcomes from near-identical list experiments placed on surveys in Turkey (2015), Venezuela (2015), and Russia (2012). Each experiment gave all respondents a list of control items to pick from (three items in Turkey and Venezuela, four items in Russia). Those respondents assigned Vote Buying Treatment received an additional item asking about being offered a gift in the run-up to the election. Those respondents assigned Coercion Treatment received an additional item asking about any threats or coercion made in the run-up to the election. In Turkey, the experiment was only administered to employed respondents.

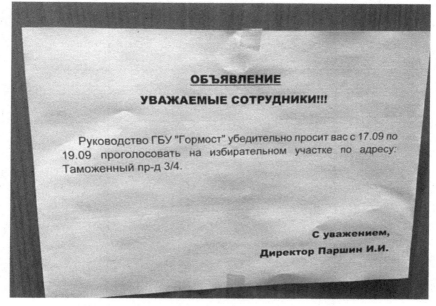

Plate 2.12

mechanism was a direct order from a superior, such that fulfilling a political task temporarily became part of the employee's job description. In these instances, a direct reference to a threat of dismissal was not mentioned, but since failure to fulfill one's duties or failure to obey directives from superiors are grounds for dismissal in most workplaces, the threat may not need to be explicit.

These orders may take the form of verbal orders, or, as KN documents clearly show, they may be written directives posted as signs, sent as emails or memoranda, or, increasingly, as text messages in workplace chats (see Plates 2.12–2.15 for examples).

In 29 percent of violation reports, employers overtly threatened dismissal if employees failed to comply. According to our interview respondents, the prospect of losing one's job is usually sufficient to induce compliance, so actual firings seem rare. However, they are not unheard of. Marina, one of our focus group participants in Zlatoust, gave the following account:

My brother was fired. When he was working at a factory, he called me one day: "Marin, they are telling us to vote for this one guy, but I want to vote

60 WORKPLACE POLITICS

Plate 2.13

for this other guy." I don't know how it happened exactly, but he ended up voting for who he wanted and they fired him. I was shocked; how could they find out? But he ended up unemployed.[28]

The circulation of such stories, even if many are rumors, likely helps reinforce compliance, especially given the severe consequences of losing one's job. Indeed, Marina reported that she no longer believed her ballot was secret after her brother told her this story.

---

[28] Focus Group Response Marina, Focus Group, Bashkirova & Partners, Chelyabinsk, Russia. October 2, 2017.

WHAT IS WORKPLACE MOBILIZATION? 61

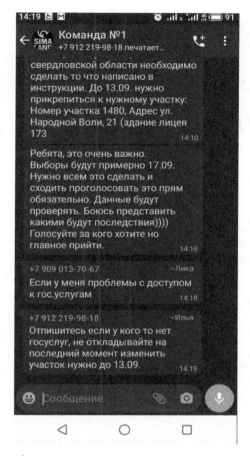

Plate 2.14

In eight percent of violation reports, employers threatened a reduction in wages or benefits. According to our interviewees and focus group respondents, the threat of withholding bonuses is fairly common. Bonuses are a significant part of total compensation in Russia, even for low-level employees. One of our focus group participants in Chelyabinsk described how it worked at his plant:

> We have an item in our contract, a points system. One of them is "participation in the life of the organization." If you don't take part in voting, they deduct points and can deduct from your bonus. And, yeah, that has happened before.

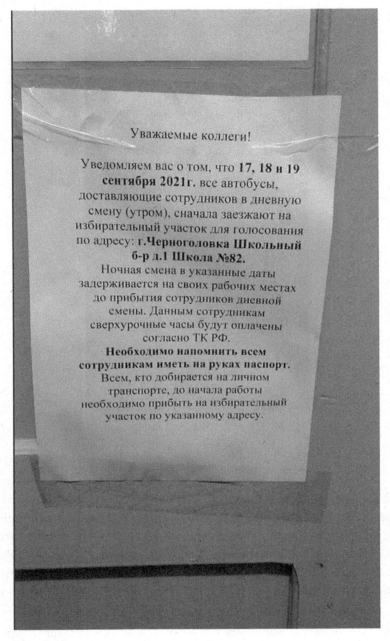

Plate 2.15

WHAT IS WORKPLACE MOBILIZATION? 63

Employers prefer to cut (or threaten to cut) bonuses rather than salary because the former is often off-book and more discretionary. This makes threats more credible.

Aside from orders, threats of firing, and wage cuts, some violation reports mentioned threats related to housing, utility provision, fines, or problems with finding another job in the future.[29] These were relatively rare. Of course, employers often avoid specifying particular sanctions, instead threatening some vague retribution. Tatyana, one of our interviewees in Satka, illustrated this while explaining how votes are mobilized in her factory:

> Management says something like: "Everyone needs to go vote." And then the line manager comes along—he brings the stick. He says something like, "I'll find something to punish you for" [if you don't vote]. And that's it. That creates this herd behavior and everyone goes to vote.[30]

Later in the interview, Tatyana reported that she once refused to vote and her supervisor wrote her up for a safety code violation.

Given the inherently hierarchical nature of the employer-employee relationship, a simple request to vote from one's boss can be perceived as potentially coercive. This is especially true if such mobilization occurs in an environment like Russia where accounts of retribution are widespread. In Satka, our focus group moderator asked respondents whether it was required to get on the bus that management provides to go to the polls. One respondent replied that it is "preferred," while a second respondent followed up, "No, but it's implicit that you should."[31]

On the whole, our data indicate that employers are much more likely to use sticks than carrots. Employers have a competitive advantage over other brokers when it comes to the effective use of such negative inducements. Indeed, this reliance on negative inducements distinguishes workplace mobilization from much of the literature on clientelist exchange, which is usually focused on positive inducements, such as vote buying. As later chapters show, this reliance on negative inducements has important implications for how we analyze this practice. In particular, the implicit and often explicit use of coercion in the workplace leads voters to view workplace

---

[29] Threats of physical violence were extremely rare (reported in only in percent of cases).

[30] Interview with Tatyana, In-depth Interview, Bashkirova & Partners, Satka, Russia. October 7, 2017.

[31] Focus Group Response, Focus Group, Bashkirova & Partners, Chelyabinsk, Russia. October 2, 2017.

64 WORKPLACE POLITICS

mobilization quite unfavorably, which, under certain conditions, limits the ability of politicians to use this tactic.

Ensuring Compliance? Monitoring and the Lack Thereof

Like other forms of clientelist exchange, workplace mobilization may confront an enforcement problem. Standard models assume that politicians enforce clientelist transactions by either punishing voters who do not vote as directed or by rewarding those who do. This requires identifying noncompliance, which the secret ballot makes difficult. Monitoring turnout is easier, but still not without challenges.

Some scholars have argued that vote brokers can monitor voter behavior by penetrating the social networks of voters (Stokes, 2005). Given the density of workplace social interactions, employers are well positioned to monitor their employees via these social networks. Sociologists have found that the workplace is a key site for the formation of "core discussion networks" (McPherson, Smith-Lovin, and Brashears, 2006). Indeed, 13 percent of respondents in our 2018 Russia survey believed their coworkers and supervisors could surmise their vote choice without being directly told.

Employers can also deploy concrete monitoring schemes. Table 2.10 codes the type of monitoring schemes (if any) reported in the 2011 KN data described earlier. Crowdsourced election violation reports are not representative of all workplace mobilization practices in Russia, but they do give a flavor of the type of monitoring techniques that employers may use. The data first show that voters are often required to obtain an absentee ballot in order to vote in the workplace or at a nearby polling station. In fact, this is one of the most common requests that Russian employers make of their employees. It is an effective mobilization technique because many Russians live far away from where they are formally registered to vote, so reminding employees to take absentee ballots is a way of ensuring that they turn out and vote. But this technique also allows employers to know where their employees are voting so that they may take attendance, a common occurrence. The KN data also contain multiple examples of employers asking their employees to provide written proof that they requested an absentee ballot.[32]

---

[32] Absentee ballots are also used in many different types of multiple-voting and ballot-stuffing schemes.

WHAT IS WORKPLACE MOBILIZATION? 65

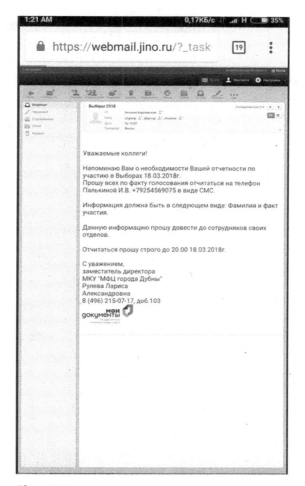

Plate 2.16

Another surprisingly common technique is simply asking employees to report back to management after they have voted. As reported in Table 2.10 our surveys found that 11 percent of employed respondents in Russia, 5 percent of those in Nigeria, and 4 percent of those in Indonesia had been asked by their employers to report back to them about turnout or vote choice. Plates 2.16–2.19 show examples of these such requests in various Russian elections. While voters could always lie, the goal of these efforts is obviously to give employees the impression that their voting behavior is or can be tracked. Employers can also ask employees to provide some evidence of electoral participation, such as stickers, calendars, magnets, or

66 WORKPLACE POLITICS

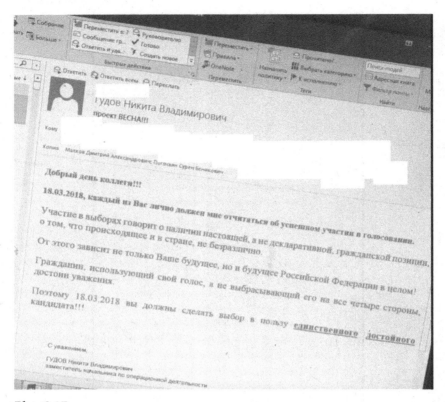

Plate 2.17

other ephemera given to voters. Some employers simply observe employee turnout directly by posting a supervisor in the precinct.

It is harder and more invasive to monitor vote choice, but examples still exist. In Russia, the most common technique was asking employees to take a photo of their ballot and send it to their supervisor. Where smartphones are increasingly ubiquitous, monitoring becomes trivial from a technical point of view.[33] But voters find this more offensive, which makes monitoring vote choice a costly endeavor that leads employers to focus on turnout mobilization.[34]

---

[33] In response, voters have been known to fake these photos by putting black string or paper in boxes on the ballot that can be removed once the photo has been taken and then vote for another candidate.
[34] Indeed, a recent review of the clientelism literature found that 82 percent of studies present no evidence of monitoring: clientelist exchange can work without extensive individual-level monitoring (Hicken and Nathan 2020).

WHAT IS WORKPLACE MOBILIZATION? 67

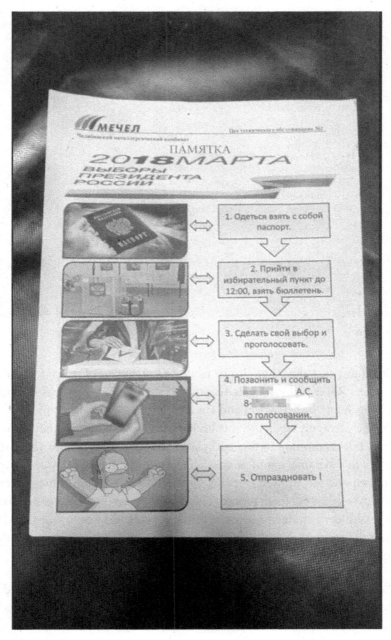

Plate 2.18

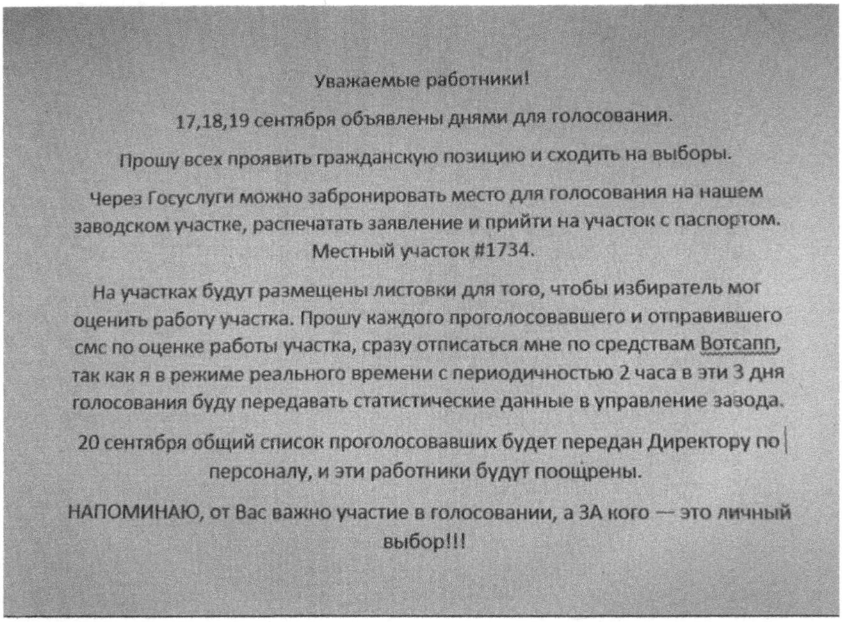

Уважаемые работники!

17,18,19 сентября объявлены днями для голосования.

Прошу всех проявить гражданскую позицию и сходить на выборы.

Через Госуслуги можно забронировать место для голосования на нашем заводском участке, распечатать заявление и прийти на участок с паспортом. Местный участок #1734.

На участках будут размещены листовки для того, чтобы избиратель мог оценить работу участка. Прошу каждого проголосовавшего и отправившего смс по оценке работы участка, сразу отписаться мне по средствам Вотсапп, так как я в режиме реального времени с периодичностью 2 часа в эти 3 дня голосования буду передавать статистические данные в управление завода.

20 сентября общий список проголосовавших будет передан Директору по персоналу, и эти работники будут поощрены.

НАПОМИНАЮ, от Вас важно участие в голосовании, а ЗА кого — это личный выбор!!!

Plate 2.19

Clientelist exchange may also be facilitated by norms of reciprocity, such that voters feel morally obligated to uphold their end of the bargain (Finan and Schechter, 2012; Lawson and Greene, 2014). Norms of reciprocity are more likely to apply when the vote broker uses positive inducements, which are much less common in the workplace. Still, our focus groups show evidence of this dynamic manifesting itself in a perhaps surprising way. Several of our respondents showed empathy for the difficult position of the supervisors who were asking them to vote. These respondents understood that their boss was under extreme pressure to turn out votes and would face sanction for not doing so. Maksim, a mid-level manager in Chelyabinsk, put it this way:

> Our director is sixty-nine and he has a yearly contract that gets renewed every year. If we vote correctly, they extend his contract. And that means stability for our organization. And for him too. Maybe it's bad. Maybe's he's tired of it already. [35]

[35] Focus Group Response Maksym, Focus Group, Bashkirova & Partners, Chelyabinsk, Russia. October 2, 2017.

But perhaps the most important point is that the perception of monitoring matters more than the reality. If voters believe they are being monitored, then they will behave as if they are being monitored, even if none occurs. In many countries, large parts of the electorate doubt the secrecy of their ballot. Afrobarometer surveys show that the share of the electorate who believe that "powerful people could find out how you voted" ranges from 11 to 47 percent of the electorate, averaging roughly 20 percent in more recent waves (Ferree and Long 2016). A 2010 survey in the United States found that 36 percent of respondents believed that it would either be "not difficult at all" or "not too difficult" for "politicians, union officials or the people you work for to find out who you voted for, even if you told no one" (Gerber et al., 2013, 5). Recent research in Ghana and the Philippines has even found that some vote brokers try to convince voters that their ballots are not secret (Ferree and Long, 2016; Cruz, 2019). As Hicken and Nathan (2020, 286) suggest, "Using intimidation to manipulate perceived ballot secrecy may be much cheaper than actually monitoring votes." In Russia, many of our respondents were specifically concerned their employer might be able to monitor voting behavior. In the 2016 Russian election study, 24 percent of respondents said that it would be easy or relatively easy for their employer to find out if they voted.

Uncertainty about whether employers can monitor voting behavior should increase compliance, particularly where the costs of noncompliance are high. Job loss, decreases in benefits, and cuts in salary would be

Table 2.10 Monitoring Schemes Employed in Workplace Mobilization Violation Reports

Scheme	Number	%
Absentee Ballot Scheme	325	23.4
No Monitoring Mentioned	278	20.0
Asking Employee to Report	210	15.1
Supervisor Posted at Polling Place	184	13.2
Photo Verification	60	4.3
Passport Details	42	3.0
Other/Unspecified Monitoring	291	20.1

Source: Golos Karta Narusheniya. Election Violation Reports catalogued during the 2011 State Duma election campaign. The strategies are not mutually exclusive.

70 WORKPLACE POLITICS

devastating to many voters. In our interviews and focus groups, we asked respondents why they and their colleagues complied with mobilization requests. Many, such as Mariya in Chelyabinsk, pointed to fear of the worst, even when the worst wasn't explicitly threatened:

> **Moderator:** Do I understand correctly that there haven't been instances when management has punished someone for not voting? So why do people comply then?
>
> **Mariya:** Right now we are having the most atrocious layoffs. And, just think, if there are two people and one of them is creating problems for management, that is the one they will fire. And people have their own problems. Some people are single parents.[36]

Or consider how Tatyana in Satka viewed her situation:

> **Moderator:** I'm simply trying to understand. Do you want to vote because management asks you to or do you vote because they tell you there will be negative consequences if you don't?
>
> **Respondent:** Well, they hint at it.
>
> **Moderator:** Tell me what they say.
>
> **Respondent:** Well, they say that you have to fulfill your duty as a citizen. They always say that you are obliged to do it.
>
> **Moderator:** And what comes to mind, if you decided not to vote after all?
>
> **Respondent:** Maybe I would lose my bonus, or something else, how could we know?
>
> **Moderator:** So they don't specifically say what would happen [if you don't vote]?
>
> **Respondent:** No.
>
> **Moderator:** You assume something would happen?
>
> **Respondent:** We can imagine it ourselves.[37]

In our previous research, we have found that forms of active monitoring— such as asking employees to report back about turnout—are less common in settings where there is high job insecurity and the threat of job dismissal is so frightening (Frye, Reuter, and Szakonyi, 2019). Survey data and election violation reports both indicate that active monitoring was less common in

[36] Focus Group Response Mariya, Focus Group, Bashkirova & Partners, Chelyabinsk, Russia. October 2, 2017.

[37] Interview with Tatyana, In-depth Interview, Bashkirova & Partners, Satka, Russia. October 7, 2017.

single-company towns, where labor markets are slack and the consequences of job loss are severe. Thus, while active monitoring does occur in the workplace, it does not seem to be a necessary condition for effective workplace mobilization.

Workplace Mobilization Is Deeply Unpopular

We have shown that workplace mobilization is common and often coercive. We conclude this chapter by demonstrating that it is also deeply unpopular. This is certainly true of those who experience it. Most of our interview and focus group respondents in Russia expressed discomfort at the politicization of the workplace, even those who support the authorities. When asked about the influence of workplace mobilization on employee morale, one focus group member in Chelyabinsk responded, "Of course, it [mobilizing] shouldn't be done this way. Everyone should feel and decide for themselves—but life forces us to do otherwise."[38] Another noted that forced mobilization to vote was worse than *subbotniks*—the tradition carried over from Soviet times whereby workers volunteer on a day off for public service: "At least with *subbotniks*, they [management] do not force, they suggest… and with elections they force us, they mention dismissals, bonuses, job losses, and people do not like this."[39]

Respondents also distinguished between mobilization by employers and by party activists. While they opposed the former, they were not opposed to political mobilization outside of work by parties. When asked about mobilization by their employer, one respondent from Zlatoust remarked, "It is not right. A person should decide for themselves—to go vote or not. And even more they should decide for whom to vote." When asked how they felt about party mobilization outside of work, this respondent noted, "Well, it's their job, these people work during elections, there is nothing wrong with that."[40]

To probe this question more systematically, we asked our survey respondents who experienced workplace mobilization in Turkey a series of questions about their feelings toward these episodes. Specifically, we asked, "How comfortable or uncomfortable are you with the contact that you had with

[38] Focus Group Response Oksana, Focus Group, Bashkirova & Partners, Chelyabinsk, Russia. October 3, 2017.
[39] Interview with Ekaterina, In-depth Interview, Bashkirova & Partners, Zlatoust, Russia. October 5, 2017.
[40] Interview with Ekaterina, In-depth Interview, Bashkirova & Partners, Zlatoust, Russia. October 5, 2017.

72   WORKPLACE POLITICS

your manager or supervisor about politics? Please answer on a scale of 1–5, where 1 equals very uncomfortable and 5 equals very comfortable."

Respondents reported significant discomfort, though the extent depended on the type of mobilizational strategy. On one end, 33 percent of respondents said that it made them very or somewhat uncomfortable when their boss simply talked about politics. But most respondents (52 percent) said the experience made them indifferent, and just 15 percent said that listening to their boss discuss politics made them feel somewhat or very comfortable.

More explicit requests, however, provoked much more discomfort. Of those asked to turn out to vote by their employer in Turkey, 57 percent said that the interaction made them very uncomfortable or somewhat uncomfortable, and just 20 percent said that it made them feel somewhat comfortable or very comfortable. Sixty-one percent of respondents whose employer asked them to vote for a specific candidate said that the request made them uncomfortable, and just 13 percent said that it made them feel comfortable. The most aggressive forms of mobilization such as vote buying and intimidation induce discomfort in overwhelming majorities. Figure 2.1 reports responses across a range of mobilization tactics.

These data suggest that voters who experience workplace mobilization disapprove of it, but what about the general public? In our nationally representative surveys of the mass public in five countries, we asked respondents,

> Some people believe it is the civic duty of employers to encourage their employees to participate in civic and political life. Others think that this is unethical. What do you think about this? How acceptable are the following types of behavior on a scale of 1–4 where 1 equals completely unacceptable and 4 equals completely acceptable?

We use a double-sided question to remind respondents of the possible arguments on each side of the debate. We then included a list of three common forms of workplace mobilization, asking whether it was acceptable for employers (1) to share political information opinions about the election in the workplace, (2) to encourage employees to turn out and vote, and (3) to encourage employees to vote for a particular candidate. Note that these three questions do not invoke more coercive methods of voter mobilization, which would likely be even less popular. Figure 2.2 plots the responses across the five countries, while collapsing the 4-point scale into a binary "approval rating" for any responses of 3 or 4 on that scale.

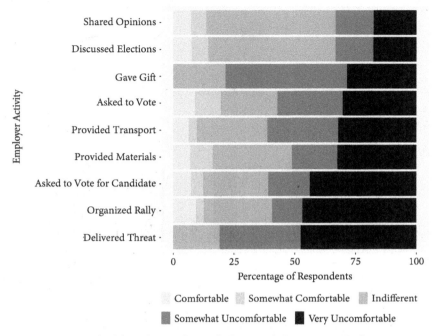

Figure 2.1 Level of Comfort with Workplace Mobilization in Turkey, 2015

Note: The figure shows the level of comfort that respondents who experienced various forms of workplace mobilization (on y-axis) felt toward the practice. Each row depicts the percentage of respondents according to each of the five levels of comfort depicted in the legend.

In all countries, only a small minority of respondents approve of the most direct forms of workplace mobilization. Most importantly, overwhelming majorities disapprove of employers asking their employees to vote for specific candidates. In Argentina, Turkey, and Russia, less than 15 percent of respondents approved of employers asking their employees to vote for a specific candidate. In Nigeria this figure was just under 30 percent. Across diverse settings, respondents opposed direct partisan appeals by employers to get their employees to support their political positions.

Voters also disapprove of employers asking their employees to turn out to vote. In Argentina and Turkey, only 30 percent of respondents approved of this tactic, with slightly higher numbers for the other three countries.[41] This question is somewhat difficult to interpret in some countries because employees may intuit the employer's candidate of choice, which makes an

---

[41] Respondents to the survey in Russia were also turned off by egregious forms of electoral subversion by party activists such as encouraging multiple forms of voting or using food or alcohol to increase turnout. However, 40 percent thought it was acceptable for party activists to hand out food packets to pensioners.

74 WORKPLACE POLITICS

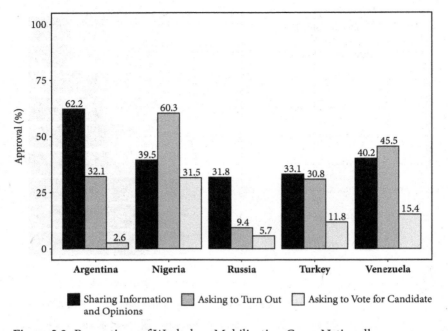

Figure 2.2 Perceptions of Workplace Mobilization Cross-Nationally
Note: This figure plots the percentage of respondents in each country survey that approved of each of the three mobilization activities carried out by employers in the workplace.

employer's explicit appeals to vote for a particular candidate unnecessary. In these cases, respondents may hear an employer's appeal to vote as an appeal to vote for a specific candidate.

Respondents expressed fewer reservations about employers communicating political information and opinions in the workplace, although here too the results are mixed. In Nigeria, Turkey, and Venezuela, majorities disapprove of this practice, while more than one-third of respondents do so in Argentina and Russia. Even this seemingly benign form of political activity is frowned upon in a broad array of political settings by large segments of the population.

Finally, we posed a similar set of question to nine hundred employed respondents in the United States after the 2020 election in an online survey conducted by YouGov. Eighty-two percent of respondents thought it was unacceptable for their employer to ask them to vote for a particular candidate, and 85 percent considered it unacceptable for the employer to ask them to attend a compulsory meeting. Both activities are legal in the United States, and both are fairly common, but employees frown upon these tactics.[42] At the same time, just 20 percent of respondents considered it inappropriate for employers to ask them to turn out to vote. Respondents in the United States drew a much sharper distinction between nonpartisan get-out-the-vote campaigns and more partisan forms of mobilization than do the respondents in other countries in our sample.[43]

Opposition to these forms of workplace mobilization does not appear to reflect partisan leanings. Across all countries in our sample, supporters of different political parties opposed workplace mobilization to statistically indistinguishable degrees. These similarities held, for example, across Democrats, Republicans, and independents in the United States; Peronists and non-Peronists in Argentina; and AKP versus opposition voters in Turkey.

Some evidence from Russia also suggests that the unpopularity of workplace mobilization is reflected in official voting patterns. Poltoratskaya (2024) examines the universe of large firms— those most likely to mobilize their workers—and finds that the closer a large firm is to a polling place, the higher the official reported turnout. At the same time, this higher turnout is in part due to an increase in protest votes for opposition parties, which suggests that workplace mobilization may induce some backlash.

Across a range of diverse political and economic settings, broad segments of the public disapprove of employers mobilizing their employees in the workplace. Employees are especially opposed to any employer efforts to influence their vote, particularly when such efforts involve intimidation or threats, but in most settings they are also opposed to seemingly more innocuous attempts at mobilization, such as distributing election materials in the workplace.[44]

---

[42] In surveys from 2015, Hertel-Fernandez finds that one in four employed voters have experienced some encouragement to turn out to vote from their employer, and roughly one in two employers have engaged in some form of political mobilization in the workplace (Hertel-Fernandez, 2016). In our online surveys from 2020 and 2021 we found higher rates of workplace mobilization, with roughly one in two employed respondents reporting that they had experienced some form of workplace mobilization. We also found that employees were as likely to be mobilized on behalf of Democrats as of Republicans in 2018 and 2020. This finding departs from Hertel-Fernandez's work showing that employers mobilized on behalf of Republicans much more frequently. This change may reflect the Democratic Party's slower response to changes introduced in the *Citizens United* decision in the Supreme Court in 2010.

[43] The greater support for nonpartisan get-out-the-vote efforts may be due to the greater legal protections afforded workers in the United States relative to the other countries in our sample.

[44] Hertel-Fernandez (2017, 246–247) also finds that large majorities in the United States oppose various forms of workplace mobilization. More than three-quarters of respondents thought that it should be illegal for employers to hire or fire employees for supporting particular issues or particular candidates. Strong majorities also believed that employers should be barred from asking rank-and-file workers to support particular candidates (64 percent) and from asking employees to support bills in Congress or state governments (59 percent). In Hertel-Fernandez's study, partisan differences were also negligible, as Democrats and Republicans opposed these measures in equal numbers.

76 WORKPLACE POLITICS

This distinguishes workplace mobilization from other mobilizational strategies, which most voters either shrug at (in the case of simple partisan get-out-the-vote efforts) or are sometimes ambivalent about (in the case of vote buying). As we explore in later chapters, voter disdain for workplace mobilization places limits on its widespread use and also leads to novel hypotheses about the types of settings where it occurs.

Data Validity and Social Desirability Bias

Studying workplace mobilization with survey data presents special challenges. Respondents may be reluctant to answer questions about workplace mobilization or may provide misleading answers due to fear that revealing their opinion might bring negative repercussions. This may be especially true for the more coercive forms of mobilization, such as when threats are used to get voters to the polls, and in settings where political freedoms are limited. To the extent that this occurs in our surveys, it would suggest that the practice is even more common than our descriptive findings suggest and it would bias against finding most of the results that we present in subsequent chapters.

But this concern should also be put in perspective. Some forms of workplace mobilization—such as the manager holding a political rally in the workplace, endorsing a candidate, asking employees to vote, or distributing campaign materials—are public matters that should give respondents some confidence that they can answer truthfully. In addition, being mobilized by your employer differs from vote buying in important ways that should make respondents more willing to respond honestly. In most cases, being mobilized by one's employer is not an illegal activity, as is the case with selling one's vote. Because respondents do not have to implicate themselves in an illegal act by admitting their experience with workplace mobilization, they have fewer incentives to dissemble than with other forms of electoral subversion, such as vote buying. In addition, in some countries, like Russia and Ukraine, workplace mobilization is often discussed in the media.

Survey research in Russia conducted during our study indicates that preference falsification may be less common than often perceived (Rosenfeld, 2023; Frye et al., 2017). For example, Frye et al. (2017) find little evidence that voters dissemble when asked the politically sensitive question of whether they approve of President Putin's job as president. Survey research on equally sensitive topics using data from Russia have

WHAT IS WORKPLACE MOBILIZATION? 77

Table 2.11 Survey Question Missingness Rates (%)

Survey	2016	2018
Education	0.64	0
Economic Situation	2.89	0.6
Income	40.35	61.4
Level of Happiness	5.31	
Party: Positive Inducement	3.22	
Party: Negative Inducement	3.38	
Party: Asked to Vote	2.57	
Party: Asked to Vote for Candidate	2.73	
Putin Approval	0.8	1.8
United Russia Support	2.25	
Level of Social Trust	4.98	
Interest in Elections	6.91	
View of Electoral Integrity	11.9	12.6
Country Moving in Right Direction	22.83	15.6
Workplace: Discussed Election	3.54	2.4
Workplace: Distributed Materials	3.05	2.4
Workplace: Encouraged to Attend Rally	3.38	2.4
Workplace: Provided Transport	4.18	2
Workplace: Asked to Vote	3.54	2.2
Workplace: Positive Inducement	2.57	1.6
Workplace: Negative Inducement	2.89	2.2

This table shows the percentage (%) of missing responses for various economic, political, and mobilization questions on the 2016 and 2018 Russian Population Surveys. Sample is subset to only employed workers. Blank means question was not asked. Zero means that no one refused to answer the question.

appeared in the *American Political Science Review*, *American Journal of Political Science*, *American Economic Review*, and *American Journal of Sociology* in recent years. Indeed, recent work has shown that respondent self-censorship is surprisingly low in many authoritarian countries, particularly those with national executive elections (Shen and Truex, 2021).

One way to gauge self-censorship is through survey nonresponse rates (Shen and Truex, 2021). In order to examine this in the context of workplace mobilization, we calculate the percentage of respondents who refused to answer various questions related to politics and electoral mobilization on the 2016 and 2018 Russian postelection surveys. We choose these two surveys because of the similarities in questions asked about both party and workplace mobilization. The sample is subset to only employed workers, for whom workplace mobilization is relevant.

78 WORKPLACE POLITICS

There is little evidence that respondents are particularly wary of answering questions about workplace mobilization. As Table 2.11 shows, only 2 to 4 percent of workers refused to answer either affirmatively or negatively about different activities taking place in the workplace. Importantly, there is only slight variation in nonresponse rates for more sensitive questions, such as the use of positive (vote buying) or negative (threats) inducements. We also see that nonresponse rates about workplace mobilization are broadly comparable to those observed when respondents are asked about their contact with party activists. In Russia, respondents seem most hesitant to share information about their income, and rarely appear hesitant talking about their political views and experiences during the period under study.

Thus, most of the analyses that we run in this book use direct questions since they are easier to analyze in a multivariate framework. But we also use indirect question techniques, such as the list experiment when analyzing the most coercive forms of workplace mobilization, in order to help account for these potential biases.

Conclusion

In this chapter, we have used a variety of data sources to show that workplace mobilization is common, takes a variety of forms, is frequently coercive, and is widely disdained by voters. As we shall see, these empirical regularities are critical to identifying the conditions under which politicians and employers use workplace mobilization. But before turning to those questions the next chapter explores a fundamental question that was left unanswered in this chapter: is workplace mobilization effective at actually getting voters to the polls?

3

Is Workplace Mobilization Effective?

Come election time, politicians can choose to mobilize voters via a number of intermediaries. Why would a politician choose one broker over another? And, in particular, why would a politician choose to rely on employers to mobilize votes? Much of this book is taken up with answering these questions. But we begin by addressing the fundamental question of whether workplace mobilization is effective. Politicians are likely to choose vote brokers who can mobilize large numbers of votes at relatively low cost. Employers, we argue, make attractive vote brokers precisely because they are highly effective at this task. In many settings, employers' leverage over employees gives them a powerful stick to influence and induce certain political decisions, including that of whether to turn out and vote.

In this chapter we combine focus group data, observational survey data, and framing experiments to argue that mobilization by employers increases voter turnout and therefore can help politicians win elections. Importantly, we find that workplace mobilization is correlated with higher turnout in a range of settings. And using survey experiments in Russia and Venezuela, we find that the average voter is more likely to respond to turnout appeals from employers than they are to appeals from party activists. In subsequent chapters, we develop a series of theoretical arguments to explain why politicians choose specific types of firms to mobilize and why employers choose specific types of workers to mobilize, but here we focus on demonstrating the effectiveness of employers at getting voters to the polls.

Why Are Employers Effective Vote Brokers?

To understand why employers are often effective brokers, it is helpful to analyze workplace mobilization as a form of clientelist exchange. Scholars have developed different theories of what makes clientelism work. The traditional view is that successful clientelism results from an instrumental exchange (Kitschelt and Wilkinson, 2007; Scott, 1972; Stokes, 2005).

Workplace Politics. Timothy Frye, Ora John Reuter, and David Szakonyi, Oxford University Press.
© Oxford University Press (2025). DOI: 10.1093/9780197802045.003.0003

80 WORKPLACE POLITICS

Brokers induce voter compliance through the conditional use of future rewards and punishments (Calvo and Murillo, 2013; Gingerich and Medina, 2013; Mares, 2015; Rueda, 2017). By exploiting voters' own self-interest, brokers convince voters to engage in political behavior that they might otherwise not undertake. A voter's behavior is then contingent on the expectation of future rewards or punishments. As we argue here, different types of brokers are likely to vary significantly in the extent to which they are able to motivate such instrumental compliance.

An alternative view posits that brokers leverage voters' feelings of intrinsic reciprocity or moral obligation (Finan and Schechter, 2012; Ravanilla, Haim, and Hicken, 2022). Some scholars argue that vote buying is most effective at mobilizing votes when targeted individuals derive pleasure from helping those politicians or brokers who offered them material compensation. Vote buying becomes self-enforcing when clients feel a strong obligation to return favors to their patrons (Lawson and Greene, 2014). A related view is that vote-buying conveys information about candidates. In this view, politicians offer handouts to inform voters about their ability to deliver particularistic services after the election (Keefer and Vlaicu, 2008; Kramon, 2016). The goal may not be to mobilize individual votes, but instead to foster perceptions of competence and trustworthiness.

Both informational and reciprocity-based theories have produced important insights, but they are less useful in helping us understand differences across classes of brokers. All brokers, it would seem, might use clientelism to convey information about politicians, and intrinsic reciprocity is a characteristic that is likely to vary more across clients (or societies) than across patrons. In addition, both informational and reciprocity-based theories of clientelism struggle to explain the use of negative inducements such as intimidation or threats to withdraw benefits, which are an important component of clientelist mobilization in much of the world. As such, we treat workplace mobilization as a form of political clientelism that is rooted in instrumental exchange between brokers and voters.

To enforce instrumental exchange, brokers must be well positioned to credibly offer or threaten consequential inducements. Where does this leverage come from? We argue that what matters most in determining leverage is the extent to which clients are structurally dependent on patrons for some benefit—economic, political, or social—that is important to their well-being.

The more a client has to depend on a patron, the more likely a "captive electoral base" will emerge (Holland and Palmer-Rubin, 2015). Clients that rely heavily on brokers have less autonomy to defect from clientelist bargains (Kramon, 2016; Medina and Stokes, 2007). Resisting the entreaties of clientelist exchange often requires outside options: voters must have other ways to secure the benefits that brokers provide, whether they be jobs, income, or access to state services. Without these other avenues, brokers occupy a monopolistic position in meting out rewards and punishments, resulting in high levels of voter compliance. This reading of dependence draws on a number of older definitions of clientelism that assume some degree of social, economic, or political hierarchy between patrons and clients (Lemarchand, 1972; Scott, 1972). Such asymmetries have played a less prominent role in some recent treatments of clientelism (Stokes, 2011), but we argue that this consideration of hierarchy is crucial for understanding the origins of leverage.

Brokers who command consequential sources of leverage over clients will be more effective at enforcing clientelist exchange. Some types of brokers have structural advantages that give them significant leverage over clients. Landlords, for example, can credibly threaten to evict (Scott, 1972). Tribal leaders, by virtue of their social standing, can credibly threaten meaningful social sanction (Lemarchand, 1972). Local strongmen and gangs can credibly threaten physical coercion (Acemoglu, Robinson, and Santos, 2013; Sidel, 1999). Low-level government officials can threaten withdrawal of social benefits (Mares and Young, 2019).

Employers—our focus—wield consequential levers of influence over their employees in most conceivable settings. They can offer significant positive inducements such as increases in wages or benefits. But their real advantage is in the size of the negative inducements they can deploy. Employers can withhold wages, trim benefits, or even fire workers. These punishments become particularly painful when workers have few other outside options for finding employment.[1]

Party activists, by contrast, usually lack such sticks. In most cases, they cannot credibly threaten sanctions that would approach the magnitude of job loss. Moreover, the modest positive inducements that they more

---

[1] In this way, our work is related to the literature on the economics of coercion (see, for example, Acemoglu and Wolitzky, 2011; Chwe, 1990), To be sure there are vast differences between workplace mobilization and studies of coercive labor practices, such as slavery, One common link, however, is that employers have the option of not only pay but also coercion to motivate their workers.

commonly offer also pale in comparison to the benefit of job security. Activists have to invest significant resources to gain anything approaching the degree of leverage that employers have by virtue of their own position. Stokes (2011) describes British parties in the nineteenth century collecting information on voters' debts, crimes, and infidelities to use as leverage in their individual leverage to get citizens to the polls

Employers also have a comparative advantage in making their inducements credible. Bosses are often engaged in repeated, long-term interactions with their employees. Workers know that they will have to interact with their bosses in the future and that they cannot avoid punishment by evading or ignoring their employers. Such iteration instills an understanding that defiance of their employers' wishes could result in punishment or exclusion from future benefit streams (Hicken, 2011; Stokes, 2005). Enforcing the clientelist bargain is by no means costless for employers, who may experience productivity or reputational consequences from punishing workers based on their political activity. Rather, we argue that it is easier to enforce these bargains in the workplace than in other settings. Voters are unlikely to find sizable threats by party activists to be very credible—and if they encounter the activist only infrequently, promises of future benefits will ring hollow.

Employers are also well positioned to solve the monitoring problems that sometimes stymie clientelist exchange. Under the secret ballot, politicians may struggle to determine whether voters are casting their ballots as directed. Turnout-based clientelism makes this an easier problem to solve, since monitoring turnout is easier than monitoring vote choice (Nichter, 2008). But monitoring turnout is not costless. Vote brokers still need to gather information on whether voters turned out. At the very least, they need to imply to their clients that this information is being gathered.

Even though monitoring is not strictly necessary for clientelism to function, the ability to monitor clients has been shown to increase the effectiveness of clientelism (Larreguy, Marshall, and Querubin, 2016; Stokes, 2005). Where does monitoring capacity come from? First, close proximity between brokers and clients improves the amount and quality of information used to track client political behavior (Brady, Schlozman, and Verba, 1995; Hicken, 2011). Dense social networks transmit political information and cues as well as facilitate group monitoring (Cruz, Keefer, and Labonne, 2016; Cruz, Labonne, and Querubin, 2017). Second, repeated interactions help decrease

IS WORKPLACE MOBILIZATION EFFECTIVE? 83

monitoring and enforcement costs. When clientelist exchanges take place as a one-shot game, brokers lose the ability to observe which voters comply with their end of the bargain. Hicken (2011) argues that repeated interactions help brokers learn what works over time with different sets of voters, and then brokers can calibrate the size of offers that need to be made.

Socially embedded brokers, such as neighborhood and civil society leaders, have advantages on this dimension. But since many people's social networks are intertwined with their workplace, employers share similar advantages. Sociologists identify the workplace as a key site for the formation of "core discussion networks" (McPherson, Smith-Lovin, and Brashears, 2006). Coworkers can be confidants for some employed voters. Indeed, evidence from a March 2018 postelection survey in Russia confirms this: 13 percent of respondents believed their coworkers and supervisors could surmise their vote choice without being directly told.[2] As noted earlier, repeated interactions facilitate employers' ability to gather detailed information on their employees' political behavior. By interacting on a near-daily basis regardless of electoral cycles, employers have more opportunities to learn whether their employees vote in elections, attend political rallies, or contribute to campaigns.

Stokes (2005) has argued that grassroots parties with tentaclelike organizations that penetrate the social networks of voters are able to successfully monitor voter behavior. In such settings, parties may have monitoring capacity that matches that of employers. But as an empirical matter, such organizations are often missing in much of the developing world (Hale, 2005; Van de Walle, 2007; Mainwaring, 1999). Political leaders often do not prioritize long-term party development, preferring to activate brokers and networks only during preelection periods. After the polls close, party cells often lay dormant. The number of full-time activists capable of gathering information and sustaining interactions with voters is minimal. Given the built-in social networks that exist in the workplace, employers may be even better placed to monitor voters in much of the developing world.

Thus, to summarize, we argue that employers have structural advantages that give them significant leverage over a typical employed voter. When it

---

[2] In contrast, nearly 60 percent of respondents believed their family members could guess who they voted for, while just under 30 percent thought their close friends and 9 percent thought their neighbors could do so.

84 WORKPLACE POLITICS

comes to monitoring, however, their relative advantages depend more on contextual factors, but in most settings, their monitoring capacity is likely greater than that of parties.[3]

Observational Evidence That Workplace Mobilization Is Effective

In the following sections we examine evidence of workplace mobilization's effectiveness. Our primary focus is on how workplace mobilization affects turnout. Though much of the literature on clientelism focuses on attempts to influence vote choice, recent work shows that using selective incentives to induce turnout is very common (Nichter and Palmer-Rubin, 2015; Gans Morse, Mazzuca, and Nichter, 2014; Nichter, 2008). Turnout is much easier to monitor than is vote choice, and as Chapter 2 demonstrated, voters find exhortations to vote for a particular candidate particularly distasteful. Given this, turnout appeals by employers are more common than are appeals to vote for a particular candidate. As the previous chapter showed, employed respondents in a range of countries are far more likely to report being asked to vote by their employer than they are to be asked to vote for a particular party. Our focus group participants in Russia suggested that their employers did not need to specify which party they should vote for; it was tacitly understood.

Sometimes vote choice can be monitored, and employers are well positioned to do this, but employers in the countries we study appear more often to simply mobilize turnout without expending effort on post-hoc monitoring of vote choice. As we discussed in Chapter 2, the fear of losing one's job combined with concerns about ballot secrecy appears to motivate worker compliance in the absence of intrusive monitoring. Even if the likelihood of discovery is low, the consequences of job loss can be so severe that voters would not risk voting their conscience, especially if their preferences are weak. And, of course, when workers and politicians are politically aligned, then monitoring is unnecessary and there is no risk to mobilizing turnout. If politicians and employers can accurately predict

---

[3] Politicians face a trade-off in relying on parties that can mobilize all voters with weaker tools and employers who can mobilize employees with stronger tools. Whether parties or employers are more effective in turning out voters in the aggregate will depend on contextual factors, such as the share of the population that is employed. We show here that employers are relatively more effective than other brokers in mobilizing a typical voter, conditional on being employed.

how workers will vote, then mobilizing loyal voters to turn out is clearly advantageous.

Similarly, in settings where the mobilizing party enjoys majority support, then mobilizing turnout will generally be advantageous. In the autocracies we study, turnout is also valued in its own right because it helps to demonstrate the regime's strength and legitimacy.[4] Thus, mobilizing turnout can be a rational political strategy under a range of conditions.

Determining the effectiveness of workplace mobilization is an empirical challenge. But our focus groups and surveys are able to shed some light on the question. To start, our focus groups and the electoral violation data from Russia both indicate that one of the most common techniques used by employers in that country is to order employees to vote. This simple fact is prima facie evidence of workplace mobilization's effectiveness. While some employees may disobey a direct order from their superior, this is likely rare. To the extent that employers can simply mandate that their employees vote, this is an effective strategy for generating votes.

A number of our interview and focus group respondents were clear that fear of sanction motivated compliance. When asked whether employees feared losing their jobs or bonuses for not following vote orders, focus group participants agreed that this was the underlying concern. As Tamara, one of our focus group participants in Satka, put it, "Everyone goes if management asks. It's better to go. It's better not to risk it."[5] Or consider this frank exchange from one of our interviews in Satka:

MODERATOR: What do you think: why do some people vote as management asks, but others don't?

TATYANA: We all do what we're asked.

MODERATOR: Why?

TATYANA: Well, let's start with the fact that nobody is eager to lose their job and who knows what that [losing one's job] might result in? No one knows.

MODERATOR: So you all go?

TATYANA: Yes, we all go.[6]

---

[4] This can also be true in authoritarian regimes with low voter turnout. In Russia, for example, the regime's electoral strategy hinges on depoliticizing the public sphere. Then, at election time, it seeks to mobilize just enough turnout to legitimate the outcome. The mobilization of workers is essential to this strategy.

[5] Focus Group Response Tamara, Focus Group, Bashkiriova. & Partners, Satka, Russia. October 6, 2017.

[6] Interview with Tatyana, In-depth Interview, Bashkirova & Partners, Satka, Russia. October 7, 2017.

86 WORKPLACE POLITICS

Another way of evaluating workplace mobilization's effectiveness is to examine whether those who report being mobilized are more likely than the average voter to turn out to vote. Hertel-Fernandez (2018) finds such an association in the United States. In Table 3.1, we present regression analyses that examine this correlation in Russia (2014), Venezuela (2015), Nigeria (2015), Turkey (2015) and Ukraine (2012). In these models (3.1), the dependent variable is equal to 1 if the respondent reported turning out and zero otherwise. The key independent variable is equal to 1 if the respondent reported that their employer asked them to turnout, and 0 otherwise. The models also control for basic demographic variables, the employment status of the respondent, and whether the respondent worked in the public sector (a powerful determinant of workplace mobilization).

In four of these five countries, workplace mobilization is positively correlated with reported turnout and the relationship is statistically significant. In Turkey, the absence of an effect is largely due to a ceiling effect. Baseline reported turnout (over 90 percent) is already very high in the survey, making it difficult to detect marginal effects. The substantive effect sizes vary in the other four surveys, but all are substantial.[7] In Ukraine, which has the largest effect size, being asked by an employer to turn out is associated with a seventeen-percentage-point increase in the probability of having reported voting. The corresponding figure in Russia is 14 percent; in Nigeria, 9 percent; and in Venezuela, 8 percent.

In Russia and Venezuela, we can conduct the same exercise and use the same models to test the effectiveness of other types of brokers. Table 3.2 shows these results. Although being mobilized by a party activist is also positively correlated with turnout, the magnitude of the effect is actually slightly smaller than it is for employers. These differences should not be overinterpreted as Wald tests do not indicate that the differences between the coefficients are statistically significant. But the models suggest, at a minimum, that employers are just as effective as party activists when it comes to mobilizing voters. On the other hand, government officials and neighborhood leaders do not appear to have the same type of ability to get voters to the polls in these settings.

Of course, studying the effectiveness of workplace mobilization in this fashion has significant drawbacks. Mobilizational appeals are not randomly

---

[7] Note that the substantive effect sizes on the control variables should not be compared across models, due to the different scales used in different surveys.

Table 3.1 Workplace Mobilization and Turnout

	Russia		Venezuela		Nigeria		Ukraine		Turkey	
	(1)	(2)	(3)	(4)	(5)	(6)	(7)	(8)	(9)	(10)
Employer Asked to Vote	0.139**	0.118**	0.087**	0.089*	0.104***	0.101***	0.175***	0.158**	0.049	0.050
	(0.051)	(0.054)	(0.037)	(0.041)	(0.028)	(0.028)	(0.060)	(0.057)	(0.063)	(0.060)
Economic Status	0.009	0.013	0.009	0.009	−0.003	−0.003	0.022*	0.022*	0.013	0.013
	(0.013)	(0.013)	(0.012)	(0.012)	(0.004)	(0.003)	(0.012)	(0.012)	(0.011)	(0.011)
Male	−0.058***	−0.041*	−0.019	−0.020	0.049***	0.050***	0.005	0.013	0.008	0.007
	(0.019)	(0.021)	(0.041)	(0.041)	(0.018)	(0.018)	(0.019)	(0.018)	(0.012)	(0.012)
Age (log)	0.282***	0.273***	0.139*	0.140*	0.165***	0.159***	0.306***	0.303***	0.158***	0.163***
	(0.031)	(0.032)	(0.067)	(0.064)	(0.033)	(0.033)	(0.030)	(0.030)	(0.022)	(0.024)
Education	0.017*	0.015*	0.032*	0.033*	0.0003	−0.001	0.012*	0.010	−0.014*	−0.011
	(0.009)	(0.008)	(0.016)	(0.015)	(0.007)	(0.007)	(0.006)	(0.007)	(0.007)	(0.008)
Employed	0.047**	0.003	−0.029	−0.027	−0.045**	−0.060***	−0.004	−0.031	0.038	0.043
	(0.017)	(0.018)	(0.056)	(0.053)	(0.018)	(0.022)	(0.021)	(0.025)	(0.022)	(0.025)
Public Sector Employee		0.134***		−0.006		0.041		0.089**		−0.045
		(0.021)		(0.027)		(0.025)		(0.043)		(0.045)
R^2	0.082	0.091	0.056	0.056	0.112	0.113	0.102	0.105	0.067	0.068
Observations	3,956	3,942	1,220	1,220	2,795	2,795	1,958	1,952	1,285	1,285
Region Fixed Effects	✓	✓	✓	✓	✓	✓	✓	✓	✓	✓

***$p<0.01$, **$p<0.05$, *$p<0.1$ This table analyzes the factors affecting whether respondents voted in recent national elections. The wording for the Economic Situation and Education variables differ slightly across surveys, and point estimates cannot be directly compared. All models use OLS and clustered standard errors on region.

Table 3.2 Other Brokers and Turnout

	Russia			Venezuela			
	(1)	(2)	(3)	(4)	(5)	(6)	(7)
Party Broker Asked to Vote	0.114***		0.095**	0.050			0.067**
	(0.039)		(0.036)	(0.033)			(0.024)
Government Official Asked to Vote		0.118	0.085				
		(0.085)	(0.081)				
Neighborhood Leader Asked to Vote					−0.019		−0.036
					(0.038)		(0.035)
Communal Council Asked to Vote						−0.011	−0.031
						(0.033)	(0.034)
Employer Asked to Vote			0.123**				0.083*
			(0.045)				(0.037)
Economic Status	0.009	0.008	0.009	0.008	0.008	0.009	0.008
	(0.014)	(0.013)	(0.013)	(0.012)	(0.012)	(0.012)	(0.012)
Male	−0.057***	−0.058***	−0.056***	−0.020	−0.015	−0.019	−0.019
	(0.019)	(0.019)	(0.019)	(0.040)	(0.039)	(0.041)	(0.039)
Age (log)	0.282***	0.284***	0.282***	0.136*	0.131*	0.135*	0.134*
	(0.032)	(0.031)	(0.031)	(0.068)	(0.068)	(0.068)	(0.068)
Education	0.017*	0.018*	0.017*	0.035*	0.035*	0.034*	0.032*
	(0.009)	(0.009)	(0.009)	(0.016)	(0.017)	(0.017)	(0.016)
Employed	0.053***	0.055***	0.048***	0.004	0.005	0.008	−0.032
	(0.015)	(0.015)	(0.016)	(0.046)	(0.046)	(0.047)	(0.056)
R^2	0.082	0.081	0.084	0.053	0.048	0.049	0.061
Observations	3,956	3,956	3,956	1,228	1,224	1,228	1,216
Region Fixed Effects	✓	✓	✓	✓	✓	✓	✓

***p<0.01, **p<0.05, *p<0.1 This table analyzes the factors affecting whether respondents voted in recent national elections. The wording for Economic Situation and Education variables differ slightly across surveys, and point estimates cannot be directly compared. All models use OLS and clustered standard errors on region.

assigned, and brokers selectively target individuals. This makes it hard to assess the causal effect of clientelist appeals in an observational setting. On their own, these correlations are only suggestive. In the next section, we extend this analysis with experimental approaches that are better suited for making causal claims.

Two Framing Experiments on Brokered Mobilization

We can have more confidence in the correlations uncovered above if they are shown to be consistent with experimental data on workplace mobilization. Adopting an experimental design that randomly assigned voters to receive different types of appeals from different brokers is impractical and would raise ethical concerns about electoral interference. To address these difficulties, scholars have resorted to a series of indirect experimental approaches, including treating voters with informational campaigns (Collier and Vicente, 2012; Vicente, 2014) and framing experiments (Lawson and Greene, 2014; Weitz-Shapiro, 2014). We adopt the latter approach.[8]

In order to gain better purchase on the possible causal impacts of workplace mobilization on voter turnout, we placed framing experiments on a 2014 survey in Russia and a 2015 survey in Venezuela. Russia and Venezuela are prominent authoritarian regimes that hold elections at regular intervals. Clientelism is common in both countries, and several different types of brokers—employers, local officials, neighborhood leaders, hospital directors, council heads, schoolteachers, and party activists—are regularly employed in both (Albertus, 2015; Allina-Pisano, 2010; Forrat, 2018; Handlin, 2016; McMann, 2006).

However, the two countries also differ in analytically useful ways. Russia is a postcommunist country, with a long history of politics in the workplace (Friedgut, 1979; Remington, 1984); Venezuela, by contrast, does not have a history of communist rule, so employers cannot draw on legacies of workplace mobilization. Second, parties in Venezuela have stronger grassroots organizations than in Russia, which are put to great use to

---

[8] The assumption that all respondents were equally like to receive each treatment allows for randomization and better causal inference, but may be more plausible for some types of respondents than others. We relax this assumption in the observational analysis above, but at the usual cost of weaker causal inference.

90   WORKPLACE POLITICS

mobilize voters during elections (Handlin, 2016). This makes Venezuela a particularly hard case to test our argument. Finally, the two countries differ with regard to economic structure. Although private sector employment strictly dominates in both countries,[9] Venezuela at the time of the survey was experiencing a much higher rate of unemployment and poverty than Russia. These differences allow us to explore whether broker effectiveness depends on particular historical legacies, political party development, or economic structure.

Our survey in Russia consisted of 4,200 face-to-face interviews conducted in twenty regions that held regional (executive and/or legislative) elections in September 2014.[10] Surveys were carried out in October 2014, three weeks after the elections. The base sample included 3,360 respondents, as well as an additional oversample of 840 employed.[11]

Our survey in Venezuela included responses from 1,400 face-to-face interviews in nine regions of the country. We used a stratified sampling procedure based on geography and habitation to achieve a nationally representative sample.[12]

For our main analyses, we implemented a framing experiment using a factorial design in which we manipulate (1) the type of vote broker and (2) mobilizational technique. Each respondent was asked the following question:

Imagine that during the next election campaign [voter broker here] approaches you and [technique here]. Given this, how likely would you be to vote in these elections?[13]

Respondents were asked to rate their likelihood of voting on a 5-point scale ranging from "definitely will not vote" to "definitely will vote." As is common, we rely on self-reported turnout intentions in the absence of

[9] Roughly 70 percent of employed respondents in Russia and 80 percent of employed respondents in Venezuela work outside the government.
[10] A list of regions as well as an explanation of the sampling approaches is available in Marques and Remington 2017.
[11] Of these oversampled respondents, we required that no fewer than 240 individuals were working in heavy industry, oil/gas extraction, and mining. This somewhat complicated sampling design was chosen for a parallel project on the determinants of workplace mobilization. The sample is not nationally representative, but our goal is not to estimate the incidence of clientelism across Russia.
[12] The country was divided into thirty-six strata based on these two criteria, from which 173 sample points were randomly selected. In addition, we oversampled 400 employed respondents distributed proportionally from the sample points.
[13] In Russia, the question specified the next State Duma campaign.

Table 3.3 Survey Experiment Coverage

	Asked You to Vote	Indicates There Will Be Negative Consequences for You If You Do Not Vote	Offers You a Gift, Money, or Reward for Voting	Tells You That Your Firm or Organization Will Suffer If Turnout among Employees Is Low
Panel A: Russia Survey				
Your Employer	344	344	374	372
A Party Activist	336	353	360	362
A Government Official	339	337	352	331
Panel B: Venezuela Survey				
Your Employer	96	132	113	114
A Party Activist	94	133	113	118
A Neighborhood Leader	125	118	120	124

a publicly available voter file. Self-reported turnout intentions are likely inflated but still provide valuable information. Moreover, the bias in self-reported turnout should be constant across each treatment and control condition, allowing us to capture meaningful variation in the responses.

Respondents were randomly assigned to one of twelve combinations of broker and mobilizing technique as depicted in Table 3.3.[14] In the Russia survey, each group comprised between 331 and 372 respondents, while in the Venezuela survey, each group comprised between 94 and 133 respondents. Covariate balance checks indicate that the randomization was successful for both surveys.

We invoke three brokers in the experiment. In Russia we used employers, party activists, and government officials, while in Venezuela we used employers, party activists, and neighborhood leaders. As discussed previously, employers are common vote brokers in Russia and Venezuela and are the main subject of our research. The next treatment references party activists because they are the vote brokers most frequently discussed in the literature and are also common in both countries. Surveys have found

---

[14] Respondent characteristics such as employment status were not factored into the randomization procedure; every respondent had an equal probability of being assigned to treatment.

party officials in Russia to be key sources of information and material inducements for voters (Usmanova, 2008). In Venezuela, the Bolivarian Movement and its Partido Socialista Unido de Venezuela (PSUV) have developed extensive grassroots structures to direct government spending (Handlin, 2016). Our surveys confirm the active roles parties play during elections; roughly 27 percent of Russians and 26 percent of Venezuelans interacted with a party activist during their countries' electoral campaign.

For the Russian survey, we included local government officials as the third broker because they are common intermediaries, especially outside major cities, where the heads of local districts are frequently tasked with mobilizing rural voters. In Venezuela, clientelist exchange is often brokered by so-called neighborhood leaders who are recruited by parties to mobilize candidates.[15] Access to the *Misiones*, or government-run social programs, often hinges on an individual's relationship with these neighborhood organizations. This is the third broker we included in the Venezuela experiment.[16]

We included four mobilizational techniques as treatments.[17] We included one appeal rooted in positive inducements, two appeals related to negative inducements, and one simple mobilizational appeal. The positive inducement explicitly mentions the use of a "gift, money, or reward" in exchange for voting in elections. In doing so, we follow much of the literature, which often measures vote-buying using survey prompts that communicate a general payoff in return for political support (Corstange, 2018; Gonzalez Ocantos, Jonge, and Nickerson, 2014).

The first negative inducement frame focused on individualized threats. We conceptualize this individualized threat as a person exchanging political support in order to maintain the status quo and prevent the loss of something of value. The second negative treatment focused on collective threats against the voter's workplace or organization. Would political support not be offered, the loss would be inflicted on both the respondent and other

---

[15] The exact phrasing was "persona de su urbanización/barrio que tenga mucha influencia," a phrasing that could encompass various types of neighborhood social leaders, including those affiliated with regime-affiliated "communal Councils."

[16] University professors, hospital superintendents, and school directors are also prominent brokers, but their targets are a limited segment of the population. In order to preserve statistical power, we must necessarily limit the number of brokers assigned as treatments.

[17] Our concern was that a focus on one type of strategy, such as turnout-buying, might result in biased results at the broker level. Using four strategies helps allay concerns that specific inducements are driving differences in broker effectiveness.

members of their collective. Finally, we also include a treatment in which each broker asks the voter to turn out.

It is important to note that employers asking their employees to vote can be construed as a form of implicit coercion, though a weaker form than if a direct threat is involved. In many cases, power asymmetries in the employer-employee relationship make these entreaties implicitly coercive. Indeed, our surveys indicated that a majority of respondents in both countries take a negative view of this type of workplace mobilization.

Our design is best suited to comparing the *relative* effectiveness of brokers and inducements. However, we conceive of the 'simple ask' treatment by party activists as the baseline. We are aware of no studies that find being asked to turn out by a party activist depresses turnout. Most find the opposite. Thus, any effects relative to this baseline category should be low estimates of broker effectiveness. In any case, our main focus is on the relative effectiveness of different brokers across the fixed set of strategies used.

We should also note that our outcome measures turnout intentions, not actual turnout. Our scenarios are hypothetical and we do not observe actual voting behavior. At the same time, the main effect of the hypothetical prompt should be to increase variance in responses and increase the number of non-committal ("Maybe I would vote, maybe I would not") responses, since we are asking respondents to speculate about future behavior. This should make it harder to find a statistically significant effect for a given treatment. Moreover, while most Russians and Venezuelans do not directly experience clientelism in every election, these practices would be quite familiar to the average citizen.

Results: Comparing Effectiveness across Brokers

Figure 3.1 shows the main results of the survey experiment. Because the employer treatment is less relevant for nonemployed voters, we limit the sample in our main analyses to the subset of respondents who reported that they were employed.[18] Given our theoretical focus on brokers, we primarily address the interpretation of those results. The y-axes of the panels in Figure 3.1 show the mean response on the turnout propensity scale

---

[18] Our main results are robust using the full sample. We also run regressions that control for the employment status of the respondent. The main results are substantively and statistically similar.

94 WORKPLACE POLITICS

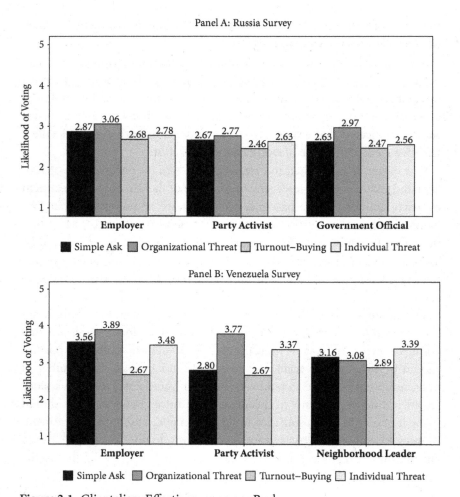

Figure 3.1 Clientelism Effectiveness across Brokers
The panels display the difference in the likelihood of voting among all respondents to the survey experiments. Voting likelihood is measured on a 5-point scale, with a value of 5 indicating "definitely will vote" and a value of 1 indicating "definitely will not vote." Mean values for each treatment group are found above each bar and are organized according to which broker was responsible for voter mobilization. The samples are subset to only employed respondents.

(responses range from 1 to 5). The first and most important result is that the average respondent in both countries is more responsive to mobilizational appeals by employers. Because we use a factorial design to assign respondents to treatment, we can simplify the presentation of the individual broker (and strategy) treatments. Figure 3.2 plots coefficients for the treatment groups relative to the "Party Activist" treatment for the Broker

IS WORKPLACE MOBILIZATION EFFECTIVE? 95

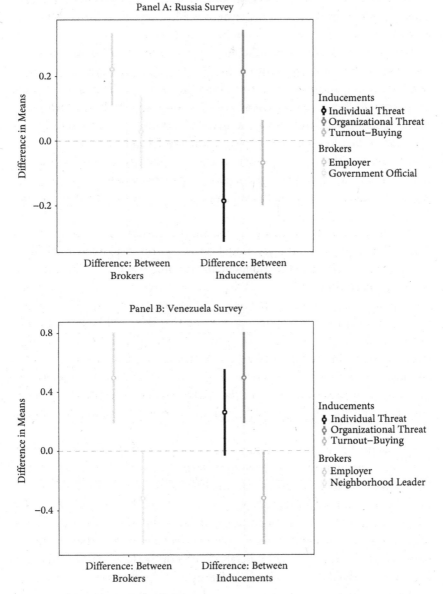

Figure 3.2 Differences in Means
This picture displays the differences in means between brokers and between inducements. Each dot displays the difference in means from each treatment and the "Party Activist" treatment for the Broker coefficients, and the "Simple Ask" treatment for the Inducements coefficients. Each dot has 95 percent confidence intervals. The samples are subset to only employed respondents.

coefficients and the "Simple Ask" treatment for the Inducement coefficients. The figures demonstrate that the employer advantage over the two types of activists is statistically significant in both countries.

Among those who received the employer treatment in Russia, the mean response on the 5-point scale of *Turnout Propensity* was 2.85, while the mean response among those who received either the party activist treatment or the government official treatment was 2.43. The difference is 0.21, which is statistically significant, and translates into a 4.2 percentage increase (.21/5) in *Turnout Propensity* over non-employer brokers. However, since the turnout propensity variable is an ordinal scale, this quantity cannot be directly interpreted as a 4.2 percentage increase in the probability of turning out. Rather it makes more sense to evaluate effects across the range of *Turnout Propensity*.

One simple way to do this is by examining changes in predicted probabilities from an ordered logit model, in which the dependent variable is *Turnout Propensity* and the independent variable is a binary indicator for whether the respondent received the employer treatment. Table 3.4 shows these quantities. Here we see that receiving the employer treatment increases the likelihood of the respondent answering that they will be likely to turn out (response category 4 or 5) by 5 to 6 percentage points. Similar effect sizes are found in the Venezuela experiment: respondents who receive the employer treatment are 9.3 percent more likely to answer that they would turn out than those who receive the party activist treatment. The difference between the employer and neighborhood leader treatments is even larger.

These effect sizes are substantial. As many turnout studies demonstrate, it is very difficult to increase turnout by large amounts (Green and Gerber, 2015). Modest but precisely estimated effect sizes are the rule in this literature. Our results indicate that employer-based clientelist appeals have sizable effects on reported turnout in our framing experiment. We also find that the other brokers are roughly comparable to party activists in their ability to mobilize voters. Government officials slightly outperform party activists in Russia, while neighborhood leaders slightly underperform party activists in Venezuela. These differences are less precisely estimated, and we interpret them in more detail here.

While employers outperform party activists in both countries, party activists appear considerably more effective in Venezuela. Party mobilization

IS WORKPLACE MOBILIZATION EFFECTIVE? 97

Table 3.4 Predicted Probabilities by Broker Treatment

	Russia	Venezuela
Panel A: Probability of Voting (%)		
Employer	28.6	54.2
Party Activist	22.5	44.9
Government Official	23.1	
Neighborhood Leader		40.9
Panel B: Probability of Not Voting (%)		
Employer	35.7	24.4
Party Activist	43.5	32.1
Government Official	42.7	
Neighborhood Leader		35.7

This table presents the predicted probabilities from individual ordered logit models that regress the respondents' likelihood of voting in the survey experiment on binary indicators for each Broker treatment status. The probabilities in Panel A displayed are the total of the predicted values for outcomes 4 and 5 (with 5 signifying "efinitely Will Vote"). The probabilities in Panel B displayed are the total of the predicted values for outcomes 1 and 2 (with 1 signifying "Definitely Will Not Vote"). The sample is subset to only employed respondents.

has a much longer history in Venezuela, which could make these prompts more realistic for Venezuelan respondents. It may also be the case that Venezuelan party activists are more credible representatives of the state than they are in Russia. This would increase the credibility of their promise of an inducement.

Although our focus in this chapter is on the relative effectiveness of brokers, the survey experiments also shed light on how well different types of selective inducements function for mobilizing voters. First, across both surveys, organizational threats strongly outperform individual threats—and all other types of inducements. Russian respondents who received the organizational threat treatment were eight percentage points more likely to respond that they were likely or very likely to vote; in Venezuela, those who received this treatment were fourteen percentage points more likely to respond similarly.

These findings make sense in light of the theoretical propositions sketched earlier. For one, organizational threats are more credible than inducements toward individuals. As other scholars have pointed out, monitoring a collective's voting behavior is easier than monitoring an individual's voting behavior (Kitschelt and Wilkinson, 2007). It is straightforward to observe the voting returns of a municipality or small town. Monitoring the voting behavior of some other collectives—for example, firms, schools, hospitals—is more difficult, but the task may be simplified if employees live close together and correspond loosely to one or small number of precincts, as is often the case with large firms. Much of the theoretical and empirical literature envisions electoral clientelism as a dyadic relationship between a broker and a client or between a party official and a broker. But voters are often members of collective organizations, such as firms, neighborhood associations, or social groups, and brokers can make rewards for voting conditional on support or punishment for a particular collective of which a voter is a member.

Perhaps surprisingly, we also find that providing gifts, patronage (turnout buying), or both is a relatively ineffective way of mobilizing voters, even compared to simply asking voters to turn out and irrespective of the broker used. These findings largely accord with recent studies arguing that without strong monitoring capacity, electoral handouts often do not change electoral outcomes (Guardado and Wantchékon, 2018).

Another explanation for this nonresult in Russia is that the median voter is too wealthy for preelectoral gifts to make much of an impact. In fact, we do find evidence that poorer respondents in both surveys respond to positive inducements by turning out to vote. In supplementary analyses we interact the turnout-buying treatment with indicators for education and income. In general, the less educated and less wealthy respondents are, the more effective are all types of inducements, including attempts at turnout-buying.

Variation across these inducements also may help explain the relative effectiveness of other brokers we employ in the experiment. The survey results indicate, for example, that government officials in Russia derive their mobilizing power mainly from making organizational threats, which is reasonable because these officials' leverage comes from budget allocations that typically are alloted to organizations rather than individuals. Officials are less able to use inducements that potentially require increased monitoring capacity, such as wielding positive and negative inducements to individuals. This makes sense, given officials' limited penetration of social networks and visibility in neighborhoods. On the other hand, we find that party activists in Venezuela command more leverage through organizational threats, while neighborhood leaders enjoy more success mobilizing voters when more monitoring capacity is required.

Conclusion

Mobilizing votes is costly, so politicians turn to vote brokers who are good at getting people to the polls. Employers are one such effective broker, which is why politicians so often turn to them. Because employees are often dependent on their employers for their livelihood and well-being, the latter have significant leverage over the former. This leverage translates into real mobilizational advantages. In addition to the leverage they wield, employers are also competent brokers because they are often engaged in repeated interactions with their employees, which makes their clientelist offers credible, and because they have significant monitoring capacity.

In few settings can party activists offer the significant inducements available to employers. Party-based clientelism requires considerable investments in mobilizational infrastructure. Thus, even where many voters are unemployed, politicians will find it advantageous to mobilize via the existing hierarchies of the workplace. For example, in Russia, even though only 53 percent of the population is formally employed, a full 10 percent of the population reported being mobilized by an employer during the 2016 State Duma elections. Fourteen percent were mobilized by a party activist. In Venezuela, our survey indicated that just 37 percent of the adult population was formally employed. And yet 18 percent of the total sample experienced mobilization by employers. Twenty-six percent experienced mobilization by party activists. Thus, in both countries, the sheer extensiveness of workplace mobilization makes the practice significant, even if many (or most) voters are outside the formal economy. In Russia, the regime's electoral strategy hinges on depoliticizing the public sphere. Then, at election time, it seeks to mobilize just enough turnout to legitimate the outcome. The mobilization of workers—especially in the state sector—is essential to this strategy. Our work highlights an important tool that autocrats can use to generate the voter turnout that helps legitimate their rule.

The findings in this chapter thus indicate that workplace mobilization can be a very effective way of mobilizing votes. If this is the case, one may wonder

100 WORKPLACE POLITICS

why the practice is not even *more* widespread. Indeed, Chapter 2 showed that even in the countries where workplace mobilization is most prevalent, fewer than half of workers are induced to vote by their employers—and in some settings, firms, and countries, the practice is quite rare. To answer this question, one must also consider the costs that the practice imposes on those who choose it. In turn, this can help us understand why the practice is more common in some settings than in others. We take up these questions in the next chapters.

4

Why Do Employers Mobilize?

On March 12, 2018, Yuri A. Kabanov, head of the Sivinskii Municipal Rayon in Permskii Krai, sent a letter with the subject line "On Rendering Assistance" that related to all enterprises and major businesses in the district.[1] The letter opens with some boilerplate about the importance of the upcoming elections before noting that Putin's regional election committee had assigned Sivinskii rayon a minimum turnout plank (i.e., level) of 70 percent that local authorities were expected to achieve. Kabanov notes that this is a "very serious plank, that cannot be achieved without your [the directors'] help." The letter goes on to note that directors can help if they

> actively participate in the mobilization of district residents on March 18 and maximally increase turnout by getting your employees to vote. For this, you only need to do a little: find the right words for each of your employees in order to convince them to come to the polls, to convince them about the importance of their vote for the President of Russia.

Kabanov then recommends some techniques for getting employees to vote and informs employers that the rayon administration "would be grateful if your designated people find the opportunity to report to us about the turnout of your employees (about the number who voted at specific times)." The document provides specific times when these figures can be reported and provides contact numbers for reporting turnout figures. The letter then closes in a polite, almost apologetic, tone: "We would like to thank you in advance for your understanding and for your readiness to work with us on the mobilization of turnout in our district. We will be grateful if you could inform us in advance about any suggestions you may have. We are ready for any dialogue."

---

[1] A copy of this letter is provided in Plate 4.1 the end of this chapter (*Karta Narusheniye* ID 40791, March 16, 2018). Rayons are the lowest-level administrative district in Russia, akin to a municipality or in rural settings, a county.

Workplace Politics. Timothy Frye, Ora John Reuter, and David Szakonyi, Oxford University Press.
© Oxford University Press (2025). DOI: 10.1093/9780197802045.003.0004

102 WORKPLACE POLITICS

Directives like this are common in Russia.[2] They illustrate a crucial fact about workplace mobilization: employers often mobilize at the behest of politicians or state officials. The power dynamic between these politicians and the employers that mobilize for them is central to the story we tell in this book.

Few studies in political science examine workplace mobilization in depth, and those that do tend to focus on relations between employers and workers (Ziblatt, 2009; Mares and Zhu, 2015; Hertel-Fernandez, 2018). Here we explore an equally important piece of the puzzle: relations between politicians and employers. We show that workplace mobilization can be costly and uncomfortable for employers. Since the costs of workplace mobilization are real, employers often must have incentives to mobilize their employees. We argue that politicians can provide inducements—negative or positive, implicit or explicit—that incentivize employers to mobilize their workers. In Russia, the primary focus of this chapter, these inducements are typically provided by the regime and its agents. This chapter provides empirical evidence that (1) employers perceive the costs of mobilization, (2) the state incentivizes employers to mobilize, and (3) employers respond to these incentives by mobilizing their employees. In this way, we are able to conceive of workplace mobilization as a bargain struck between employers and politicians.

Why Employers Are Reluctant to Mobilize Their Employees

For firms, mobilizing employees requires organizational and financial resources. Organizing rallies at the firm, printing and distributing campaign materials, and getting out the vote all require time, money, and effort. Leaked documents from Russia's KN database indicate that the task of mobilizing employees in large firms entails a months-long planning process across multiple departments with layers of managerial oversight.[3] The process can involve a series of meetings, written reports, and extensive data gathering. One such leaked document from the industrial giant RosTex shows that the

---

[2] We have gathered a number of such communications that were leaked to the press, and we share some in this chapter.

[3] See, for example, *Karta Narusheniye* ID 39575, January 19, 2018; *Karta Narusheniye* ID 42336, March 8, 2018; *Karta Narusheniye* ID 2976, November 20, 2011; and *Karta Narusheniye* ID 40625, March 14, 2018. All original *Karta Narusheniye* reports cited in this book are available at https://www.kartanarusheniy.org/.

process of planning for mobilization during the March 2018 elections began over six weeks prior to voting day.[4] In January and February, the following twenty tasks were assigned to all branches of the firm:

1. Forming an executive committee on mobilization
2. Forming databases of all employees to be contacted
3. Designing a plan for controlling and monitoring supervisor work with employees
4. Designing a plan for controlling and collecting data on turnout
5. Conducting trainings for supervisors on how to mobilize
6. Developing a "media plan for social, cultural, and other events" during the "mobilizational period"
7. Holding informational meetings with voters
8. Holding meetings of managers with employees (in February)
9. Issuing "personal" invitations from managers to employees
10. Distributing request from the CEO
11. Printing mobilizational flyers
12. Forming an "analytic" group to control quality and compliance
13. Monitoring media mentions about the firm's mobilizational efforts
14. Formulating a press plan for covering the firm's mobilizational efforts internally
15. Conducting meetings on the refinement and editing of voter lists
16. Forming a committee on coordination with "public opinion leaders"
17. Distributing messages from "public opinion leaders" to employees
18. Forming a special subcommittee on work with veterans,
19. Gathering lists of veterans,
20. Conducting meetings with veterans

After this preparatory work was completed, the branches executed the planned events, meetings, and exhortations to vote on election day. The planning document indicates that the entire process was closely monitored, with fifteen separate written reports and databases compiled to oversee its progress.

Unfortunately for employers, the costs of mobilization can go far beyond organizing. As Chapter 2 described, some firms also reward their workers with vacation time, monetary bonuses, or gifts (such as food or alcohol) in

---

[4] *Karta Narusheniye* ID 39575, January 19, 2018.

exchange for their political participation. Of course, as we have noted, many employers rely on negative inducements, such as threats or cajoling, but these methods are also far from costless. As subsequent chapters show, such practices upset workers, damage workplace morale, and undermine productivity. Every minute an employee spends at a political event or a supervisor spends discussing politics with their subordinate is one not spent performing their primary responsibilities at work. In sum, politics on the shop floor can prove distracting, time-consuming, divisive, and demoralizing.

Employers admit as much when asked about the practice. Our 2017 firm survey included a question asking why some employers might choose *not* to mobilize their workers during elections. Respondents were given a list of seven possible answers, asking them to rank up to three as the most important reasons employers like them might refrain from getting involved with electoral politics.[5] Table 4.1 lists answers according to popularity. Among the most popular responses were that workplace mobilization "requires time and effort" (78 percent of respondents) or "requires money" (60 percent). Sixty-five percent responded that employees do not like it. A large portion of respondents (71 percent) also cited productivity concerns over employees being distracted from their duties during campaign efforts.

Table 4.1 Why Don't Employers Like Yours Mobilize?

Response	Percent (%)
(1) It requires time and effort.	77.9
(2) They consider it unacceptable.	72.9
(3) Employers are not interested in politics.	72.5
(4) It distracts employees from work.	70.8
(5) Employees do not like it.	65.1
(6) It requires money.	59.5
(7) Other firms in the region are already mobilizing.	38.8

This table shows the percentage of respondents from the 2017 Russian employer survey selecting choices about why firms don't mobilize their workers. Respondents could pick up to three of the choices or decline to answer.

[5] Note the indirect wording used in this question. Asking respondents about how "firms like theirs" would respond is done to reduce social desirability bias and is frequently used in firm surveys to measure corruption.

WHY DO EMPLOYERS MOBILIZE? 105

Firms may also be reluctant to participate overtly in politics because of their normative views on the practice. Even in Russia, there are social norms against employers getting involved in politics. As Table 4.2 demonstrates, many employers simply find mobilization "unacceptable." We probe these preferences further with a separate question on the firm survey asking respondents to rank common political activities on a 1–4 point scale, with 1 indicating Not Acceptable and 4 indicating Completely Acceptable.[6]

Table 4.2 presents the marked dispersion in responses. A majority of respondents thought that asking employees to turn out and vote (values of 1 or 2, totaling 56 percent) was morally unacceptable, though the responses were almost evenly divided over the full 4-point scale of acceptability. Other more intrusive forms of workplace mobilization drew even harsher rebukes from employers. Large majorities oppose endorsing a specific party/candidate (82 percent) and threatening employees with dismissal (78 percent).[7] For Russian employers, politicizing the workplace comes with significant costs and risks.

Table 4.2 How Acceptable Is Workplace Mobilization (%)?

	Not Acceptable			Completely Acceptable
	1	2	3	4
(1) Asking employees to turn out and vote	32	24	24	19
(2) Asking employees to vote for a specific candidate or party	51	31	14	5
(3) Informing employees that if a certain party lost, there would be negative consequences for the firm	47	31	16	7

This table shows the percentage of survey respondents from the 2017 Russian employer survey who answered at each level on a 4-point scale about how acceptable the listed activities are for firms to perform during elections.

[6] Some of this opposition to workplace mobilization may be politically motivated, since the practice is closely associated with the incumbent Russian government.
[7] In Chapter 7, we discuss the wider electoral implications of such negative views of workplace mobilization.

106 WORKPLACE POLITICS

Workplace Mobilization as a Transaction

For the reasons sketched earlier, many employers find workplace mobilization burdensome or distasteful. Politicians cannot necessarily count on their ideological supporters in the business community to voluntarily take up the mantle of getting their employees to the polls. To be sure, some employers do this of their own accord. In the United States, for instance, voluntary workplace mobilization appears to be common (Hertel-Fernandez, 2018). When David Siegel, a longtime Republican donor and CEO of the country's largest time-share company, wrote to his seven thousand employees in 2012 warning them that he would have to lay off workers if Barack Obama won the election, he made it clear that the letter reflected his own views about the impact of supposedly higher taxes. In those same elections, Georgia Pacific, a subsidiary of Koch Industries, sent a similar letter to all of its thirty thousand employees, warning them of the consequences of an Obama victory and appending a list of endorsed candidates.[8] Major corporations in India, such as Coca-Cola, Dabur, and HDFC Bank, make considerable efforts to motivate their employees to register and vote during national elections. In the words of one human resources officer describing his company's motives, "Election day is extremely important as it gives us an opportunity to share our political ideology."[9]

But in many other countries, pressure from politicians or the state is the norm. This is especially true in Russia, where the Russian government routinely persuades, cajoles, and induces companies to mobilize on behalf of regime parties and candidates.[10] Leaked directives from state officials shed light on how the process works.[11] For instance, in the run-up to the 2018 presidential elections, several major news outlets gained access to documents showing that the Nizhegorodskaya Oblast' regional ministry of industry had issued directives to all major enterprises instructing

---

[8] Greenhouse, Steven, "Here's a Memo From the Boss: Vote This Way," *New York Times*, October 26, 2012.

[9] Gurtoo, Himani Chandna. "Go out and vote, cool companies tell their employees" *The Hindustan Times*, December 2, 2013.

[10] Our surveys reveal that Russian opposition parties are much less likely to command the influence or resources to pressure companies in this manner, though there are exceptions in certain regions.

[11] See, for example, *Karta Narusheniye* ID 39892, February 14, 2018; *Karta Narusheniye* ID 39747, February 5, 2018; *Karta Narusheniye* ID 39747, May 20, 2016; *Karta Narusheniye* ID 39747, November 21, 2011. See also "V Kanske Rukovoditelyam Predpriyatiy Poruchili Oprosit' Sotrudnikov Pered Vyborami." *TBK*, June 27, 2021.

them to hold "motivating" meetings with employees. These instructions also included specific guidelines on how to apply coercion and how to avoid overusing it.[12]

Leaked directives, such as the one that opened this chapter, also help clarify the incentive structures facing politicians and employers. Many of these directives provide extensive instructions for employers on how to mobilize their employees (such as by compiling lists of potential voters and helping employees vote away from their home precinct).[13] Directors were also given specific instructions about how to report back to authorities about their planning activities.[14] Larger firms are sometimes even assigned a unique contact in the administration to help them with mobilization.[15]

Of course, in order to prevent leaks, government officials often avoid issuing written instructions, instead transmitting directives orally. Judging by press reports and leaked recordings, a common technique is for a minister, mayor, or other official to gather major directors or industrialist organizations and address them jointly.[16] Consider, for example, the leaked recording of a January 2018 address by the governor of Vladimir Oblast', Svetlana Orlovskaya.[17] In the recording, obtained and published by a regional newspaper, Orlovskaya can be heard telling directors,

A lot of serious work depends on you. The presidential elections—this is an important and key task for the country. And your task is to get your employees to come vote. .... There needn't be any resentment here. Elections are serious work: to engage the public, mobilize them so that they come and vote. ... I am asking you to carry out good mobilizational work, so that people come out. And naturally, so that they come out, you should tell them that the future of your enterprise is being decided. We relate to you as partners.

[12] Ivanov, Maksim, and Mariya Karpenko. "Yavis' ne Zapylis" *Kommersant.* March 7, 2018; Miller, Liza, Maksim Ivanov, Andrey Repin, and Aleksandra Vikulova, "Regiony Vstupili v Borbu za Yavku," *Kommersant,* January 25, 2018; Davydov, Ivan, "Nasvstrechu Vyboram," *New Times,* January 26, 2018.
[13] *Karta Narusheniye* ID 40298, March 4, 2018; *Karta Narusheniye* ID 40332, March 6, 2018.
[14] *Karta Narusheniye* ID 39741, February 5, 2018.
[15] *Karta Narusheniye* ID 39892, February 18, 2018.
[16] See "Vybory 4 Dekabrya 2011 goda i sostoyanie politcheskoi sistemy v rossii," Analytic Report of the Public Council "Honest Choice" Moscow, December 2011, p. 214; Ivanov and Karpenko. "Yavis' ne zapylis."
[17] *Karta Narusheniye* ID 39619, January 24, 2018.

108 WORKPLACE POLITICS

Officials often give specific turnout levels that employers are asked or expected to hit.[18] But just as often, the message in these recordings is more implicit. Take, for example, a secretly recorded video that went viral on YouTube shortly before the 2011 Russian parliamentary elections. In the video, the mayor of Novokuznetsk, a major industrial city in Siberia, is seen addressing a gathering of the directors of the city's largest enterprises. The mayor, Valerii Smolevo, asks business leaders to encourage their workers to vote for United Russia and to discredit opposition parties. In this semipublic setting, Smolevo does not mention specific sanctions that enterprises would face if they failed to mobilize the vote for UR, but the message was clear to all:

> We need to carry out these elections in the proper manner so it won't be painful or uncomfortable. You are all smart people; you are all directors. You saw the recent United Russia congress; you saw that, on Friday, the governor gathered a team to discuss preparations for the parliamentary elections on December 4. It's clear to everyone that United Russia should win.

The video is also remarkable for the detail of Smolevo's message that enterprise directors are expected to convey to their employees:

> It [United Russia] is the only real force, actually a ruling party, that is actually doing something real. If you look at other opponents currently in the Duma, no one should expect any sort of real help or deeds from them. Everyone should understand that. Everything that is done by the authorities in the country, and in the city, needs to be tightly connected to United Russia.[19]

Sometimes authorities turn to more heavyhanded tactics, such as threatening to withdraw subsidies or tax privileges, or in the case of state enterprises, personnel actions. But on the whole, the regime prefers to avoid such hamfisted methods—especially after the 2011–2012 election cycle, in which blatant fraud and intimidation produced a societal backlash that catalyzed a nationwide protest movement. In fact, ahead of the 2016 elections, several governors were reported to have received reprimands from the Kremlin for

---

[18] See "Glava Surguta Sidorov poprosil rukhovoditelei predpriyatii goroda organizovat' yavku na vybory mera," Ura.ru, July 27, 2010.
[19] "Glava Novokuznetska o vyborakh v GosDumu," YouTube, October 5, 2011.

WHY DO EMPLOYERS MOBILIZE? 109

applying heavy-handed tactics in their mobilizational efforts. In one case, the governor of Samara Oblast', Nikolai Merkushkin, was dressed down by the head of the Central Election Commission (and eventually fired) because too many fraud complaints were coming out of Samara.[20] But the coup de grâce, and his eventual firing, came because his abusive approach to organizing workplace mobilization had alienated too much of the local business community.

We asked our focus group and interview respondents whether their firm directors were induced to mobilize in some way by the authorities. Consider the following excerpt from our Chelyabinsk focus group, which included a mid-level manager, Maksim, whose proximity to management gave him special insight on this question:[21]

> Maksim: Of course, otherwise, there would no point in contriving all this propaganda, you understand.... I know for sure that if the firm has a tender [for a state contract], then they will get privileges... If everyone votes, doesn't matter if it is for someone in particular or just high turnout, the firm will be closer to the state and it will have better chances of winning this or that tender in the future.
>
> Elena (1): In state enterprises, it's just the director. I don't know how, maybe financial support personally for the director.... but I don't think it helps the enterprise. It's for him personally, but I don't think it goes to the organization. I am not talking about the employees, but about upgrades or something like that. I think it all stays with him.
>
> Elena (2): Well, after all, there are some administrative questions that have to be solved with a large paper bag,[22] and if the enterprise voted for the necessary candidate—these questions will be easier to solve in the administration.
>
> Maksim: Elena said it right. There is only so much in the municipal budget, and those who cooperate with the state will be more likely to get financing, if we're talking about state enterprises. As for whether that goes to the organization or the director, that's already a separate problem.

Maksim's and Elena's suspicions are confirmed by documents from the KN archive, which demonstrate that politicians in Russia attempt to

---

[20] Korchenkova, Natal'ya, and Andrey Ivanov, "Nikolaya Merkushkina zhdyot slozhnyi razgovor," *Kommersant*, August 27, 2016.

[21] Focus Group Response Maksim and Elena, Focus Group, Bashkirova. & Partners, Chelyabinsk, Russia. October 3, 2017.

[22] This is a reference to bribes and corruption.

110 WORKPLACE POLITICS

gauge the effectiveness of employers' mobilizational efforts. The authorities commonly request that employers provide records of their employees, so that these records can be checked against voter rolls. Employers are also asked to report on turnout levels among their employees, usually by requesting that employees report to management after they voted. This scheme helps in monitoring voter behavior, but it also helps politicians gauge managers' efforts. One of the most common requests that employers make of their employees is to take absentee ballots and vote in a specific precinct. Concentrating all of the firm's votes in a single or small number of precincts makes it easier for politician to measure turnout levels in the firm. Indeed, the instructions that politicians give to firms often include specific instructions to organize this type of absentee voting.[23]

The findings from our 2017 firm survey corroborate the notion that the Russian state induces firms to mobilize. In that survey, we flipped the question from Table 4.3, this time asking respondents why "firms like theirs" might *choose* to mobilize. The distribution of responses in Table 4.3 is informative. Relatively few cited either personal support for a candidate or political party or civic duty as their motivation. Instead, most respondents report that employers' decisions to mobilize are motivated by their interactions with the authorities. Seventy percent of respondents reported that employers mobilized either because they wanted to "strengthen relations with authorities" or because they feared the reaction of authorities if the firm had low turnout.

Table 4.3 Why Do Employers Like Yours Mobilize?

Response	Percent (%)
(1) They want to strengthen relations with authorities.	55.4
(2) They want to support a specific candidate or party.	39.9
(3) They consider it their civic duty.	31.6
(4) They fear the reaction of authorities if there is low turnout.	15.7

This table shows the percentage of respondents from the 2017 Russian employer survey selecting choices about why firms mobilize their workers. Respondents could pick up to three of the choices, or decline to answer.

---

[23] *Karta Narusheniye* ID 39741, February 5, 2018.

Framing Experiment

To probe more deeply how employers respond to inducements from the authorities, we placed a simple framing experiment on the 2017 firm survey that prompts respondents to consider the degree to which relations with the government factor into their decision to mobilize their workers. We randomly divided the sample of 690 firms into two equal-size control and treatment groups. Respondents in the control group were asked to rate the likelihood that their firm's management would speak to employees about the importance of voting during the next elections. The outcome was measured on a 5-point scale, with higher values indicating a higher likelihood of speaking to employees. The treatment group was given the same prompt, but was then told that their governor or a party leader specifically asked them for help in generating turnout.

The exact wording of the question follows. This format allows us to experimentally induce a realistic but hypothetical situation for respondents, whereby government or party officials are entreating them to engage in mobilization. The treatment prompt does not suggest coercion on the part of the government, but clearly invokes a scenario in which the government is trying to get employers to mobilize their workers.[24]

Treatment (50% of sample): *Suppose that your regional government or a representative of a political party asked the leadership of your firm (organization) to help mobilize employees to vote in elections.*

Question: How likely would it be that the leadership of your firm (organization) would speak with its employees about the importance of voting during the next elections?

01. Very unlikely
02. Somewhat unlikely, but possible
03. 50/50
04. Somewhat likely
05. Very likely
09. Hard to answer

---

[24] Balance checks show that the treatment was administered randomly. We regress treatment status on a vector of firm characteristics using logistic regression. We include interviewer fixed effects in all models, both in the balance checks and in the regressions below. Unfortunately, our survey firm assigned questionnaires either to treatment or control status before distributing them to interviewers. This created an imbalanced sample across interviewers, and some questionnaires were ultimately not used. But within each interviewer, firms were properly randomized. When controlling for interviewer effects, the joint likelihood ratio tests indicate that treatment assignment is not correlated collectively with these confounders.

112   WORKPLACE POLITICS

Table 4.4 shows the results of the experiment. Model 1 regresses the treatment indicator on the outcome variable, while including interviewer fixed effects, as discussed in footnote 24. The treatment effect is positively and statistically significant at the 0.10 level. Firm managers who were told, in this hypothetical scenario, that their governor has asked them to ensure turnout among their employees are 15 percent more likely to report that they would ask their workers to turn out. This effect is more precisely estimated in Columns 2 and 3, as we add both covariates and region fixed effects. Firm directors who receive the treatment about governors coordinating workplace mobilization are much more likely to respond that they would speak to their employees during a hypothetical election. In Model 4, we explore the results without interviewer fixed effects. In this imbalanced sample, our main result is imprecisely estimated (see footnote 24).

Table 4.4 Framing Experiment about Mobilization

	(1)	(2)	(3)	(4)
Treatment	0.15*	0.234**	0.198*	0.038
	(0.084)	(0.101)	(0.105)	(0.105)
Firm Size		0.087*	0.092*	
		(0.048)	(0.046)	
Firm Age		-0.021	-0.040	
		(0.088)	(0.088)	
State-Owned Enterprise		0.369**	0.419**	
		(0.187)	(0.182)	
Immobile Assets		0.015	-0.074	
		(0.151)	(0.143)	
Firm Sells to State		0.214**	0.167	
		(0.106)	(0.102)	
Firm Offers Benefits to Workers (count)		0.078**	0.069*	
		(0.037)	(0.032)	
Firm Mobilized Workers		0.932***	0.979***	
		(0.190)	(0.185)	
Region Fixed Effects			✓	
Interviewer Fixed Effects	✓	✓	✓	
Observations	670	615	615	670

***p<0.01, **p<0.05, *p<0.1 This table presents the results from the framing experiment in the 2017 Firm Survey about who mobilizes. The outcome variable is a 5-point scale measuring likelihood of engaging in workplace mobilization. Standard errors are clustered at the region level.

On the whole, we interpret these results as evidence that firm directors are responsive to state pressure and are more likely to mobilize when they receive such encouragement. However, a drawback of this survey experimental approach is that the scenarios are hypothetical, so our conclusions must be tentative. The next section uses administrative data to examine the potential exchange relationship between firms and the state.

Workplace Mobilization and Public Procurement in Russia

Workplace mobilization is costly, so politicians must, implicitly or explicitly, incentivize firms to mobilize their workers. Such motivation can take a variety of forms, including rewards of subsidies, regulatory relief, tax exemptions, threats, and so on. Firms in Russia undoubtedly understand that being in the good graces of the regime is helpful. In this section, we probe a specific type of potential reward system by analyzing public procurement data. Our aim is to determine whether firms are more likely to be rewarded with (or retain) public procurement contracts if they engage in vote mobilization.

As the next chapter demonstrates clearly, firms are not selected at random to mobilize their workers, so we cannot simply compare procurement outcomes between firms that do and do not mobilize. Overcoming these issues requires an empirical approach that accounts for preexisting differences between mobilizing and nonmobilizing firms. In this section, we use a difference-in-differences strategy to accomplish this goal.

Variable Measurement

The first task is to identify a sample of firms with varying levels of workplace mobilization. Though data on the ownership and balance sheets of Russian firms are abundant, devising verifiable indicators of workplace mobilization is not possible. Firms do not report political activity to tax authorities, and using aggregate measures of precinct turnout is infeasible because employees do not necessarily live in the same precinct where a firm is located.

Instead, we use the 2017 Russian firm survey, which, as described earlier, asks directors whether their firm engaged in any of six campaigning activities in the runup to the 2016 Duma elections. We then code a binary indicator

114   WORKPLACE POLITICS

for the 33.4 percent of firms that mobilized their employees using this broad definition. This indicator distinguishes the control and treatment groups in our empirical setup.

Although the firm survey is rich in details about firm outcomes and interactions with politicians, asking firm directors to reflect simultaneously on their participation in the runup to elections and relations with the government raises questions about the direction of causality. Analysis of cross-sectional data cannot reasonably show that workplace mobilization is the product of a quid pro quo between firms and politicians, rather than a simple reflection of long-established ties. For example, if mobilizing firms also report having received financial subsidies from the government, we cannot establish whether the mobilization itself unlocked that benefit or some other characteristic or political activity led both to mobilization and the subsidies.

We therefore need data on firm financial relations with the government that are measured over time. Ideally the officials responsible for this assistance should be subordinate to regional governors, who typically assume primary responsibility for organizing campaign efforts. Although firms could receive any number of financial benefits for participating in workplace mobilization, most of these are impossible to study systematically. Data on region-level subsidies and direct firm transfers are not collected, thereby complicating our efforts to track which firms receive what types of money.

However, since 2011 the Russian government has made available information on all federal, regional, and municipal public procurement contracts through a single online portal.[25] Totaling over one trillion dollars in volume, this database has been used extensively by both journalists and academics studying efficiency and corruption in Russia's mammoth procurement system (Best, Hjort, and Szakonyi, 2023). Seeking access to public procurement contracts has become a defining characteristic of firms engaging in political activity, from funneling campaign contributions to gubernatorial candidates to directors running for office themselves (Szakonyi, 2020). For each contract, the procurement data include detailed information on the government customer, goods or services purchased, and the supplier.

---

[25] Russian State Procurement Portal: Zakupki.ru.

Our firm survey contained information on the name, sector, and location (region) of each firm. With the help of research assistants, we used these three pieces of information to identify each respondent firm's unique tax identifier (INN). Of the 690 firms surveyed in the summer and fall, tax IDs were located for 662 (96 percent). Once these identifiers had been assigned, we connected surveyed firms to their procurement activity from 2011 to 2018. The next section includes further discussion of how we operationalize these data.

Modeling Specifications

We use a simple difference-in-differences approach to measure the effect of mobilizing during the 2016 Duma elections on subsequent access to state procurement. The estimating equations are straightforward. First, we separate the sample into those firms that acknowledged that they had engaged in workplace mobilization and those that did not. Next, we limit the sample to a six-month window before and after the elections to narrow our identification to the mobilization itself (and not any other shocks during the period). The analysis sample is thus a balanced panel dataset of 7,944 firm-month observations (662 firms over the 12 months from April 2016 to March 2017).

Our primary outcome variables are three binary indicators for whether a given firm won procurement contracts from any federal, regional, or municipal government in each month during the period. From 2011 to 2018, roughly 21 percent of firms surveyed appear in the official data as suppliers in contracts to the federal government, 18 percent to regional governments, and 17 percent to municipal governments. In any given month, roughly 6 percent of these firms signed contracts with government bodies at any of these levels. Note that these official figures are somewhat lower than the self-reported numbers from the survey (47 percent of surveyed firms answered that they sold products or services to the state). The discrepancy may be due to firm directors mischaracterizing their sales to the government by including state-owned enterprises (SOEs) in their responses. Data on SOE contracts are not made public to the same degree, meaning our analysis is undercounting firm-level public procurement contracts. As a robustness check, we show that our results are robust to only including firms that self-reported sales to the state.

116 WORKPLACE POLITICS

In addition to these binary outcomes, we collect data on the total volume of procurement at each level of government for each month as well as the percentage of contracts procured using electronic auctions. This latter measure can be interpreted as a proxy for transparency and competition; electronic auctions help reduce informal favoritism and corruption by requiring price as the main criterion for selecting winners and decreasing the opportunities for officials to award contracts to connected firms (Szakonyi, 2021).

We account for possible selection effects biasing our results in two ways. First, we restrict the sample of firm-months to only firms that won any contracts at all over the 2011–2018 period from the level of government in question. For example, for models where the outcome is a binary indicator for a firm winning a federal government contract in a given month, only firms that won at least one contract at any point from 2011 onward would enter the sample. This step ensures that only firms with experience contracting with the government are analyzed, helping to narrow our focus.

Next, in all specifications we include both firm and month fixed effects. The former produces within-firm comparisons: the models compare procurement outcomes before and after the 2016 Duma elections (and the workplace mobilization that did or did not happen in each firm). The latter controls for seasonality during the procurement process. Much of Russian government spending occurs in the final three months of the calendar year as institutions attempt to spend their budgets before they lose them. This can cause strange spending patterns and introduce problems if the types of goods and services bought come from firms more likely to participate in workplace mobilization. Month fixed effects help control for these trends.

Figure 4.1 checks the key identifying assumption of parallel trends underlying this empirical approach. In each panel, the x-axis indexes months during the twelve-month period surrounding the 2016 elections. The y-axis plots the mean percentage of firms that won contracts from the federal government (Panel A), regional governments (Panel B), and municipal governments (Panel C). The lighter line shows these averages for firms in the control group which did not mobilize for the September 2016 Duma election; the darker line captures those that did. The vertical dotted line through the middle of the plot marks the timing of the election exactly halfway through the period under analysis.

Importantly, for all three plots, the lines for the treatment and control groups are essentially parallel in the runup to the September elections. Though the means exhibit some noise and fluctuations, we do not see consistent evidence that the two groups of firms (mobilizing or not) experienced

WHY DO EMPLOYERS MOBILIZE? 117

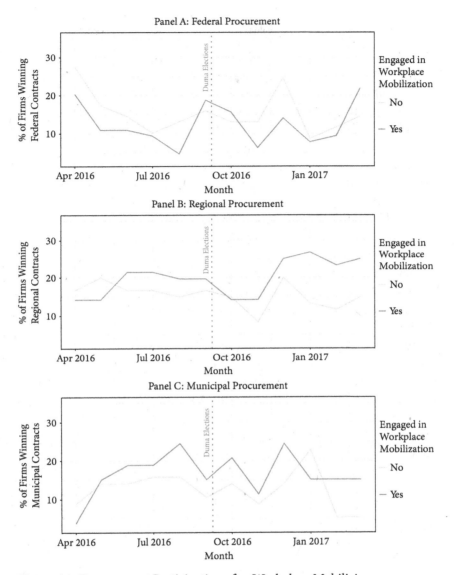

Figure 4.1 Procurement Participation after Workplace Mobilizing
This figure shows the percentage of firms that won federal, regional, or municipal procurement contracts in each month, broken down by whether they participated in workplace mobilization in the 2016 State Duma elections. The sample is restricted to only firms that won any contract at each respective level per the Goszakupki data from 2011 to 2017.

differential trends in the months prior to the election. Mobilizing firms on average are more likely to access public procurement contracts (which is consistent with the findings from upticks or downturns in their sales to the government during campaigns).

118 WORKPLACE POLITICS

Empirical Analysis

Figure 4.1 not only demonstrates the existence of pretreatment parallel trends, it also sheds light on the actual treatment effect of workplace mobilization on downstream procurement outcomes. Firms that mobilize their workers appear to enjoy greater access to regional procurement after the election. Panel B shows a marked uptick in the probability of mobilizing firms winning any regional contract beginning roughly two months after the Duma elections occurred. This differential between mobilizing and nonmobilizing firms persists for the rest of the calendar year and into early 2018. We do not see a similar gap for either municipal or federal procurements; in both panels, the plots show basically parallel lines through the twelve-month period, with no difference between the pre- and postelection periods.

Table 4.5 more precisely quantifies these effects using a standard difference-in-difference model on firm-month panel data. We interact an indicator for whether a firm mobilized workers with another for whether the month was after September 2016 (the date of the election). For each model, we restrict the sample to only firms that had won at least one contract through the level of government operationalized in the outcome. Including both firm and month fixed effects absorbs the constituent parts of that interaction; we use multiway clustered errors on firm and month. The models show no postelection bump with regard to federal or municipal government for mobilizing firms, but a clear increase in access to procurement at the regional level (Column 4). That we see the most significant effects on regional procurement is not surprising since regional, rather than federal or municipal, authorities are primarily responsible for organizing workplace mobilization. Mobilizing firms are roughly 10 percent more likely to secure regional procurement contracts after the election. These results are robust to including firms that had regional contracts according to the Goszakupki data and those that self-reported in the survey that they sold to the state. This suggests that regional governments with state contracts reward firms who that mobilized their workers are rewarded after the elections by regional governments with state contracts.

Next, in Table 4.6, we explore several possible mechanisms that may be driving the results. Under the difference-in-difference setup with firm fixed effects, the preferred way to investigate heterogeneity is through triple interactions (difference-in-difference-in-differences) of firm characteristics with

Table 4.5 Workplace Mobilization and Procurement: Regression Results

	Any Contract (1)	Federal (2)	Municipal (3)	(4)	Regional (5)	(6)
Mobilized Workers* Postelection	0.028	0.011	0.019	0.097***	0.032**	0.018***
	(0.037)	(0.053)	(0.061)	(0.034)	(0.013)	(0.007)
Firm, Month Fixed Effects	Yes	Yes	Yes	Yes	Yes	Yes
Procurement Experience	Any	Federal	Municipal	Regional	Regional + Survey	Any
Observations	2,388	1,596	1,320	1,392	4,104	7,680

This table analyzes the effect of workplace mobilization on procurement outcomes. The outcome is a binary indicator if a firm won any type of procurement contract at various levels (Columns 1–6). Columns 1–4 restrict the sample to only firms that won a contract at that level of government, while Column 5 includes firms that won a contract in the official data and that reported selling to the state in the Firm Survey. Column 6 includes all firms in the data. Standard errors are clustered on firm.

Table 4.6 Workplace Mobilization and Procurement: Mechanisms

	(1)	(2)	(3)	(4)	(5)	(6)	(7)	(8)
Mobilized Workers* Postelection	0.060	−0.043	0.021	0.028	0.047	0.011	0.057	−0.022
	(0.041)	(0.110)	(0.040)	(0.049)	(0.273)	(0.189)	(0.088)	(0.096)
Mobilized Workers* Director Supports UR		−0.016						
		(0.038)						
Mobilized Workers* Director Supports UR* Postelection		0.155						
		(0.113)						
Mobilized Workers* State-Owned Enterprise			−0.062*					
			(0.032)					
Mobilized Workers* State-Owned Enterprise* Postelection			0.167**					
			(0.069)					
Mobilized Workers* Difficulties Finding Workers				−0.018				
				(0.040)				
Mobilized Workers* Difficulties Finding Workers* Postelection				0.080				
				(0.122)				
Mobilized Workers* Firm Age (log)					−0.003			
					(0.018)			
Mobilized Workers* Firm Age (log)* Postelection					0.002			
					(0.043)			

	(1)	(2)	(3)	(4)	(5)	(6)	(7)	(8)
Mobilized Workers* Government Support					0.111 (0.098)			
Mobilized Workers* Government Support* Postelection					0.027 (0.192)			
Mobilized Workers* Number of Benefits						−0.019* (0.010)		
Mobilized Workers* Number of Benefits* Postelection						0.006 (0.017)		
Mobilized Workers* Sales Growth								0.007 (0.009)
Mobilized Workers* Sales Growth* Postelection								0.019 (0.021)
Firm, Month Fixed Effects	✓	✓	✓	✓	✓	✓	✓	✓
Observations	1,392	1,224	1,344	1,380	1,392	816	1,392	1,380

***p<0.01, **p<0.05, *p<0.1 This table shows DiD triple interaction models predicting whether firms received regional procurement contracts. All constituent terms are included in the models, though only double and triple interactions are shown. Standard errors are clustered on the firm.

the binary indicators for mobilization and the postelection period. Though trickier to interpret, this approach ensures that we are adequately controlling for many firm-level factors driving endogenous selection into workplace mobilization. Each column shows the main DiD interaction and then the DiDiD estimates using variables that we have argued affect the costs and benefits of engaging in workplace mobilization. All interaction variables are measured using the survey.

We see that state-owned enterprises as well as firms that offer benefits to their workers are much more likely to see an increase in region-level procurement after the Duma elections around which they engaged in workplace mobilization. These firms are more dependent on state contracts for their revenue and thus more likely to curry favor with the regime by mobilizing during elections. Our results suggest that these firms are amply rewarded for mobilizing on behalf of the state.

Access to state procurement is just one way that firms may be incentivized to mobilize their workers. Governments have numerous levers at their disposal, both positive and negative, to induce firms to get involved during elections. However, much of this carrot-and-stick game gets decided behind closed doors, with data never being released about the compensation (or punishment) handed down in exchange for political obedience. We know, though, from surveying firm directors that these incentives matter, and the results here provide concrete evidence for one channel of influence.

4.4 Conclusion

This chapter has shown that workplace mobilization is not costless for employers. Employers must be given incentives to mobilize their employees at election time. In Russia, there is ample evidence that the state uses carrots and sticks to encourage employers to mobilize their workers. Data from both a firm survey and public procurement contracts are consistent with these reports. We provide evidence that firms respond to state pressure to mobilize their workers. We also show evidence of the concrete rewards they sometimes receive for mobilizing. This implies that workplace mobilization can be analyzed as the product of bilateral exchange between politicians seeking votes and firms that can supply votes. The next chapter theorizes this exchange relationship more deeply in order to better understand when and where workplace mobilization occurs.

WHY DO EMPLOYERS MOBILIZE? 123

АДМИНИСТРАЦИЯ
СИВИНСКОГО МУНИЦИПАЛЬНОГО РАЙОНА
Ул. Ленина, д. 66 , с. Сива, 617240
Тел. (34277) 2-12-38, факс (34277) 2-12-38
E-mail:siv-adm@permkray.ru
ОКПО 04038040, ОГРН 1025902153639
ИНН/КПП 5949400379/593301001

12.03.2018 № 833

На № _____ от _____

Об оказании содействия

Руководителям предприятий,
организаций, учреждений,
бизнес структур

Уважаемые коллеги!

Приближается 18 марта – единый день голосования, День выборов Президента России. От гражданской позиции каждого жителя Сивинского района будет зависеть будущее всей страны, будущее района, наших семей и детей.

Будущее России зависит от сильного и уважаемого в мире Президента, а его авторитет и рейтинг будет впрямую зависеть от поддержки россиянами его кандидатуры на предстоящих выборах. Для Сивинского района краевым штабом установлен высокий процент явки – 70%, это очень серьезная планка, которую без Вашей помощи не достичь.

Мы с Вами можем активно поучаствовать в мобилизации явки жителей нашего района 18 марта на избирательные участки и повлиять на максимальное увеличение процента этой явки за счет голосования Ваших работников. Для этого необходимо сделать совсем немного: найти самые нужные слова для каждого вашего работника, чтоб убедить его в необходимости прийти 18 марта на избирательный участок, убедить каждого в важности его голоса за Президента России.

Уважаемые руководители! Убедительно просим не остаться в стороне от выборов и взять вопрос голосования Ваших работников на личный контроль. Очень рекомендуем назначить в Ваших подразделениях ответственных за явку ваших работников на избирательные участки, за мониторинг явки и взаимодействие со штабами по выборам сельского поселения и района. При необходимости рекомендуем применить такую форму контроля как обзвон работников по телефону, либо попросить каждого самостоятельно сообщить о своем голосовании вышестоящему руководителю.

Будем очень признательны, если назначенные Вами люди найдут возможность сообщить о явке Ваших работников (о количестве проголосовавших на конкретное время) в районный штаб при главе района.

Plate 4.1

124 WORKPLACE POLITICS

2

Первое контрольное время:
с 13.30 до 14.00
Второе контрольное время:
с 16.30 до 17.00
Телефоны для связи:
2-13-00 Кабанов Юрий Алексеевич
2-16-69 Миронова Наталья Борисовна
2-14-00 Чадова Татьяна Борисовна
Заранее благодарим Вас за понимание и готовность к совместной работе по мобилизации явки избирателей района. Будем благодарны, если Вы заранее проинформируете о своих предложениях. Готовы к диалогу.

С уважением,
руководитель районного штаба по выборам,
глава района Ю.А. Кабанов

Plate 4.1 *Continued*

5

Who Mobilizes?

Employers often have powerful tools to mobilize their workers, and politicians often have strong incentives to encourage them to do so, but these efforts do not unfold automatically. Because workplace mobilization is costly for managers and politicians, many are loathe to engage in this practice. Indeed, in most of the settings we study, the majority of firms do not mobilize their workers. This leads to the broader question at the heart of our book: Why do some firms mobilize their workers during elections, while others do not?

To identify when workplace mobilization occurs, we develop a straightforward theoretical framework that considers the costs and benefits of workplace mobilization for politicians, firm managers, and workers. We argue that workplace mobilization is especially likely where politicians exercise greater leverage over firm managers, and where, in turn, managers exercise greater leverage over their employees. This leverage often emanates from the availability of outside options for employers and employees. Workplace mobilization is thus deeply rooted in power relations among politicians, managers, and their employees. In the empirical portions of this chapter, we focus most of our attention on relations between politicians and managers, while Chapter 6 takes up in more detail the question of manager-employee relations.

We also find that workplace mobilization occurs where the costs of transacting between politicians and managers are lower. When politicians and managers have close personal or organizational ties, they are more likely to reach and abide by an agreement about how to share the costs and benefits of workplace mobilization. Thus, workplace mobilization is not only is forged by relative power relations but also stems from the nature of personal elite relationships.[1]

---

[1] In Chapter 7 we explore how the institution of free media alters the impact of these power relations.

Workplace Politics. Timothy Frye, Ora John Reuter, and David Szakonyi, Oxford University Press.
© Oxford University Press (2025). DOI: 10.1093/9780197802045.003.0005

126   WORKPLACE POLITICS

Incentive Problems of Workplace Mobilization

Workplace mobilization creates two incentive problems that are at the core of our argument. Because managers and workers rarely engage in workplace mobilization of their own accord, politicians need to motivate managers to pressure their workers, and in turn, managers need to motivate their workers to go to the polls. This is a standard incentive problem in many principal-agent settings where a principal fears that without providing sufficient incentives, the agent will not do what the principal would like.

One key factor in overcoming this problem is leverage, often measured as the availability of outside options. In our case, where politicians have sufficient leverage over their managers, they can more easily compel managers to accept terms that favor the politician, and, in this case, make workplace mobilization more likely. Similarly, where managers have sufficient leverage over their workers, they are better positioned to compel workers to turn out to vote. Where politicians and managers have outsize leverage over their bargaining partners, they are often able to strike deals that make workplace mobilization more likely. In our empirical analyses that follow, we trace how variations in the relative leverage held by politicians, managers, and workers influence the likelihood of workplace mobilization.

However, even where politicians have great leverage over managers and managers have great leverage over workers, transaction costs and commitment problems may stymie efforts to conduct workplace mobilization. Because it takes time, energy, and resources to bargain over the terms of workplace mobilization, in some cases, politicians and employers may find it is not worth the effort.

In addition, because agreements between managers and workers and between workers and managers to engage in workplace mobilization are not enforceable in court, all parties to the agreement must rely on their expectation that other parties will not renege on their arrangement. This is problematic because the exchange of threats or promises for turning out to vote takes place at different times.

Workplace mobilization is replete with these credible commitment problems. Managers may promise to expend effort to mobilize workers in hopes of getting benefits from the state, but then renege on this effort in expectation that the politician will find it difficult to observe their behavior. Politicians may threaten to punish managers who do not mobilize their workers, and managers may promise to punish workers, but after an election, neither politicians nor managers may follow through on punishments because actually delivering the punishment is costly. Anticipating that the threat is unlikely to be delivered, managers and workers may not comply with the agreement in the first place.

Similarly, politicians may promise managers that if they mobilize their workers on election day, they will receive benefits from the state after the election. However, once managers have gotten their workers to the polls, politicians have little incentive to fulfill their end of the bargain. Because managers may anticipate that politicians will renege on their promises, they may be reluctant to mobilize their workers.

In many settings, personal relationships and organizational ties can help reduce transaction costs by increasing levels of knowledge and trust among participants. In this case, politicians and managers who know each other well and belong to similar organizations like parties and business associations may find it much easier to strike and enforce agreements to engage in workplace mobilization. Thus, key to our argument are variables that shape the relative leverage of the parties that engage in workplace mobilization and the transaction costs of striking and enforcing an agreement on workplace mobilization.

Theoretical Framework

Like many models of brokered vote mobilization, our approach starts from the premise that politicians must provide brokers with incentives to mobilize (Stokes, Dunning, and Nazareno, 2013; Camp, 2017; Brierley and Nathan, 2022). However, employers are atypical vote brokers because vote mobilization is not their primary function. In addition, employers are unusual because they are well placed to use both positive inducements and coercion, which can make them particularly effective at getting out the vote. Thus, our model draws inspiration from the literature on the economics of coercion, in which employers use a mixture of both pay and pressure to motivate their workers (Baland and Robinson, 2008; Acemoglu and Wolitzky, 2011; Chwe, 1990).

In this respect our approach is close to that taken by other studies of workplace mobilization, such as Mares and Zhu (2015) and Hertel-Fernandez (2018). However, our work differs from existing models of workplace mobilization by theorizing not only the relationship between employers and voters but also the relationship between employers and politicians.

We analyze workplace mobilization under a standard principal-agent logic in which a politician (principal) uses positive or negative inducements to encourage a manager (agent) to expend effort to mobilize their workers to vote (cf. Jensen and Meckling, 1976 and Gailmard and Patty, 2012). Politicians seek to mobilize as many votes as possible at the lowest price.[2] Managers, for their part, recognize that mobilization imposes substantial costs on them; Chapter 4 outlined its effects on productivity, morale, and profitability. As compensation, managers thus try to maximize the benefits they receive from the state.[3] With limited resources but also a range of possible firms to tap, politicians will target their inducements toward those that can be bought off or pressured at the lowest possible cost while still ensuring that voters get to the polls.[4]

We focus on two parameters that affect the cost of inducing a firm manager to mobilize and thus which firms get mobilized. First, variation in the leverage that the politician has over the manager will influence the price at which the manager sells their effort, and hence the likelihood that the firm will mobilize its workers. The politician's leverage is linked to the outside options available to the manager. In other words, how dependent is the manager on the state for the benefits being offered? Or how vulnerable is the firm to punishment from the state for not complying with a politician's request?

We expect politicians to focus on firm managers who have few outside options should they refuse the contract offered by the politician. For example, politicians have greater leverage over managers of state-owned enterprises (SOEs) because they can be removed by the politician far more easily than can managers of private sector firms. SOE managers often serve

---

[2] Our approach differs from models of voter mobilization that foreground information transmission as the primary motivation. For example, Mares and Young (2019) argue that coercive mobilization against welfare recipients can be understood as a signal to voters opposed to this policy. Similarly, Kramon (2017) argues that vote buying signals a politician's intention to support a political group rather than as a means of buying support. In this chapter we train our focus on power relations, but in Chapter 7 we explore how workplace mobilization generates information for voters who are not mobilized.

[3] In cases where politicians hold significant leverage, firms may try to minimize the risk of negative inducements rather than maximize benefits.

[4] There still may be a risk that each side reneges on the contract—for example, by shirking. Our reading of the Russian case suggests that this problem is acute, but solvable. Politicians regularly monitor firm effort by requiring that firm managers report on their mobilization efforts (datasets, passport details, etc.). Employees are also commonly made to use absentee ballots and vote at specified polling stations, allowing managers, and the politicians they report to, to monitor mobilization effort. When politicians cannot apply such monitoring tools, they may assign them a high cost of mobilization, taking into account the probability of reneging.

at the whim of elected and government officials and are easily replaceable as political conditions change (Ennser-Jedenastik, 2014; Mi and Wang, 2000; Szarzec, Totleben, and Piątek, 2022). Moreover, having been fired, the manager may have few options to work in the state sector again.

Politicians also may have greater leverage over firms that depend on sales to the state or subsidies for their revenue. Firms vary greatly in the degree to which their goods and services are consumed directly by public agencies. Some even design their production lines or invest in innovation specifically to meet government needs (Caravella and Crespi, 2021; Aschhoff and Sofka, 2009). By withholding public procurement contracts, politicians can affect the financial flows to these firms and even threaten them with bankruptcy if they do not comply with political directives (Grossman and Helpman, 2001). Firms with a more diversified customer base, especially those that can easily market their products to private sector firms or sell directly to consumers, are much less vulnerable to threats of economic loss from being cut off from access to state contracts.

We expect politicians to also have greater leverage over managers of firms with specific assets who find it difficult to shift to other jurisdictions or to other lines of production (Bates, 2014; Williamson, 1983; Frieden, 1991). Many firms are dependent on location-specific assets such as factories, buildings, or the presence of raw materials; politicians can more easily pressure these companies to mobilize given the difficulty of them moving production. Put another way, managers who run state-owned firms, depend more on the state for sales, and have specific assets will all be more likely to be targeted by politicians and thus engage in workplace mobilization.

This discussion of relations between politicians and managers yields three hypotheses.

Hypothesis 1 State-owned firms will be more likely to mobilize their workers.

Hypothesis 2 Firms that are financially dependent on the state will be more likely to mobilize their workers.

Hypothesis 3 Firms in sectors characterized by specific assets will be more likely to mobilize their workers.

Another key factor that determines the cost of mobilization for the politician is the ease with which employers can mobilize votes. The costlier it is for employers to mobilize votes, the harder it is for politicians to convince

130 WORKPLACE POLITICS

them to do so. Manager leverage over employees reduces the costs to managers of mobilizing their employees. Just as the politician's leverage over managers influences the likelihood of workplace mobilization, so too does the manager's leverage over their workers. One key source of leverage for employers is the presence of alternative options in the labor market (Acemoglu and Wolitzky, 2011; Mares and Zhu, 2015; Hertel-Fernandez, 2018; Mares and Young, 2019). If labor markets are slack and workers cannot find employment in a suitable alternative position, then they are likely to find threats of punishment to be more persuasive. Fearing a loss in status, a cut in pay, or a pink slip, employees usually accede to their managers' wishes. Slack labor markets reduce the costs to the manager of mobilizing their workers and thereby decrease the cost that politicians have to pay to induce mobilization by employers. This increases the likelihood of workplace mobilization.

Similarly, workers who are highly dependent on their firms not only for wages but also for the provision of social goods at below market prices are more likely to be dependent on management. Management has more leverage over these employees, because any disruption in relations with their employers would have severe negative repercussions for the employee. When the firm provides workers with multiple fringe benefits, managers have a broader menu of potential inducements at their disposal (Friebel and Guriev, 2005).

Another factor that affects the cost of mobilizing votes is the size of the firm. The marginal cost of each mobilized vote declines as the workforce grows, which means that managers in large firms can "sell" more votes to the politician at a lower cost per vote. Thus, firms with more workers are more cost-effective sites for workplace mobilization. In Russia, both our focus group and interview data and the crowdsourced election fraud reports indicate that individualized appeals to voters are much less common than collective appeals (e.g., firmwide emails, announcements at a rally, and official directives). Survey data from Venezuela follow this pattern as well. Because the cost per voter of contacting a voter is lower in large firms than in small firms, we should expect mobilization to be especially likely in the former.

This is true for most other mobilizational techniques as well. For example, the costs of transporting an additional voter to the polls via bus decline with each voter until the seats on the bus are filled. It may also be easier for politicians to overcome commitment problems in large firms, as monitoring the mobilization efforts of managers can be done by aggregating

WHO MOBILIZES? 131

turnout statistics; politicians can track turnout and vote totals in electoral districts where employees live. It is more difficult for managers of large firms to explain away shortfalls in turnout in their electoral districts than it is for those of small firms. Politicians and managers therefore should favor mobilizing firms with more employees. Note that this prediction is at odds with the clientelist literature, which emphasizes that monitoring is likely to be more effective in small communities.

Hypothesis 4 Firms in slack labor markets are more likely to mobilize their workers.

Hypothesis 5 Firms that provide their employees with significant nonwage benefits will be more likely to mobilize their workers.

Hypothesis 6 Firms with more employees will be more likely to mobilize their workers.

Relative leverage is an important determinant of workplace mobilization, but so are the transaction costs associated with striking and abiding by an agreement to exert the necessary effort and resources to get workers to the polls. Thus, we also focus on variables related to the ability of the politician and the manager to overcome obstacles to making the exchange of inducements for voting. Because politicians and managers exchange positive and negative inducements for votes, each side must be assured that the other will hold up their end of the bargain. Workplace mobilization is, therefore, more common when managers and politicians expect to have ongoing relations and can monitor each other's fulfillment of the agreement. When exchanges are repeated and grounded in trust, parties to the agreement can identify potential partners more quickly, rely less on costly schemes to monitor implementation of the agreement, and more quickly agree on terms (Kreps, 1990; Beccerra and Gupta, 1999; Dyer and Chu, 2003).

Hypothesis 7 Firm managers who have close personal contacts with politicians will be more likely to mobilize.

Similarly, when managers belong to organizations that engage regularly with politicians, opportunities increase for monitoring and information sharing, which can help ensure that the exchange of effort for inducements occurs without incident. For example, when managers and politicians belong to the same party organization, managers should be more likely to mobilize their

132 WORKPLACE POLITICS

workers. In Russia, in the late 2000s and 2010s, representatives of most major enterprises in the region were members of United Russia's (UR) regional political council, a leadership/advisory body that would meet periodically to discuss key political issues facing their region. In such settings, UR leaders would undoubtedly expend fewer resources building channels of communications, collecting information on firms' capacity to mobilize, and assessing the correct material exchange needed to cement the bargain when transacting with firm managers who are UR members.

This logic is somewhat different from standard treatments of partisanship in vote mobilization models that emphasize the content of party preferences rather than the personal ties generated by elite-level party organization. Cox (2009) and Nichter (2008), for example, argue that voters whose partisan preferences are easier to predict and are closer to those of the mobilizing politician will be less costly to mobilize. This suggests that politicians should target "core" employers rather than "swing" or opposition-supporting employers. It is cheaper to induce managers who are ideologically aligned with the politician to mobilize because the ideological and moral costs of mobilizing are lower for those employers. In Russia, however, the primary party that engages in the practice, United Russia, is a catch-all party with little ideological coherence. Here party membership promotes mobilization not via ideological affinity, but rather by the generation of personal ties that help to overcome commitment problems. In our empirical tests, we are able to separate these two explanations by distinguishing directors who are party members from those who are just supporters of the ruling party.

Hypothesis 8 Firm directors who are members of the ruling party will be more likely to mobilize workers.

Because business associations provide similar opportunities for building trust, reducing monitoring costs, and sharing information as do political parties, we might expect workplace mobilization to be more likely in firms whose managers are members of business organizations. One possible counterpoint is that firms organized into business associations may be able to extract more from the politician and therefore raise the cost of buying their effort. In settings such as Russia where business organizations enjoy some success lobbying (Pyle, 2006; Pyle and Solanko, 2013; Yakovlev and Govorun, 2011), they might be able to drive up the cost of workplace mobilization for politicians. However, business associations are voluntary and far from all firms are members. Associations increase the probability

WHO MOBILIZES? 133

of politician-employer agreements being secured by lowering transaction costs and facilitating information exchange. Both sides have incentives and resources to make a deal: firms in business associations want to maximize benefits while preventing nonmembers from arranging side deals with politicians, while politicians would prefer to contract at scale with many firms rather than hammer out individual arrangements.

Hypothesis 9 Firms that are members of business organizations will be more likely to mobilize their workers.

In sum, workplace mobilization is more likely when it is less costly for politicians to organize it. These costs are lower both when politicians have leverage over managers and when managers have leverage over their employees. They are also reduced when the costs of monitoring and transacting with employers are low. By focusing on a host of variables related to the influence of leverage and transaction costs of engaging in workplace mobilization, we hope to gain a better understanding of which firms are likely to try to get their workers to the polls.

Research Design

We use our two surveys of firm managers in Russia to examine these hypotheses (described in Chapter 2). Surveys of firm managers offer several advantages for studying the determinants of workplace mobilization. While some forms of workplace mobilization take place in public and are reported in the media, many forms of mobilizing employees are informal and not captured in financial or registration documents, or media reports. Surveys can help capture a broader range of firm activities than a content analysis of media outlets. Although government administrative data might offer more precise measures of firm size and sector, these records cannot be used to identify which firms mobilize their workers, nor can they provide a full picture of firms' political connections or labor market conditions.[5] Employee surveys are helpful in this regard (we analyze them in the next chapter), but employees often have imperfect knowledge of firm finance and structure. Firm management is better positioned to provide this information. Company managers have firsthand knowledge of firm operations,

---

[5] In the prior chapter, we connected survey responses of firm managers with administrative data on state contracts to explore how firms benefit from mobilizing their workers. But our measure of workplace mobilization still comes from interviews with directors.

134　WORKPLACE POLITICS

characteristics, and political activities and are ideal sources of information for the task at hand.

One concern with this data is that some directors may be hesitant to discuss their political activities with interviewers. If this was true, some of our estimates of workplace mobilization may be capturing the lower bounds of this practice. To help address these issues, in the next chapter we analyze surveys with employees. By using surveys of firm managers and workers, we are able to balance the biases and different sources of information that the two groups bring to the study of workplace mobilization. But since employees have much less accurate information about firm operations and decision-making, we treat firm surveys as our primary data source for analyzing firm-level variation in workplace mobilization.

The six-year gap between the surveys also helps us test whether any patterns uncovered in the data are specific to a certain set of political or economic conditions. Russia was much more politically competitive at the federal and regional level and somewhat less repressive in 2011 than in 2017. In addition, President Putin's approval rating was substantially higher in 2017 than it was six years earlier in large part due to the annexation of Crimea in 2014, which produced a prolonged rally-round-the-flag effect in Russia (Hale, 2018; Frye, 2019). Differences in Russia's political environment across these two periods allow us to assess the robustness of our findings.

Outcomes

In both surveys, we asked directors about a wide range of political activities that may have occurred in their workplace prior to elections, as shown in rows 1 to 10 of Table 2.5. In 2011 we asked a smaller set of questions but expanded our list in 2017 to better capture the full range of mobilizational techniques that employers use, such as providing transportation to the polls and holding rallies.

Overall, we find that a large share of employers engaged in some form of workplace mobilization. At the bottom of the table, we calculate the share of directors who answered yes to any of the questions shown in the top ten rows. By this calculation, roughly one-fifth (21.7 percent) of employers mobilized their workers during the 2011 elections. Summing over the same set of rows from the 2017 firm survey (the "Consistent" totals row in the table), we find that roughly one-third of (large) employers mobilized that year. When we take into account the new questions posed to employers, we see that nearly two in five employers in 2017 brought politics into the workplace. As noted here—and consistent with our earlier argument—the higher rate of workplace mobilization in 2017 is likely due to the skew toward larger firms in the 2017 sample.

Our main measure of workplace mobilization is calculated based on these two totals. We create a dichotomous variable that takes the value of 1 if a director reported engaging in any of the activities shown in Table 2.5, corresponding to the percentages shown in row 12 (Any Employer Mobilization).[6]

Predictors

For ease of comparison, we aimed for consistent coding across the two surveys when operationalizing our main predictors. In most cases, we were able to ask the same question on each of the surveys. Our first three hypotheses suggest that firms with greater dependence on the state will be more likely to mobilize. We code state-owned firms with a binary indicator if the respondent reported that the federal, regional, or municipal government had a minority or majority stake in the enterprise. We also coded binary indicators for whether the firm sells its products or services directly to the government. To assess the impact of variation in asset specificity, we use the self-reported sectoral classification of the enterprise and code a binary indicator that equals 1 if the firm operated in a sector characterized by specific assets: natural resource extraction and heavy industry. Figure 5.1 shows how workplace mobilization varies by sector; the practice is most common in heavy industry and the extractive sector, less common in the service sector.[7]

---

[6] Although the battery of questions changes slightly over time, we prefer to include the full set of activities for our 2017 measure. The results are robust to just using the "Consistent" totals measure.

[7] Our measure of asset specificity focuses on natural resources and heavy industry, the latter capturing a range of types of factories that are immobile and difficult to switch to other lines of production. This coding approach follows other observational work that exploits more detailed data on asset redeployability to derive measures of specificity (Kim, 2018). As for the Russian case, utilities may be included as well but form only a small portion of our sample, are a diverse group of entities, and are also state-owned, which we capture in the analyses. Transportation includes a wide range of firms that are usually mobile and can ship multiple types of products. Construction firms are also mobile and can operate in a wide range of markets, so also fall outside of our definition.

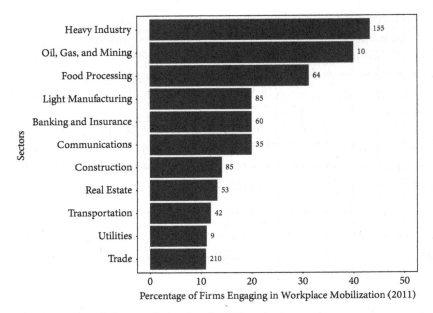

Figure 5.1 Workplace Mobilization by Sector
This figure shows the percentage of firms that engaged in workplace mobilization broken out by sector. Data come from the 2011 Russian employer survey.

Our fourth, fifth, and sixth hypotheses concern the costs to employers of mobilizing employees. To measure manager leverage, we employ variables that tap the firm's relationship with its labor force. Measuring labor market conditions is challenging for a variety of reasons discussed in the next chapter, and our survey of firm managers unfortunately lacks a precise measure of labor market tightness. As a proxy, we use a question that asks respondents to rate (on a 5-point scale) whether a deficit of skilled workers created an obstacle to running their business. To ensure comparability across the surveys, we collapsed this variable into a binary indicator if respondents saw this deficit as somewhat (4) or very much (5) detrimental to their operations. Although this question focuses on high-skill workers, who are not the usual targets of workplace mobilization, labor market tightness is likely correlated across skill levels.

To measure nonwage benefits (H5), we asked directors whether their firm provided nonwage benefits (typical benefits include housing, subsidized transportation, childcare, and medical insurance) to its workers; we code a binary indicator that captures the 51 percent of firms that answered that some type of benefit was provided. In the 2017 survey, respondents were asked to select from a list of possible nonwage benefits their firm could provide;[8] we create a count measure based on how many benefits each respondent selected in total. Finally, to measure firm size (H6), we take the logarithm of the reported number of employees.

Our next set of hypotheses focused on the transaction costs associated with workplace mobilization. We argued that personal ties between directors and government officials help lower these transaction costs. To measure personal ties, we code a binary indicator for whether a firm director is personally acquainted with either the mayor of their municipality or their regional governor. Mayors and regional governors have primary responsibility for mobilizing the United Russia vote in their jurisdictions. To examine the hypothesis about membership in business organizations, we include a variable indicating if the enterprise was a member of any business association. While business associations are not overtly political in Russia, most have close relations with the state. Associations cooperate closely with government officials and rarely if ever depart from government-chosen priorities (Chebankova, 2013). We also capture the partisan allegiance of the firm manager with a binary measure that indicates whether the firm director supported or was a member of the ruling party, United Russia.

We control for the age of the firm (measured by the logged number of years in existence), as well as for its recent performance (measured by whether it had made any large-scale investments in the previous twelve months).

Models and Results

We analyze each firm survey separately, using linear probability models to simplify the interpretation of coefficients.[9] Each model includes region fixed effects and standard errors that are clustered at the region level. Our analyses are correlational and, as such, should be treated with the necessary

---

[8] Respondents were asked about health insurance, pensions, child care, professional training, material help, company-provided holidays, and housing.
[9] Results are robust to using logit models.

138 WORKPLACE POLITICS

caveats and limitations concerning endogeneity. These concerns are particularly pronounced for variables that reflect choices made by management (e.g., having connections with the governor, paying nonwage benefits to employees). Our models are presented in a stairstep fashion such that each table begins with a reduced-form model that only includes the firm's more ascribed (and exogenous) traits. In subsequent models, we add variables that reflect management decisions. After presenting the results, we discuss several specific sources of potential endogeneity.

The main results are presented in Tables 5.1 (2011 Employer Survey) and 5.2 (2017 Employer Survey). First, we see strong and consistent support for the notion that state-dependent firms are more likely to mobilize their workers (H1). The coefficient on state-owned enterprise is positive and statistically significant in almost all models in both 2011 and 2017. In model 1, state-owned firms are almost twenty percentage points more likely to mobilize their workers. We also see that firms that sell to the state are more likely to mobilize.

Because *State-Owned Enterprise* and *Firm Sells to State* are highly correlated, it is difficult to separate their effects in fully specified models. In the 2011 firm survey, *State-Owned Enterprise* falls short of significance in Model 4, which includes the full battery of political variables. This outcome makes sense, given that the directors of state-owned enterprises are also much more likely to have relationships with regional or local officials. Still, *Firm Sells to State* remains significant in this model. The opposite is true in some of the fully specified 2017 models—*State-Owned Enterprise* remains significant, but *Firm Sells to State* drops below statistical significance. Thus, our results strongly indicate that state dependence matters, but in fully specified models, we are unable to distinguish the effect of being state-owned from the effect of selling to the state.

Our models also indicate support for the hypothesis that firms with specific assets are more likely to engage in workplace mobilization. The variable is positive and statistically significant in all models from the 2011 survey. The 2017 survey excluded service sector firms—those with the least specific assets—so that survey is not a good testing ground for this hypothesis. Nonetheless, the variable is positive in all models and approaches statistical significance in several.

The models provide some modest support for the hypothesis that workplace mobilization is more common in settings where employers have more leverage over workers. In all models, offering nonwage benefits to workers is

WHO MOBILIZES? 139

Table 5.1 Employer Mobilization, 2011 Survey

	(1)	(2)	(3)	(4)
Firm Size	0.059***	0.047***	0.043***	0.037***
	(0.009)	(0.010)	(0.012)	(0.012)
Firm Age	−0.019	−0.024	−0.018	−0.030
	(0.018)	(0.018)	(0.019)	(0.020)
State-Owned Enterprise	0.193**	0.196**	0.138*	0.096
	(0.078)	(0.083)	(0.078)	(0.078)
Specific Assets	0.113***	0.090***	0.097***	0.084**
	(0.031)	(0.031)	(0.037)	(0.038)
Firm Experiences Difficulties Finding Workers	−0.058*	−0.039	−0.044	−0.042
	(0.030)	(0.030)	(0.034)	(0.035)
Firm Sells to State		0.142***	0.137***	0.129***
		(0.033)	(0.037)	(0.038)
Firm Invested in Previous Year		0.019	0.032	0.027
		(0.027)	(0.031)	(0.033)
Firm Offers Benefits to Workers (binary)		0.070**	0.063	0.048
		(0.034)	(0.039)	(0.041)
Director Supports UR			0.170***	0.149***
			(0.040)	(0.040)
Director Has Personal Contact with Politicians				0.156***
				(0.047)
Firm Is Member of Business Association				0.018
				(0.057)
R^2	0.208	0.255	0.319	0.343
Observations	747	689	537	512
Region Fixed Effects	✓	✓	✓	✓

***p<0.01, **p<0.05, *p<0.1 This table analyzes a binary indicator for whether firms engaged in any of the seven activities listed in Table 2.1 that were asked in the 2011 survey. All models include region fixed effects and robust standard errors.

positively associated with workplace mobilization. This finding comports with our argument that the employers' leverage increases when workers depend on their employers not just for wages but for important social benefits.[10] This variable is statistically significant in all specifications in the 2017 survey, but falls short of significance in some of the more fully-specified 2011 models.

[10] Some nonwage benefits are regulated by region-level legislation, which we control for by including region fixed effects.

140 WORKPLACE POLITICS

Table 5.2 Employer Mobilization, 2017 Survey

	(1)	(2)	(3)	(4)
Firm Size	0.080***	0.051**	0.053**	0.036
	(0.020)	(0.020)	(0.023)	(0.023)
Firm Age	0.039*	0.023	0.019	−0.011
	(0.022)	(0.024)	(0.025)	(0.024)
State-Owned Enterprise	0.288***	0.248***	0.228***	0.173**
	(0.065)	(0.068)	(0.069)	(0.069)
Specific Assets	0.084*	0.056	0.089*	0.030
	(0.049)	(0.050)	(0.053)	(0.048)
Firm Experiences Difficulties Finding Workers	−0.025	−0.024	−0.019	−0.002
	(0.036)	(0.036)	(0.038)	(0.036)
Firm Sells to State		0.070**	0.025	0.009
		(0.036)	(0.038)	(0.036)
Firm Invested in Previous Year		−0.020	−0.011	−0.016
		(0.028)	(0.030)	(0.027)
Number of Benefits		0.060***	0.043***	0.027**
		(0.011)	(0.012)	(0.011)
Director Supports UR			0.240***	0.203***
			(0.044)	(0.042)
Director Has Personal Contact with Politicians				0.330***
				(0.050)
Firm Is Member of Business Association				0.126***
				(0.046)
R^2	0.261	0.309	0.347	0.446
Observations	631	609	515	490
Region Fixed Effects	✓	✓	✓	✓

***p<0.01, **p<0.05, *p<0.1 This table analyzes a binary indicator for whether firms engaged in any of the seven activities listed in Table 2.1 that were asked in the 2017 survey. All models include region fixed effects and robust standard errors.

We also see a negative association between *Firm Experiences Difficulties Finding Workers* and workplace mobilization. This relationship is statistically significant (at the .1 level) in the reduced model in 2011, but not in other models. As noted earlier, this measure focuses on skilled workers. Skilled workers are in high demand in Russia, so workplace mobilization does not usually focus on them. And if the correlation between the labor market conditions of skilled and unskilled workers is weak, then this measure may underperform. In the next chapter, we introduce better measures of labor market conditions using surveys of workers.

WHO MOBILIZES? 141

Finally, our models provide strong support for the notion that workplace mobilization is more likely in large firms.[11] A director of a firm with six hundred employees is more than twice as likely as a director of a firm with ten employees to report permitting a political event in the workplace. This finding is intriguing in light of the clientelism literature, which suggests that clientelist exchange is more prevalent in small settings and tight-knit communities because brokers find it easier to monitor compliance in those settings. Our findings indicate that politicians consider more than just monitoring costs when they decide how to mobilize voters: they also take into account the economies of scale associated with mobilization.[12]

The results also provide support for the argument that bargaining costs affect the decision to engage in workplace mobilization. Firm managers who had personal contacts with politicians were 16 percent more likely to mobilize their workers. As a robustness check (not shown), we also find that directors who had experience serving in government were more likely to encourage their workers to go to the polls.

We then find that firms that are members of business associations are much more likely to mobilize their workers. As noted earlier, politicians find it cheaper to engage with multiple firms simultaneously in the efforts to get out the vote.

Finally, our analyses show that the partisanship of the manager matters as well. Column 3 in both tables shows that UR-affiliated directors mobilized their workers at a higher rate.[13] This finding holds even while controlling for the firm's level of state dependence. In supplemental analyses, we explored this hypothesis further by focusing on membership in United Russia. In our surveys we asked directors not only if they supported United Russia but if they were formal members of the ruling party. Party members are more likely than mere supporters to be involved in regional party structures such

[11] The coefficient is not significant in the 2017 firm survey, but that survey only focused on large and very large firms, so it is not an appropriate dataset for testing this hypothesis.

[12] Unfortunately the 2017 firm survey did not include information on the actual revenue or profitability of the enterprise. But all of the firm-level results shown in Tables 5.1 and 5.2 are robust to including controls for relative growth in revenue (compared to previous years) and whether the firm was located in a capital city, where different types of political mobilization might be expected to occur alongside workplace mobilization.

[13] The sample size is reduced by including this variable for director affiliation, most likely because the respondent in the survey is sometimes not the firm director and they may not know the actual director's political leanings. These results are robust to including a control for not performing listwise deletion and instead controlling for whether data on director political affiliation are available. Likewise our results are robust to just subsetting to respondents who are the firm directors and not another member of the management team.

142   WORKPLACE POLITICS

as political councils (*politsovety*) that meet regularly. Given the hierarchical nature of United Russia, firm mobilization within ruling party structures is likely to entail much lower transaction costs. Our data are consistent with this notion. When we subset our data to include only UR supporters (i.e., a sample that includes both formal members and mere sympathizers), we see that UR members are much more likely to mobilize than are nonmembers. Given that United Russia is a relatively nonideological party, this suggests that a firm's organizational ties to United Russia give rise to higher rates of workplace mobilization.[14]

Limitations

The preceding analyses are consistent with our argument but should be interpreted with some caution, given the observational nature of our data and the endogeneity bias common to this mode of analysis. This bias is likely most severe in our analyses of the impact of personal relations between politicians and managers and the partisan ties of managers. Parsing the direction of the relationship in these cases is particularly challenging as the process of engaging in workplace mobilization may shape the personal relations between firm managers and politicians. In addition, workplace mobilization itself may influence the partisan views of the managers. Thus, making strong claims here is difficult.

Other variables such as ownership structure, asset specificity, and the slackness of the labor market are more difficult (but not impossible) for politicians to manipulate in service of short-run political aims (e.g., facilitating workplace mobilization). One deeper endogeneity issue is that politicians might try to create economies dominated by state ownership, slack labor markets, and specific assets in order to maximize not just workplace mobilization but also their ability to intervene in firms for political purposes. This is in line with Acemoglu and Wolitzky (2011), who argue that coercion is used to limit outside options for workers in labor markets. Such efforts, if they were to occur, unfold over the long term and would not be inconsistent with the theoretical framework we offer here.

---

[14] These results on manager partisanship are also robust to including manager gender, age, and education as controls, helping to address possible concerns that manager support for United Russia may be cofounded by other demographic characteristics also potentially related to the use of workplace mobilization. Instead, we find that regime support is the only statistically significant predictor at the manager level of whether the firm mobilizes its workers.

Another endogeneity concern is that the types of employers that are vulnerable to state pressure are also more likely to mobilize because they have an inherent ideological preference for the regime. While state-dependent directors could exhibit an ideological preference for the regime, it is difficult to see why directors of large firms would be more likely to have this preference once we control for government financial support, sector, and ownership structure. Empirically, we attempt to mitigate this endogeneity concern by controlling for the vote preference of directors in our firm models. Thus, conditional on ideological preference, we find that directors of certain types of firms are more likely to engage in voter mobilization.

Conclusion

Power relations among politicians, firm managers, and employees are central to understanding political mobilization in the workplace. In settings where employers have leverage over managers, workplace mobilization is likely to be more common. In this chapter, we have shown evidence of this, demonstrating that workplace mobilization is more common in (1) state-owned firms, (2) firms that sell to the state, and (3) firms with specific assets. Workplace mobilization is also more common in settings where firm managers can mobilize votes cheaply. Where slack labor markets give firm managers leverage over employees, workplace mobilization becomes less costly for employers and therefore more common. This chapter has provided some preliminary evidence of this, while the next chapter examines manager leverage over employees more deeply. We also find that workplace mobilization is much more common in large firms, where economies of scale reduce the marginal costs of each additional mobilized voter. Finally, where the costs of bargaining between firm managers and politicians are lower, workplace mobilization is more likely to occur. Workplace mobilization is also made easier where politicians, managers, and workers have organizational or personal ties that reduce opportunism during bargaining. Consistent with this perspective, we have found that workplace mobilization is more likely in firms where firm managers have connections with regional governors and where they are members of business associations.

By identifying the conditions under which workplace mobilization occurs, we identify a novel reason why politicians are often loathe to introduce economic reforms that would liberalize labor markets. Economic liberalization increases the autonomy of employers from the state and thereby raises the costs of mobilizing votes. Similarly, by keeping labor markets rigid and tying workers to specific employers, politicians can increase their leverage over managers and workers at election time. Such strategies are economically inefficient, but they also have political benefits.

In addition, by identifying the most common sites of workplace electoral subversion, our analysis provides some microfoundations to arguments about the economic bases of transitions from autocratic rule. Boix (2003) and Acemoglu and Robinson (2006) identify asset specificity as a key obstacle to democratization but do not provide microlevel tests of their arguments. Our findings are consistent with this view, but we posit a different mechanism. Firms in sectors with low asset specificity may subvert democracy not just because they fear redistribution under democracy but also because they are vulnerable to pressure from the autocrat.

6

Who Gets Mobilized?

In 2004, millions of Hong Kong residents went to the polls to elect half the city's Legislative Council. With more seats now chosen by voters, these elections marked a gradual step forward in the city's democratization. Demonstrations earlier that summer saw hundreds of thousands of people take to the streets to condemn the imposition of new internal security measures and demand the right to elect all their politicians.[1] Pro-democracy candidates were hopeful about their chances of securing a majority in the council and pushing for even more democratic reforms, such as universal suffrage.

In Beijing, leaders nervously watched these developments. To fight what they saw as a direct threat to their hard-line rule, pro-Beijing groups turned for help to some of the most powerful local actors in Hong Kong: large corporate enterprises and financial institutions. The influence these firms, both state-owned and private, had over their workers' private lives was immense. Workers were told by their bosses to provide lists of the addresses and contact information of all eligible voters in their family, and threatened with "trouble" if they didn't comply.[2] Human rights activists described a "culture of fear" in the workplace, as bosses muzzled any political dissent.[3]

Across the island, employees were also told directly who to vote for and then had to use relatively new technology (for the time) to relay their ballot choice to management. As one worker at a clock factory remarked,

> A senior staff member of my company asked me to vote for pro-Beijing candidates, instead of pro-democratic candidates. To make sure I have done that, he told me to take pictures of my completed ballot sheet with my

---

[1] Bradsher, Keith, "Throngs Go to Polls in Key Vote for Hong Kong: Beijing Puts Pressure on Companies to Ensure Result It Wants," *International Herald Tribune*, September 13, 2004.

[2] Human Rights Watch, "Hong Kong: Elections Marred by Intimidation," September 9, 2004.

[3] Workplace mobilization became so controversial that pro-Beijing groups embarked on an eight-week, $30 million publicity campaign to assuage voter concerns about intimidation in the workplace. Chan, Carrie, "Push for Clean Elections," *South China Morning Post,* June 22, 2004. See also Human Rights Watch, "Hong Kong: Elections Marred by Intimidation."

Workplace Politics. Timothy Frye, Ora John Reuter, and David Szakonyi, Oxford University Press.
© Oxford University Press (2025). DOI: 10.1093/9780197802045.003.0006

146   WORKPLACE POLITICS

mobile-phone camera ... He told me that if we voted for pro-democrats, our company's business would be in trouble.[4]

In the end, pro-Beijing candidates retained their grip on the Legislative Council during the elections, and the use of workplace mobilization has since become a persistent feature of election campaigns in Hong Kong. For example, during the 2016 Legislative Council Elections, press reports indicated that state-owned enterprises handed out lists with the names of recommended candidates and asked employees to call their managers after voting.[5] Employees in Hong Kong often come under severe pressure from their managers to toe a pro-Beijing line, or otherwise face dire personal consequences.

From Hong Kong to Nigeria to Russia, understanding relations between politicians and firms is central to workplace mobilization. Having explored this theme in the last two chapters, we now turn our focus to the second leg of our theory: relations between firm managers and their employees. Employers are more likely to mobilize their employees when the cost of successfully getting them to the polls is low. Thus, we argue that employers who have more leverage over their employees are more likely to engage in workplace mobilization. We focus on two types of leverage. First, workers in slack labor markets (e.g., where jobs are scarce and unemployment is high) are more likely to experience workplace mobilization. The threats and beseechments of employers will carry greater weight in such settings, because alternative employment is harder to find., which makes it easier for employers to get workers to the polls. Their counterparts in tight labor markets have much greater bargaining power vis-à-vis their employers and are less vulnerable to electoral pressure.

We also argue that employees in the state sector are more likely to be mobilized by their employers. Among other factors, state-sector employees generally have fewer transportable skills and less attractive exit options than do their peers in the private sector, which gives managers in the state bureaucracy powerful leverage over their workers. In addition, in countries where political patronage is common, the political views and partisan ties of state sector employers can be important determinants of career advancement,

---

[4] Ng, Michael, "Warning on Poll Pressure," *The Standard*, May 14, 2004.

[5] "Vote This Way: Chinese State-Owned Firms Reportedly Hand Out Instructions to Staff on How to Vote in Hong Kong Elections," *South China Morning Post*, September 4, 2016.

giving state employees less ability to resist mobilization by their employers (Oliveros, 2021).

In this chapter, we use qualitative data from focus groups, as well as survey data and experiments from Russia and six other countries. To explore how labor market conditions and state-sector employment influence the likelihood of workplace mobilization. These data show how employers assess the vulnerabilities and exit options of their workforce when deciding whether to engage in workplace mobilization.

A Shift in Perspective

This chapter shifts our empirical perspective to the worker. We have gained valuable information by exploring workplace mobilization from the perspective of firm managers. Employers are uniquely positioned to understand the needs and characteristics of their firm, and only managers can report on their interactions with politicians. But understanding how workers perceive workplace mobilization is crucial for understanding the broader implications of the practice. In addition, shifting to the worker's perspective also expands our scope of analysis, allowing us to study workplace mobilization in the public sector and in countries outside of Russia. Many countries have high levels of public employment, so it is important to study the practice in the state sector.

Finally, the worker's point of view is helpful in correcting biases introduced by surveying employers. Even well-intentioned employers may have difficulty gauging how workers experience workplace mobilization. Emails that seem innocuous from the employer's point of view may appear coercive or threatening to employees. For less well-intended employers, the coercive nature of workplace mobilization may be precisely the point. We learn a great deal from surveys of employers, but it is essential to explore the views of workers. We do so in this chapter and the next.

Labor Market Conditions and Workplace Mobilization

Our theory suggests that labor markets shape the use of workplace mobilization. As Chapter 2 showed, workplace mobilization is generally disliked by employees, who view the practice as an intrusion into their private lives.

148 WORKPLACE POLITICS

Politicizing the workplace thus carries an important set of costs for employers. Forcing workers to engage in political activity against their wishes harms employee morale, up to the point where mobilized workers may seek other employment.

Slack labor markets reduce these costs. Where jobs are scarce and unemployment is high, workers have fewer exit options and are more likely to accede to management's wishes than are their peers in tight labor markets. Knowing that their workers cannot easily find other jobs, employers can more easily and effectively levy threats of job loss, demotion, or wage cuts for those who do not toe the political line.

Our focus groups and interviews illustrate the precarious situation in which workers often find themselves. Consider, for example, the following exchange from our focus group participants in Zlatoust, a single-company town in the Urals. After the moderator asked whether management had intimated that there would be negative consequences for them if they did not vote, respondents reflected on the difficulty of making ends meet in Zlatoust and the anxieties that this created when they faced political pressure from their bosses:[6]

MARINA: They took our bonuses away.

OLGA: Well, on the internet they were talking about how they would take bonuses away from the kindergarten teachers if they didn't go vote and verify it with a photo. The whole internet was plastered with that.

NINA: What, do they get big bonuses in the kindergartens?

OLGA: Well, the salary is small, so the bonus counts for something.

MARINA: Bonuses can be different amounts. Let's say the salary was 10000 rubles and the bonus is 1500, that's not nothing. Even if it's just 500 rubles. I remember when I got my job and they refused to give me my bonus because I didn't go vote. And it was *my* bonus. We get a bonus once a year and they didn't give it to me. It's not like they didn't give it to me, it's more like they took money away from me.

MODERATOR: Do you think people are afraid of that?

MARINA: They are where I work.

OLGA: Nowadays, salaries are so low that people are afraid of everything.

SERGEI: People are afraid of everything now. Afraid of losing their salary, big or even small, because they won't find another one. So it's easy to scare people.

[6] Focus Group Responses, Focus Group, Bashkirova & Partners, Zlatoust, Russia. October 4, 2017.

WHO GETS MOBILIZED? 149

MODERATOR: Svetlana, what do you think?

SVETLANA: Completely agree.

OLGA: This is especially true at some sort of state enterprises. People are afraid of being fired there because the state enterprises at least work somehow and how are you going to find another job? It doesn't matter if you have a good education or not.

SVETLANA: If you don't like it, there is a whole line of people waiting to take your place.

In situations of economic precarity, workers often calculate that it is better to toe the line than to risk punishment. Ekaterina, one of our interview respondents in Zlatoust, highlights this point:[7]

EKATERINA: The boss gathered us up, and the candidate came to us during the day, there was a speech, and then the boss said that we had to vote for this and that candidate without question.

MODERATOR: You were told in no uncertain terms whom to vote for?

EKATERINA: Yes. They asked us to vote for Vainshtein, if I remember correctly.

MODERATOR: Were you promised anything in exchange for your vote?

EKATERINA: No, we weren't promised anything. On the contrary, they told us that if we didn't go [to vote]—then we could lose our bonuses or be punished in some other way.

MODERATOR: Did you believe the threats?

EKATERINA: Well, everyone values their work right now. We all went to vote. They ordered us, and we gathered in line like geese and went. We decided it's better not to risk it.

These remarks underscore how employers can use their power in the labor market to compel workers to engage in political activity. In places with few economic opportunities, employers need not be explicit about the potential consequences for workers who do not fall in line. Employees understand their vulnerability, and even if they find workplace mobilization morally repugnant, they value continued employment over such objections.

However, when employers face difficulties replacing workers, they may be less likely to pressure their workers to engage in political activity out

---

[7] Focus Group Response Ekaterina, Focus Group, Bashkirova & Partners, Zlatoust, Russia. October 4, 2017.

150 WORKPLACE POLITICS

of fear of those workers quitting and taking another position. Workers who can easily find other jobs also may feel empowered to disregard any attempts by management to engage them politically. Take, for example, Tatyana, a twenty-six-year-old factory worker in Satka who recounted in our interview that she had refused her boss's requests to vote. When the moderator asked why she thought people complied, she offered the following interpretation of her coworkers' thought process and an explanation of her own:[8]

> Well, people have their own ideas, that's one thing. But at the same time, some people are not afraid. For example, me. Frankly speaking, if I didn't go, I wouldn't be afraid of losing my job. I don't think there's a specific job that I need to hang on to—I mean, I could just go work in a store; maybe that's not what I want exactly, but I'd find another job for myself. I'll go to the unemployment office or something else, but there will be an opportunity. I am not hanging on to my job for dear life.

Tight labor markets or employees who think they have outside options therefore constrain employers politically by reducing the credibility of the threats they use to cajole their workers around elections.

Our data are especially appropriate for assessing the impact of labor market conditions on workplace mobilization. We begin by looking at all four survey waves conducted in Russia (2011, 2014, 2016, and 2018), as described in Chapter 2. For our primary measure of employer leverage, we coded whether the respondent lives in one of Russia's 333 single-company towns, or *monogoroda*. Single-company towns—settlements that are economically dependent on a single enterprise—are common in countries around the world, including Australia, Chile, India, Canada, the United States, Japan, Argentina, and Indonesia.[9] In the post-Soviet space, such settlements are especially common due to the economic geography of Soviet central planning. A prominent feature of state-led industrialization in the Soviet Union was the rapid creation and settlement of hundreds of new cities centered around a large factory, often in far-flung locations near important natural resources. In Russia, these *monogoroda* are defined by the federal government as any municipality where a single enterprise or group of interlinked enterprises provide more than 50 percent of the city's industrial output.

---

[8] Interview with Tatyana, In-depth Interview, Bashkirova & Partners, Satka, Russia. October 7, 2017.
[9] See Borges and Torres (2012) for a comparative overview.

WHO GETS MOBILIZED? 151

The Russian Government has identified 333 such towns in Russia, accounting for 10 percent of the country's population.

A number of scholars have described the vulnerabilities that workers in single-company towns face (Gaventa, 1982; Borges and Torres, 2012; Crowley, 2015). Employer leverage is heightened in such settings because losing one's job at the main enterprise would have grave consequences. When an employee spoils relations with the director of the main enterprise in a single-company town, fewer openings are available to apply for after losing their job. Threats are made more credible in single-company towns because the labor market is more often slack. This vulnerability is made all the more severe because many people in single-company towns are dependent on the firm not just for their livelihood but also for social provisions such as housing, transportation, access to recreational facilities, preschool, and health care. In fact, this social dependence may make nonemployed individuals in single-company towns more vulnerable to coercion than nonemployed respondents elsewhere. Our focus groups, as well as press accounts, indicate that employers typically make collective mobilizational appeals to the entire workplace, rather than targeting individual employees within workplaces. Employers therefore need to infer the vulnerability of a workforce based on easily observable, collective characteristics of the workforce. The location of a firm in a single-company town is one such useful indicator.

To explore the impact of labor market conditions, we use a linear probability model that estimates the likelihood a respondent experienced any of the following forms of political mobilization by employers: discussing elections at work, sharing political opinions, endorsing a candidate at work, distributing campaign materials at work, providing transport to the polls, asking employees to attend a rally, asking employees to vote, or asking employees to vote for a specific candidate.[10] All models control for the respondent's sex, age, education, and income, as well for the size of the respondent's city of residence and for employment in the state bureaucracy or a state-owned firm. The first column reports the results for respondents who work in the state bureaucracy as well as those who work in private firms. We do not include sectoral fixed effects here, as doing so would remove state employees from the analysis. In reported in Table 6.1, we report results only for those working in nonstate firms and include fixed effects for the economic sector. Standard errors are clustered at the regional level.

[10] In the supplementary appendix, we also estimate similar models with a dependent variable that taps only whether the respondent was asked to vote. Results are similar.

152 WORKPLACE POLITICS

Table 6.1 Workplace Mobilization in *Monogorods*

	Mobilized in Workplace		
	(1)	(2)	(3)
Male	−0.018	0.009	−0.005
	(0.018)	(0.022)	(0.025)
Age (log)	0.018	0.038	0.022
	(0.023)	(0.029)	(0.026)
Education	0.015***	0.013**	0.015**
	(0.005)	(0.007)	(0.007)
City Size	−0.035***	−0.032***	−0.031***
	(0.008)	(0.009)	(0.010)
Economic Status	0.029**	0.021*	0.021*
	(0.011)	(0.012)	(0.011)
Public Sector Employee	0.146***	0.089**	0.073*
	(0.023)	(0.035)	(0.039)
Turned Out in Recent Parliamentary Election	0.068***	0.055***	0.057***
	(0.016)	(0.018)	(0.020)
Binary Putin Approval	−0.036*	−0.024	−0.024
	(0.021)	(0.021)	(0.021)
Monogorod Resident	0.099**	0.109***	0.098***
	(0.039)	(0.037)	(0.037)
R^2	0.056	0.036	0.047
Observations	3,470	2,492	2,378
Survey fixed effects	✓	✓	✓
Sector fixed effects			✓

***p<0.01, **p<0.05, *p<0.1 This table presents results using individual-level predictors pooled across all four surveys. The outcome variable is a binary indicator for the Minimal definition of Workplace Mobilization (just those components that were asked in all four surveys). Column 1 uses the full sample of employed respondents (in government and the private sector), while Columns 2 and 3 look only at private companies. All models include survey wave fixed effects, with errors clustered on region.

We find that across all three model specifications, residents of single-company towns are roughly ten percentage points more likely to experience workplace mobilization. The magnitude of these effects is large and statistically significant, as residing in one of these towns is among the most powerful predictors of being mobilized in the workplace. When labor market conditions are tight and exit options few, employers feel more emboldened to bring politics to the workplace.

Other variables also provide some insight into our theory. As in prior chapters, we find that workers in smaller towns and rural areas are more likely to experience workplace mobilization than their peers in larger towns and cities. One interpretation is that workers in smaller towns may have

WHO GETS MOBILIZED? 153

fewer employment opportunities than those in larger towns, which would suggest a link between the job market and workplace mobilization.[11] In addition, workers employed in the state bureaucracy are more likely to be mobilized by their employers. We explore this relationship in more detail in the next section of this chapter.

Results on several of the control variables are also noteworthy. First, wealthier, more educated respondents are more likely to report being mobilized. Since those with higher socioeconomic standing (SES) might have more outside employment options and therefore be less vulnerable to pressure, this finding could be interpreted in tension with our theory. At the same time, mismatches between formal education and skill in the labor force are common in middle-income countries. It is also likely that higher-SES respondents are more likely to perceive and report workplace mobilization as such. A similar logic likely explains why workplace mobilization appears to be weakly correlated with regime support (support for Putin) in several of our models.[12] Oppositional workers are likely more attuned to workplace pressure.

Intriguingly, we also find that voter intimidation is much more common in single-company towns in Russia. To show this, we turn again to data from our 2012 list experiment on voter intimidation in Russia (see Chapter 2 for further discussion). Table 6.2 shows that coercion is far more likely in these settings. Our list experiment reveals that approximately 26 percent of respondents in single-company towns experienced electoral intimidation, compared to only 5 percent outside single-company towns (a statistically insignificant result).[13] Among employed residents of single-company towns, a staggering 44 percent of voters reported that they had felt intimidation (the share of nonemployed voters in single-company towns who felt intimidation was only 9 percent). Vote buying, by contrast, is no more likely in single-company towns. In Russia, most intimidation occurs in the workplace, and most workplace-based electoral subversion consists of coercion.

---

[11] To be sure, other interpretations are possible. For example, monitoring of voter turnout could be easier in small towns.

[12] This finding is also consistent with the simple observation that workplace mobilization targets core regime supporters who can be depended upon to vote for the regime, if they do turn out.

[13] It is worth reemphasizing that outside of single-company towns, employed respondents are still more likely to report electoral intimidation than nonemployed respondents: 13 percent of employed respondents living outside of single-company towns reported coercion, whereas 0 percent of nonemployed respondents reported coercion.

154 WORKPLACE POLITICS

Table 6.2 Single-Company Towns and the Prevalence of Negative/Positive Inducements

	(1) Control	(2) Negative	(3) Positive
Panel A: Respondent lives in single-company town			
Mean Number of Responses	1.822	2.091	1.917
Number of Observations	62	66	60
Difference from Control Group		0.268**	0.094
		(0.155)	(0.160)
Panel B: Respondent does not live in single-company town			
Mean Number of Responses	2.082	2.132	2.063
Number of Observations	476	478	473
Difference from Control Group		0.050	−0.018
		(0.052)	(0.052)

*** p<0.01, ** p<0.05, * p<0.1 This table shows means from a list experiment asking respondents about their experience with voter intimidation. Panels are subset according to whether the respondent is a resident of a single-company town (*monogorod*), where a small number of large enterprises are responsible for the majority of employment and production output. Standard errors in parentheses and stars reflect p-values as calculated using one-sided t-tests.

The practice is especially common in single-company towns where outside employment options are few.

Next, we dig deeper into other proxies for economic leverage using the survey of forty-two hundred respondents following elections to regional parliaments in Russia in 2014. Focusing on this survey separately offers several advantages and disadvantages. First, our 2014 survey included a large over-sample of employed individuals (around four hundred) that would give us the statistical power to parse the effects of fine-grained differences in employment circumstances. We also asked more questions about job market conditions and work experience in our standalone 2014 survey than we did in the omnibus surveys.

At the same time, one disadvantage of the 2014 survey is that it was carried out after regional (rather than national) elections and in the midst of the post-Crimea upsurge in regime support. At the time, the Kremlin was less concerned about low turnout in regional elections, as the post-Crimea rally-round-the-flag effect created high levels of voter enthusiasm. These two factors reduced the incentive to put pressure on workers, so the 2014 survey recorded significantly lower levels of workplace mobilization than our other surveys, which resulted in less variation on our dependent variable.[14]

One key predictor of workplace mobilization in our study is perceived job insecurity. Measuring this concept is challenging because it has multiple dimensions and official statistics on unemployment rates may not reflect how workers perceive their likelihood of job loss. Our argument suggests that the employers' decision to mobilize hinges on how vulnerable they perceive their employees to be. Measuring fears of job loss among workers is a useful proxy for this perception. To capture the multiple dimensions of perceived job insecurity, we asked respondents three questions.[15] First, to examine the perceived likelihood of job loss, we asked, "What do you think, about how likely is it that you will lose your job in the next twelve months?" Responses ranged from 0 to 100 percent. The mean response was 24 percent. One quarter of respondents reported a 0 percent chance that they would lose their job in the next twelve months, while one in three respondents reported at least a 50 percent chance of losing their job in the next year.

We also measure the perceived significance of losing one's job. In some lines of work, like construction, layoffs are common but may be short-lived and even expected as part of the job. In other sectors, layoffs can be long-lasting and cause steep declines in financial security and status. To capture variation in the significance of losing one's job, we asked respondents, "Imagine an unpleasant situation where for whatever reason, you lose your job tomorrow. About how confident are you that you could find a job as good as the one that you currently have?" Responses ranged on a 5-point scale from absolutely not confident (1) to absolutely confident (5). The average response was 2.8 with a standard deviation of 1.1.

---

[14] Our dependent variable is a composite measure of whether the respondent reported any form of workplace mobilization. The appendix shows models that restrict the operationalization only to those more clientelistic and coercive methods. Results are similar.

[15] We do not use formal unemployment rates as they are often unreliable in countries with large informal sectors, weak data-gathering institutions, and modest welfare states that provide few incentives to register for unemployment. These features are prominent in the countries in our study. In addition, unemployment rates are often reported at high levels of aggregation (region) that mask variation at lower (and more relevant) levels and often fail to capture the greater problems of underemployment and low job quality. See Dewan, Sabina, and Peter Peck, "Beyond the Employment/Unemployment Dichotomy: Measuring the Quality of Employment in Low Income Countries," WP #83, International Labor Office, Geneva, November 2007, 1–25.

156 WORKPLACE POLITICS

Finally, we asked respondents whether they had a second job. Many workers in Russia and elsewhere hold a second job as a hedge against the possibility of losing their current position.[16] Second jobs can therefore be seen as an indication of insecurity in one's primary job. Eight percent of respondents in our survey reported holding a second job.

In separate regressions in Table 6.3, we add each of the three measures of perceived job insecurity. Here again we analyze all respondents employed in the state and private sectors in the first three columns (omitting sector fixed effects), but then focus just on those working in the private sector in the rightmost three (and include sector fixed effects). The model specifications are identical to those used in the analysis of all four waves together, with standard demographic and political controls included at the individual level.

Controlling for a host of factors, we find that workers with higher levels of subjective job insecurity report higher levels of workplace mobilization. For example, in column 1, we find that workers who report a one standard deviation (.28) increase in the perceived likelihood of losing their job in the next twelve months are about four percentage points more likely to have experienced workplace mobilization. When we restrict the sample by excluding workers in the state bureaucracy in column 4, this figure increases to more than five percentage points for each increase in one standard deviation in perceived likelihood of job loss.

In column 2, we find that a one-unit change in the perceived ease of finding a similar job is associated with a four-percentage-point increase in the likelihood of workplace mobilization. This figure is slightly higher when state bureaucrats are excluded from the analysis, as shown in column 5. Finally, in column 3, we find that workers who reported holding a second job were about seven percentage points more likely to be mobilized by their employers in their primary job. In the restricted sample shown in column 6, this figure falls to 6 percent, but is imprecisely estimated.

Taken together these results suggest a relationship between perceived job insecurity and the likelihood of workplace mobilization. These results are important as they show that in enterprises across Russia—not just those located in *monogorods*—workers who experience more uncertainty about their future employment prospects are much more likely to be report being mobilized. Using three different measures of labor insecurity, as well as

---

[16] Having a second job may also mean that the respondent is trying to earn extra money because their primary employment does not offer a sufficient salary. Although somewhat distinct from job security, this type of second job also may suggest that respondents are concerned about their overall ability to earn a living wage.

Table 6.3 Labor Market Conditions

	Mobilized in Workplace					
	(1)	(2)	(3)	(4)	(5)	(6)
Constant	0.447***	0.470***	0.484***			
	(0.143)	(0.159)	(0.140)			
Male	−0.044	−0.052	−0.051	−0.082	−0.107*	−0.091*
	(0.041)	(0.039)	(0.037)	(0.048)	(0.052)	(0.046)
Age (log)	0.0005	−0.014	0.018	0.014	−0.010	0.029
	(0.034)	(0.041)	(0.033)	(0.039)	(0.054)	(0.040)
Education	0.021**	0.015**	0.014*	0.019	0.013	0.015
	(0.007)	(0.007)	(0.007)	(0.011)	(0.010)	(0.009)
City Size	−0.039	−0.039*	−0.043*	−0.023	−0.028	−0.032
	(0.023)	(0.021)	(0.021)	(0.020)	(0.021)	(0.021)
Public Sector Employee	0.085*	0.077*	0.087**			
	(0.043)	(0.037)	(0.034)			
Economic Status	0.013	−0.001	0.004	0.002	−0.010	−0.007
	(0.024)	(0.023)	(0.021)	(0.016)	(0.020)	(0.018)
Turned Out in Recent Parliamentary Election	0.085	0.084**	0.079**	0.100**	0.091***	0.074**
	(0.050)	(0.036)	(0.038)	(0.041)	(0.027)	(0.029)
Binary Putin Approval	−0.003	0.004	0.0008	−0.012	−0.008	−0.017
	(0.038)	(0.036)	(0.040)	(0.056)	(0.060)	(0.065)
Self-Reported % of Losing Job	0.172**			0.252***		
	(0.075)			(0.087)		
Difficulty of Finding New Work		0.048**			0.055**	
		(0.017)			(0.024)	
Has Second Job			0.085**			0.084
			(0.035)			(0.065)
State-Owned Enterprise				0.013	0.026	0.051
				(0.091)	(0.052)	(0.047)
R^2	0.036	0.038	0.032	0.051	0.049	0.035
Observations	990	1,237	1,341	718	907	993
Sector Fixed Effects				✓	✓	✓

***p<0.01, **p<0.05, *p<0.1 This table presents results using only individual-level predictors in the 2014 Survey. The outcome variable is a binary indicator for the Full definition of Workplace Mobilization. Standard errors are clustered on region.

WORKPLACE POLITICS

controlling for sector (and in turn asset specificity), we see that managers prey upon the most vulnerable workers to apply political pressure, without fearing job exit or other threats to production.

Workplace Mobilization in the State Sector

Workers' vulnerability can be linked to labor market conditions, but it may also be related to their sector of employment. State-sector workers are especially good targets for political mobilization. Oliveros (2021) provides numerous examples from Argentina of state employees participating in and organizing rallies, delivering benefits to supporters, and advocating for incumbents. She finds that municipal employees appointed by the mayor without civil service protections are key cogs in political machines that turn out voters. Recognizing that a loss by their political patron would put their jobs in danger, these political appointees are far more likely to engage in a range of voter mobilization efforts than are their peers. Forrat (2018) shows that public school teachers in Russia play a similar, if somewhat more nefarious role on electoral commissions.

Mobilizing in the public sector is often cheaper for incumbent politicians because they do not need to provide incentives to the firm manager to get workers to the polls. In Chapter 4 we showed that politicians often have to motivate firm managers to mobilize their workers by providing them concessions, such as privileged access to state contracts. In Chapter 5 we found that politicians are well placed to pressure firm managers who are more dependent on the state and have immobile assets. When mobilizing in the public sector, politicians can eliminate the middleman and rely on their direct subordinates to get state employees to the polls. State sector workers form part of a clearly constructed vertical hierarchy, through which management can directly pass down commands that reduce opportunities for bargaining. Whereas some private sector employers can refuse to abide by the wishes of politicians seeking votes from their workplace, mid-level managers in the bureaucracy have much less autonomy to disobey their superiors. In Russia, for example, it is common for public sector organizations to simply *require* that supervisors mobilize their employees. Plates 6.1–6.3 show a number of examples of such directives from the KN data.[17]

---

[17] Failure to comply can bring retribution from the state. For example, after the 2024 presidential elections, the mayor of Nizhny Tagil publicly announced that his administration would be checking to see whether state employees had voted. As he stated, those who "ignored" the election "had no place in state service, whatever their level of qualification." See "Mer Nizhnego Tagila poobeshchal vyyavit' negolosovavshikh byudzhetnikov" RBK, March 19, 2024.

Plate 6.1

But mobilization in the state bureaucracy is an especially attractive strategy for politicians for other reasons as well. Public sector workers often have higher wages and benefits—benefits that cannot be easily replaced in the private sector. And where public and private sector wages are similar, it is often still the case that nonwage benefits and subjective job satisfaction are higher in the public sector (Gimpelson and Lukiyanova, 2009). Public sector employees also have access to opportunities for personal enrichment through bribery and corruption (Gorodnichenko and Peter, 2007). In addition, public sector workers have stronger job protections during economic

160 WORKPLACE POLITICS

Уважаемые коллеги!

18 марта 2018 года в нашей стране проводятся выборы Президента Российской Федерации.

Учитывая важность указанных выборов, предлагаю обеспечить 100 процентное участие сотрудников вверенных вам следственных отделов в голосовании, которое будет проводится с 8 до 20 часов по местному времени.

О явке сотрудников на выборы Президента Российской Федерации необходимо письменно сообщить руководителю организационно-контрольного отдела следственного управления Дмитриевой Е.Ю. в срок до 8 часов 30 минут 19.03.2018.

Руководитель
следственного управления
генерал-майор юстиции В.В. Самодайкин

Plate 6.2

ТЕЛЕФОНОГРАММА

Начальникам отделов, отделений
служб и подразделений.

Разъяснить подчиненным сотрудникам о порядке голосования сотрудников органов внутренних дел, задействованных на службе в день проведения выборов вне своего избирательного участка.

Необходимо в обязательном порядке подать заявление, в котором указать избирательный участок по месту несения службы:
с 31 января по 12 марта 2018 года:
в любую территориальную избирательную комиссию;
в любой филиал МФЦ;
в электронном виде через «Единый портал государственных и муниципальных услуг»;
с 25 февраля по 12 марта 2018 года:
в любую участковую избирательную комиссию.

До 01 марта 2018 года руководителям доложить число сотрудников, которые будут нести службу вне своего избирательного участка и количество подавших заявления.

Руководителям обеспечить 100 % явку личного состава для голосования в день выборов.

И.о. начальника МО МВД России «Новосибирский»
капитан полиции   В.В. Палкин

«12» февраля 2017 года

Plate 6.3

downturns, and even where private sector protections are equivalent, public sector workers are more likely to have these protections enforced than are their private sector counterparts.

For example, in many countries, the state dominates employment in education and health care. Because it would be especially difficult to find similar employment outside the state sector, workers in these sectors may be more vulnerable to pressure from their managers, and therefore more likely to experience workplace mobilization. Public sector employment is generally more stable since it can be more costly for one to lose their position and the accompanying benefits. Indeed, there is evidence that workers who exhibit higher levels of risk aversion may prefer employment in the state sector (Pfeifer, 2011).

Finally, political patronage plays a key role in public sector employment in many countries, particularly those without merit-based civil service recruitment. Workers who are hired into the state sector as clients of political patrons make good candidates for political mobilization. Oliveros (2021) shows that political appointees in Argentina are far more likely to engage in political mobilization than are state employees who are not political appointees. Fearing that they may be replaced if their patron loses office, such workers need little encouragement to engage in political activity on their patron's behalf. By their nature, patronage jobs are politically contingent work. Because political patronage plays a far less pronounced role in private sector employment, state sector employees are much more likely to experience political mobilization than are their non-state sector peers.

Evidence of State Sector Employment and Workplace Mobilization

Our analyses have shown that state sector employees in Russia are significantly more likely to experience workplace mobilization. For example, in Table 6.5 we show analyses of pooled data from four surveys conducted in Russia between 2011 and 2018. The model specifications mirror those used earlier pertaining to economic leverage. In column 1, we find that state sector employees (both those working in the bureaucracy and in state-owned corporations) were fifteen percentage points more likely to experience workplace mobilization than workers employed outside the state sector, controlling for a range of other factors. This is one of the most consistent results in our analyses.

Breaking these results down further in column 2, we find that employees working in the bureaucracy are much more likely to have been mobilized

162 WORKPLACE POLITICS

Table 6.4 Mobilization by Employer Type

Employer Type	Mobilized in Workplace (%)
Local or Regional Government	50
Federal Government	49
Military/Police	49
Agricultural Enterprise	41
State-Owned Enterprise	40
Private Enterprise	31
Entrepreneur / Microenterprise	24
Other Employment	21
NGO / Social Organization	14
All Employees	36

This table shows the percentage of respondents mobilized in the workplace,
showing statistics pooled across all four surveys. Mobilized in the Workplace is a
binary indicator for the Minimal definition of Workplace Mobilization (just
those components that were asked in all four surveys).

in comparison to those working in state-owned corporations. Part of this difference can be attributed to the incentives that employers face in the two settings. Many state-owned corporations in Russia have some minority private shareholders and therefore share some cultural similarities (and compete) with firms fully located in the private sector. SOE managers may therefore be reluctant to completely politicize the workplace for fear of losing workers to private firms where political engagement is not occurring. Government bureaucrats, on the other hand, have fewer suitors for their skill sets and are more likely to owe their jobs to political patronage.

Next, in columns 3 and 4, we examine further the impact of variation in employee profession, looking first at mobilization during federal elections (using the 2011, 2016, and 2018 surveys) and then during regional elections (using the 2014 survey). Intuitively, we see that during federal elections, members of the federal bureaucracy, the military, and law enforcement are all more likely to be mobilized. These national-level civil servants receive the most pressure from their managers to turn out. Local and regional bureaucrats are next in line, with significantly higher rates of mobilization than those workers from the private sector. On the other hand, in the runup to regional elections in 2014, we see local and regional bureaucrats experiencing mobilization at higher rates. Regional incumbents have less leverage over federal bureaucrats, thus making it hard for them to activate them around elections.

WHO GETS MOBILIZED? 163

Table 6.5 State Sector Employment and Workplace Mobilization

	Mobilized in Workplace			
	(1)	(2)	(3)	(4)
Male	−0.020	−0.018	0.002	−0.045
	(0.017)	(0.017)	(0.020)	(0.031)
Age (log)	0.015	0.015	0.016	−0.007
	(0.023)	(0.023)	(0.028)	(0.044)
Education	0.014***	0.013**	0.018**	0.014*
	(0.005)	(0.005)	(0.008)	(0.007)
City Size	−0.035***	−0.035***	−0.025**	−0.040***
	(0.008)	(0.008)	(0.010)	(0.012)
Public Sector Employee	0.144***			
	(0.023)			
Economic Status	0.028**	0.028**		
	(0.011)	(0.011)		
Turned Out in Recent Parliamentary Election	0.073***	0.072***	0.088***	0.055*
	(0.017)	(0.017)	(0.021)	(0.027)
Binary Putin Approval	−0.037*	−0.037*	−0.042*	0.026
	(0.021)	(0.021)	(0.025)	(0.044)
Government Bureaucrat		0.172***		
		(0.023)		
State-Owned Enterprise		0.088**	0.128***	−0.003
		(0.035)	(0.033)	(0.043)
Federal Government			0.235***	0.040
			(0.041)	(0.055)
Local or Regional Government			0.149***	0.205***
			(0.035)	(0.058)
Military/Police			0.195***	0.088
			(0.052)	(0.065)
Entrepreneur / Microenterprise			−0.117**	−0.013
			(0.050)	(0.055)
Agricultural Enterprise			0.127	0.013
			(0.081)	(0.079)
NGO / Social Organization			−0.085	−0.404***
			(0.086)	(0.047)
Other Employment			−0.048	
			(0.119)	
R^2	0.052	0.054	0.067	0.040
Observations	3,470	3,470	2,090	1,414
Election(s)	All	All	Federal	Regional
Survey fixed effects	✓	✓	✓	✓

***p<0.01, **p<0.05, *p<0.1 This table presents results using individual-level predictors pooled across all four surveys. The outcome variable is a binary indicator for the Minimal definition of Workplace Mobilization (just those components that were asked in all four surveys). All models include survey wave fixed effects, with errors clustered on region.

Next we explore the relationship between public sector employment and workplace mobilization in other countries. We run separate models for each of the six countries where we have appropriate data (Argentina, Indonesia, Nigeria, Turkey, Ukraine, and Venezuela), but because we used the same question wordings across surveys, the specifications are nearly identical. The outcome is a binary indicator for whether a respondent experienced any of the most common forms of workplace mobilization (employers distributing campaign materials, holding rallies, arranging transportation to the polls, discussing politics at work, etc.).[18] We then include a binary indicator for whether a respondent worked in the state sector, either in the bureaucracy or in a state-owned firm. Controls in all models include gender, age, education, previous turnout, and income. Standard errors are clustered at the level of the first subnational unit (region, state, etc.) depending on the country.

Figure 6.1 presents the coefficients on state sector employment for each of the countries in our cross-national dataset. The dots indicate the point estimates, with 95 percent confidence intervals shown as bars. We find that in five of the six countries, employment in the state sector is associated with an increased likelihood of experiencing workplace mobilization

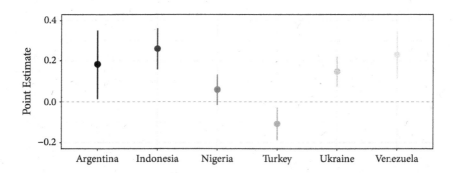

Figure 6.1 State Sector Workplace Mobilization across Countries

Note: This figure plots the coefficients on *Public Sector Employment* from models with an outcome of being employed in the workplace. Each model was estimated separately using a standard battery of controls (gender, age, education, past voting behavior, economic status, and rural residency) and subsetting the sample to only employed respondents. Standard errors were clustered either on region or province, depending on the country.

---

[18] The appendix shows models that restrict the operationalization only to more clientelistic and coercive methods. Results are similar, except that the effect of state employment in Turkey is no longer negative.

relative to employment in the private sector. Moreover, these increases are substantively large, ranging from fifteen to twenty-three percentage points.

The one exception to this pattern is Turkey, where we find a negative relationship between state employment and the likelihood of workplace mobilization. This finding is puzzling, but anecdotal evidence suggests that private government contractors are heavily involved in political mobilization in Turkey. For example, a major Turkish newspaper reported that the Ankara Municipality Water and Sewage (ASKI) office ordered its subcontractors to mobilize its more than one thousand new employees to help with election campaigning for the June 2015 parliamentary elections. Officials from ASKI bused these subcontractors to the rally, threatened them with dismissal for noncompliance, and made sure that all knew that officials were taking attendance.[19] This information leaked as the subcontractors lost their contracts after the November elections. Similarly, the Ankara municipal government used threats to compel contractors to attend election rallies and official ceremonies in support of the The Justice and Development Party during parliamentary elections in 2015.[20] It could be that state sector mobilization in Turkey is prevalent but indirect, because it operates through private subcontractors. Alternatively, high rates of mobilization in other sectors may mask mobilization in the state sector. Turnout in the parliamentary election in June 2015 was 84 percent.

In the United States as well, political mobilization by state sector employers is uncommon, but this is likely due to strong legal restrictions on the practice (Hertel-Fernandez, 2018).[21]

These findings suggest the importance of the state bureaucracy as a locus of political activity in diverse settings. Argentina, Indonesia, Nigeria, Russia, Ukraine, and Venezuela possess very different levels of economic development, historical legacies, economic structures, and patterns of employment, but we see strong evidence that state sector employees are more likely to be mobilized in the workplace than are their non-state sector peers.

---

[19] Cepni, Ozan, "Aski'de isci kiyimi," *Cumhuriyet*, April 22, 2016.
[20] "Melih Gokchek'in guvenlikchilieri!," *Sözcü*, April 19, 2015.
[21] In three of the six countries (Argentina, Nigeria, and Ukraine), we also see a positive interaction between education and state sector employment.

Conclusion

Having focused on relations between politicians and employers in Chapters 3 to 5, in this chapter we have explored how relations between employers and workers shape the prospects for workplace mobilization. We find that in a diverse range of countries, employers are especially likely to mobilize their workers in the state sector and in slack labor markets.

Narrowing our analytic lens has helped to identify how power relations influence whether employers mobilize their workers. In the next chapter, we pull back our lens and consider how the broader voting public influences the use of this tactic. Because politicians and employers may consider in their strategies the costs of electoral backlash by voters outside their firms, it is important to understand how voters view the practice. In addition, we bring institutions into the analysis by exploring the impact of the media environment on workplace mobilization. Doing so helps us understand how institutions can mediate power relations among politicians, employers, and employees and deepen our understanding of workplace mobilization.

WHO GETS MOBILIZED? 167

Appendix

Table 6.6 Workplace Mobilization in *Monogorods* (Turnout Buying)

	Employer Asked to Vote		
	(1)	(2)	(3)
Male	−0.004	0.010	−0.006
	(0.010)	(0.013)	(0.015)
Age (log)	0.030*	0.054***	0.042**
	(0.015)	(0.018)	(0.017)
Education	0.007*	0.007*	0.008*
	(0.004)	(0.004)	(0.005)
City Size	−0.008	−0.009	−0.008
	(0.006)	(0.007)	(0.007)
Economic Status	0.013	0.007	0.007
	(0.009)	(0.009)	(0.009)
Public Sector Employee	0.108***	0.076***	0.065**
	(0.018)	(0.024)	(0.026)
Turned Out in Recent Parliamentary Election	0.056***	0.050***	0.055***
	(0.015)	(0.015)	(0.015)
Binary Putin Approval	−0.042**	−0.028	−0.034*
	(0.020)	(0.020)	(0.020)
Monogorod Resident	0.122***	0.130***	0.121***
	(0.031)	(0.035)	(0.035)
R^2	0.108	0.093	0.105
Observations	3,569	2,558	2,439
Survey Fixed Effects	✓	✓	✓
Sector Fixed Effects			✓

***p<0.01, **p<0.05, *p<0.1 This table presents results using individual-level predictors pooled across all four surveys. The outcome variable is a binary indicator for the Minimal definition of Workplace Mobilization (just those components that were asked in all four surveys). Column 1 uses the full sample of employed respondents (in government and the private sector), while columns 2 and 3 just look at private companies. All models include survey wave fixed effects, with errors clustered on region.

Table 6.7 Labor Market Conditions (Restricted Measure)

	Mobilized in Workplace (Restricted)					
	(1)	(2)	(3)	(4)	(5)	(6)
Constant	0.365**	0.411**	0.420**			
	(0.150)	(0.168)	(0.148)			
Male	−0.028	−0.041	−0.042	−0.065	−0.095*	−0.083*
	(0.038)	(0.037)	(0.035)	(0.045)	(0.050)	(0.045)
Age (log)	0.009	−0.008	0.025	0.033	0.006	0.043
	(0.034)	(0.040)	(0.033)	(0.040)	(0.055)	(0.040)
Education	0.022***	0.017**	0.016*	0.018	0.012	0.013
	(0.008)	(0.008)	(0.008)	(0.012)	(0.009)	(0.010)
City Size	−0.033	−0.033	−0.037*	−0.017	−0.023	−0.027
	(0.022)	(0.020)	(0.021)	(0.019)	(0.020)	(0.020)
Public Sector Employee	0.086*	0.073*	0.083**			
	(0.044)	(0.039)	(0.036)			
Economic Status	0.016	−0.001	0.005	0.008	−0.004	−0.001
	(0.023)	(0.022)	(0.021)	(0.015)	(0.020)	(0.018)
Turned Out in Recent Parliamentary Election	0.081	0.079*	0.075*	0.097**	0.088***	0.074**
	(0.055)	(0.040)	(0.042)	(0.046)	(0.031)	(0.032)
Binary Putin Approval	0.0005	0.006	0.005	−0.007	−0.004	−0.015
	(0.040)	(0.039)	(0.042)	(0.060)	(0.064)	(0.067)
Self-Reported % of Losing Job	0.179**			0.253***		
	(0.077)			(0.086)		
Difficulty of Finding New Work		0.048***			0.057**	
		(0.016)			(0.024)	
Has Second Job			0.068*			0.069
			(0.035)			(0.077)
State-Owned Enterprise				0.011	0.025	0.048
				(0.090)	(0.051)	(0.045)
R^2	0.033	0.034	0.026	0.050	0.048	0.033
Observations	988	1,234	1,336	717	905	990
Sector Fixed Effects				✓	✓	✓

***p<0.01, **p<0.05, *p<0.1 This table presents results using only individual-level predictors in the 2014 Survey. The outcome variable is a binary indicator for the Full definition of Workplace Mobilization. Standard errors are clustered on region.

WHO GETS MOBILIZED? 169

Table 6.8 State Sector Employment and Workplace Mobilization (Restricted Measure)

	Mobilized in Workplace (Restricted)			
	(1)	(2)	(3)	(4)
Male	−0.023	−0.020	−0.002	−0.040
	(0.016)	(0.016)	(0.020)	(0.029)
Age (log)	0.031	0.030	0.024	0.015
	(0.019)	(0.019)	(0.022)	(0.038)
Education	0.008	0.007	0.010	0.011
	(0.005)	(0.005)	(0.007)	(0.006)
City Size	−0.029***	−0.029***	−0.023**	−0.027**
	(0.007)	(0.007)	(0.009)	(0.012)
Public Sector Employee	0.143***			
	(0.024)			
Economic Status	0.032***	0.031***		
	(0.011)	(0.011)		
Turned Out in Recent Parliamentary Election	0.072***	0.070***	0.089***	0.040
	(0.017)	(0.017)	(0.019)	(0.031)
Binary Putin Approval	−0.038*	−0.038*	−0.050**	0.057
	(0.021)	(0.021)	(0.025)	(0.041)
Government Bureaucrat		0.174***		
		(0.023)		
State-Owned Enterprise		0.081**	0.132***	−0.025
		(0.034)	(0.037)	(0.031)
Federal Government			0.213***	0.039
			(0.034)	(0.063)
Local or Regional Government			0.182***	0.193***
			(0.035)	(0.067)
Military/Police			0.220***	0.043
			(0.053)	(0.053)
Entrepreneur/Microenterprise			−0.049	−0.015
			(0.048)	(0.057)
Agricultural Enterprise			0.123	−0.044
			(0.084)	(0.075)
NGO / Social Organization			−0.113**	−0.357***
			(0.056)	(0.053)
Other Employment			−0.061	
			(0.118)	
R^2	0.059	0.062	0.083	0.033
Observations	3,477	3,477	2,101	1,412
Election(s)	All	All	Federal	Regional
Survey fixed effects	✓	✓	✓	✓

***p<0.01, **p<0.05, *p<0.1 This table presents results using individual-level predictors pooled across all four surveys. The outcome variable is a binary indicator for the Minimal definition of Workplace Mobilization (just those components that were asked in all four surveys). All models include survey wave fixed effects, with errors clustered on region.

170 WORKPLACE POLITICS

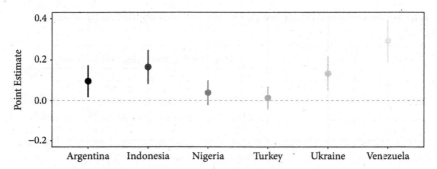

Figure 6.2 State Sector Workplace Mobilization across Countries (Restricted)

Note: This figure plots the coefficients on *Public Sector Employment* from models with an outcome of being employed in the workplace. Each model was estimated separately using a standard battery of controls (gender, age, education, past voting behavior, economic status, and rural residency) and subsetting the sample to only employed respondents. Standard errors were clustered either on region or province, depending on the country.

7
How Do Voters Respond?

We opened this book with a story from Russia's Far East illustrating the lengths to which politicians and employers will both go to hide from the general public their use of workplace mobilization. A media scandal over workplace mobilization at *Amuragrocenter* forced plant managers and the local administration to attempt an elaborate and ultimately unsuccessful cover-up.

In our research, we came across many other examples of employers who experienced popular backlash for mobilizing their workers. In 2012, the Ryazan Electrical Instrument Factory, one of Russia's largest producers of advanced radar equipment, found itself at the center of one such scandal. Multiple news outlets reported that the plant was forcing its employees to work on Sunday (election day) and vote at the factory under threat of dismissal.[1] Komsomolskaya Pravda, Russia's second largest daily newspaper, published a full-length expose that included curt denials from plant managers.[2] Faced with the scandal, plant managers rescinded their plan to have employees vote at the factory.

In the runup to the 2022 Brazilian presidential elections, a video went viral on social media showing a businessman from the state of Bahia telling his employees to put a cellphone in their bras in order to film their vote.[3] He was forced to publicly apologize and issue a retraction video. In 2016, Jennifer Anderson, the owner of an Ace Hardware store in Davis, California, wrote to her employees to "Vote Romney." When her letter appeared online, local reaction was "extremely negative" and spawned a petition and talk of a boycott.[4] In response, Anderson felt compelled to apologize for offend-

[1] See "Rabochikh ryazanskogo pribornogo zavoda zastavlyayut 4 marta golosovat' pod prismotrom nachal'stva," *Novaya Gazeta*, February 17, 2012, and "V Ryazani na zavodakh otkryvayut izbiratel'nyye uchastki, a 4 marta delayut rabochim dnem," *Rosbalt*, February 17, 2012.

[2] Chenenko, Elena, "V den' vyborov Ryazanskiy pribornyy zavod rabotat' ne budet," *Komsomolskaya Pravda*, February 17, 2012.

[3] Viapiana, Tabata, "Brazilian Companies Are Pressuring Workers to Vote for Certain Candidates and Over 1,600 Complaints Have Been Registered," *Brazil Reports*, October 28, 2022.

[4] Chun, Janean, "Jennifer Anderson, Davis Ace Hardware Owner, Apologizes for Urging Employees to Vote Romney," *Huffington Post*, November 13, 2012.

Workplace Politics. Timothy Frye, Ora John Reuter, and David Szakonyi, Oxford University Press.
© Oxford University Press (2025). DOI: 10.1093/9780197802045.003.0007

172   WORKPLACE POLITICS

ing employees and customers. Indeed, business owners and labor lawyers in the United States often cite the fear of a popular backlash by workers and the broader public as an important constraint on introducing politics into the workplace. One legal expert noted. "It just doesn't go over well in the workplace, to really be pushing hard for one candidate or the other. . . . It can backfire and it can be bad busines"[5]

Thus far, we have focused on relations between politicians and employers, and between employers and employees. But because workplace mobilization also may affect the calculus of voters who do not experience it directly, politicians who mobilize via employers must consider how these tactics will play with the broader electorate. In this chapter, using data from Russia and the United States, we examine how the general voting public responds to workplace mobilization. We find that voters are willing to withdraw their support for candidates and parties that mobilize their workers, especially when the practice is coercive. In fact, workplace mobilization elicits more opprobrium from voters than does vote buying by party activists.

Politicians who use employers as vote brokers face a trade-off: under the right conditions, workplace mobilization can increase electoral support by getting workers inside the company to the polls, but doing so can reduce support among voters outside the company who disapprove of the practice. How politicians navigate this trade-off depends in part on the structure of the economy (as noted in previous chapters), but also on the likelihood that voters will learn that a candidate has employed workplace mobilization. In contexts where media freedom is greater, voters are more likely to learn about workplace mobilization. In these information-rich settings, the gains to politicians from mobilizing workers may be outweighed by the reduction in support from voters who oppose the tactic. However, where the media are less free, workplace mobilization will be more prevalent because politicians and employers will see themselves as less likely to be punished by voters outside the workplace who may not learn that a politician has used this unpopular technique. In this chapter, we find that workplace mobilization is indeed less prevalent in Russian regions with greater media freedom. In these settings, politicians are deterred from engaging in workplace mobilization by the threat of electoral blowback among voters who disapprove of the practice.

---

[5] McGregor, Jena, "What Your Boss Can and Can't Do When It Comes to Politics at Work," *Chicago Tribune*, October 21, 2016.

This chapter highlights another key difference between employers and other vote brokers. While voters in many settings disapprove of clientelism, it appears that workplace mobilization provokes more ire than the most commonly studied forms of clientelism. Politicians must always consider not only the votes that clientelism directly generates but also the fact that using such practices may turn off some other voters (Weitz-Shapiro, 2014). This trade-off appears even more acute in the case of workplace mobilization— which makes it especially important to consider the ways that institutional context, such as the quality of democracy or the media environment, shapes patterns of electoral subversion in the workplace.

Argument

Much research on clientelism focuses on the incentives facing brokers and their clients. Studies of vote buying often explore which types of voters are more likely to be the targets of vote buying, with a particular interest in the client's partisanship, levels of income, and location. Whether brokers give gifts to swing voters or core supporters, to urban or rural residents, or to the poor or broader classes in society all comprise vibrant lines of research (Stokes, Dunning, and Nazareno, 2013). We explored these aspects of targeted workplace mobilization in previous chapters.

But clientelist mobilization can have an impact beyond brokers and their clients, particularly among other voters who are not specifically targeted. Voters in Argentina reduce their support for candidates who engage in vote buying (Weitz-Shapiro, 2014), while those in the United States punish politicians for violating democratic norms (Graham and Svolik, 2020) and electoral procedures (Carey et al., 2022). Blatantly coercive tactics, in particular the use of violence, angers voters. Using a survey experiment in Guatemala, Gonzalez-Ocantos et al. (2020) show that voters are more likely to punish candidates who had used violence in the past versus those who had engaged in vote buying.

Importantly, prior research suggests that voters may not simply forgive politicians from their own party who engage in such aggressive forms of electoral mobilization. Gutiérrez-Romero and LeBas (2020) and Rosenzweig (2021) find that voters in Kenya report a willingness to punish preelection violence even if it is committed by co-partisans. Closest to this chapter, Reuter and Szakonyi (2021) use a survey experiment to show that pro-government voters in Russia are more likely to punish a pro-government politician who engages in election subversion, such as vote buying or using coercive mobilization techniques.

However, less is known about how voters respond specifically to workplace mobilization as a particular form of electoral subversion. There is, though, good reason to believe that voters might disapprove of workplace mobilization. As previous chapters have demonstrated, employers have considerable leverage over their employees, which leads to a frequent reliance on coercion—implicit or explicit—as the core inducement that underlies workplace mobilization.

Most voters are deeply uncomfortable with such violations of personal autonomy. Even more benign forms of mobilization, such as employers sharing their political opinions in the workplace or reminding employees about the importance of voting, can be perceived by workers as disrespectful or misplaced. By communicating their political views from a position of power, bosses can be perceived as crossing an unwritten line differentiating the private and public spheres. Instead, our surveys suggest that respondents prefer an apoliticized workplace, where conversations with superiors remain centered on work, rather than potentially unrelated political and social issues. For these reasons, as Chapter 2 showed, most voters in the countries we study are critical of workplace mobilization.

Because voters disapprove of workplace mobilization, we expect it to color how they evaluate candidates and parties. Politicians, in turn, are likely to condition their decision to use workplace mobilization on the probability that they will face backlash. But such effects are, of course, also conditional upon voters learning that a politician has used this tactic. For this reason, we also need to consider how the information environment shapes the choices of politicians. Recognizing the negative connotations that workplace mobilization evokes, politicians and employers often hide their attempts at electoral subversion (Pisano, 2022). Voters who do not learn about electoral subversion are unlikely to be influenced by it.

The most likely source of information about workplace mobilization is the mass media, which suggests that the broader public is more likely to learn about the use of workplace mobilization in settings with high(er) levels of media freedom. The costs of using this unpopular tactic are therefore higher, relative to less free media environments. Where media freedom is restricted, voters are less likely to learn about the practice, and therefore the costs to politicians of using such strategies will be lower. In such settings, the gains from mobilizing voters in the workplace may outweigh the loss of votes among the general public.

As media independence grows, employer coercion becomes less attractive. Journalists, activists, and opposition party leaders who learn of this tactic will be both more capable and more willing to spread the word about such malfeasance. Voters can then punish politicians for using coercion by abstaining or voting for another party.

Furthermore, we should expect that media freedom will affect the specific types of workplace mobilization that politicians and employers adopt, should they choose to do so. The general public responds particularly negatively to more coercive forms of workplace mobilization. Employers who overtly pressure and threaten workers face much more backlash than those who engage in less coercive forms, such as voter education activities. Part of this is due to the role of media. Journalists are more likely to pick up and pursue stories that implicate politicians and employers in more egregious and offensive acts. Stories of employer malfeasance not only fit more squarely with journalists' public interest mandate, but they also attract more attention from readers and viewers. The presence of independent media should reduce workplace mobilization, but if it does occur, it will take less coercive forms where there is free media. In the following sections, we explore a number of implications of these arguments.

The Electoral Implications of Workplace Mobilization

As we demonstrated in Chapter 2, many respondents disapprove of workplace mobilization, but this does not necessarily mean that it would enter into a voter's calculus. Knowing that a voter supports or opposes a particular policy is often insufficient to identify how they will vote because voters have many goals when they enter the ballot box. They may disapprove of workplace mobilization but also take into account other factors, such as the charisma of the candidate and their own partisan preferences.[6]

---

[6] The latter point is particularly relevant in light of recent debates about polarization and negative partisanship. A number of prominent studies have argued that voters in polarized societies are willing to overlook electoral subversion by co-partisans if it helps their party defeat the opposition (Graham and Svolik, 2020). Thus, for example, voters may disapprove of the idea of workplace mobilization, but find ways to justify and excuse it when candidates and parties that they support use it. This could attenuate the reputational costs of workplace mobilization. For this reason, it is important to examine whether workplace mobilization has real electoral costs for politicians and the extent to which these costs are attenuated by polarization.

176   WORKPLACE POLITICS

To examine the political implications of workplace mobilization on hypothetical vote choice, we conducted a survey experiment on a nationally representative sample of sixteen hundred respondents in Russia in May 2018. We explored whether informing respondents about various forms of electoral manipulation, including two forms of workplace mobilization, shaped respondents' intention to vote for the incumbent.[7] We supplied all respondents with a prompt describing a hypothetical situation involving a regional governor campaigning during the next elections (see Table 7.1). In the control group, respondents received only the prompt describing the governor's promises to increase spending on various budget items, with no additional information about the mobilization tactics to be used.

As Table 7.1 shows, we then randomly assigned the rest of the respondents to receive one of four treatments in addition to the prompt that describes different types of mobilization techniques this governor used to turn out the vote. The techniques chosen indicate two common types of workplace mobilization (public sector workers in Treatment #1 and private sector workers in Treatment #2), vote buying by party activists (Treatment #3), and finally

Table 7.1 Perceptions of Workplace Mobilization

Prompt: Let's say that in the next electoral campaign, your governor promises to increase spending on roads, hospitals, and schools. He also promises to bring new jobs to the region [electoral mobilization technique here]

		Number of Respondents
Control	No new information.	327
Treatment #1	In addition, imagine that you learned that he had put pressure on state workers to vote for him in the election.	311
Treatment #2	In addition, imagine that you learned that he put pressure on employers to get their employees to vote for him in the election.	323
Treatment #3	In addition, imagine that you learned that he encouraged party activists to give small gifts to voters to vote for him in the election.	309
Treatment #4	In addition, imagine that you learned that he held a debate on television with his main political opponent.	332

[7] One limitation common to this line of research is that we rely on hypothetical questions on vote choice.

HOW DO VOTERS RESPOND? 177

the inoffensive activity of participating in a political debate, included as a placebo (Treatment #4). We are primarily interested in examining whether disapproval of workplace mobilization (especially vis-à-vis party activism) leads voters to turn away from candidates who practice it.

To that end, after receiving the question prompt (and one of the treatments depending on their random assignment), all respondents were then asked both about their willingness to turn out and whether they would vote for this gubernatorial candidate. Both outcomes were presented using a 5-point scale, with greater values indicating a greater willingness.

Most importantly, the results in column 1 in Table 7.2 indicate that voters report a willingness to punish candidates who put pressure on employers in the state bureaucracy and private sectors to mobilize their workers to vote. When told that the incumbent governor had put pressure on state employees to vote for him, respondents reduced their support for the governor by about

Table 7.2 Governor Campaigning Framing Experiment

	Support for Governor				
	All			Strong UR	Weak UR
	(1)	(2)	(3)	(4)	(5)
Workplace Mobilization: State Workers	−0.616*** (0.129)	−0.670*** (0.123)	−0.231** (0.106)	−0.793** (0.313)	−0.637*** (0.117)
Workplace Mobilization: Pressure on Employers	−0.661*** (0.140)	−0.701*** (0.129)	−0.221** (0.100)	−0.934*** (0.269)	−0.648*** (0.129)
Party: Vote Buying	−0.390*** (0.118)	−0.460*** (0.113)		−0.799*** (0.288)	−0.335*** (0.111)
Debate Participation	−0.076 (0.088)	−0.050 (0.088)	0.398*** (0.093)	−0.064 (0.204)	−0.010 (0.097)
R^2	0.050	0.264	0.219	0.389	0.262
Observations	1,474	1,447	1,164	278	1,163
Reference Group	Control	Control	Party	Control	Control
Covariates		✓	✓	✓	✓
Region Fixed Effects		✓	✓	✓	✓

This table analyzes the experiment placed on the May 2018 Levada survey asking respondents to evaluate a governor candidate who engages in different types of campaign activities. Full treatment wordings are described in Table 7.1. The reference group for each model is given at the bottom of the table. Standard errors are clustered on the region.

178   WORKPLACE POLITICS

0.62 on a 5-point scale, or about one-half of one standard deviation. The results are similar when respondents were told that the governor put pressure on private employers to turn out their workers to vote. Public aversion to workplace mobilization does not seem to depend on whether it occurs in the public or private sector. Our placebo treatment (candidates debating their political opponents) did not produce a statistically different effect from the control group.

Respondents also punish incumbent governors for getting party activists to buy votes, but, importantly, the negative effects are significantly lower than those produced by workplace mobilization. Column 3 of Table 7.2 sets the party vote-buying treatment as the reference category. Compared to party-based vote buying, both workplace mobilization treatments prompt respondents to withdraw support from the governor candidate. This difference could be caused by the negative (i.e., coercive) connotation elicited by the question's phrasing: "putting pressure." But even in Russia, a country with a long history of workplace mobilization, the general public is turned off by the practice, and more so than by parties distributing inducements.

Workplace mobilization is only costly for the regime if the number of voters turned off by the practice is greater than the number whom employers successfully mobilized. If the latter figure is larger, politicians may be willing to tolerate some level of backlash with the knowledge that they will still come out ahead electorally. One way this could happen is if partisan voters were able to forgive co-partisan politicians for workplace mobilization and maintain their support. That is, if partisanship affects the evaluations of workplace mobilization, politicians engaging in the practice might be excused by their strongest supporters and come out ahead, on balance. The voters most likely to punish them for pressuring employers would be those already disinclined to support them.

We test this proposition in columns 4 and 5 of Table 7.2 by comparing the responses of supporters of United Russia to the rest of the population. Respondents were asked to place themselves on a 10-point scale indicating their level of support for United Russia. Respondents who placed themselves at 8 or higher were coded as strong supporters of United Russia (column 4); all others are either regime opponents or weak UR supporters (column 5). Since at the time of the survey the vast majority of governors in Russia were either United Russia members or closely aligned with the regime, we can assume that most strong UR voters view the governor as their co-partisan.

Our findings suggest that strong United Russia supporters react just as vigorously upon learning that a gubernatorial candidate had pressured employees at work or bought votes. Comparing the strong versus weak regime supporters, we do not see any statistically significant differences among the coefficients for the two workplace mobilization treatments. These findings accord with recent work showing that pro-regime voters in Russia withdraw their support from regime candidates who engage in fraud (Reuter and Szakonyi, 2021). A similar dynamic is likely at play here. One takeaway is that partisanship does not save regime politicians in Russia from being punished by their voters for engaging in workplace mobilization. Instead, regime politicians risk losing some of their own supporters when they engage in workplace mobilization.

Officials in Russia seem aware of such risks and try to minimize them. A number of the leaked mobilizational directives from state officials in the KN data include language instructing officials on how to avoid backlash when mobilizing. Take, for example, a document (Plate 7.1, at the end of this chapter) produced in January 2018 by the municipal administration of Rubtsovsk—an industrial center in Altai Krai.[8] The document contains a section entitled "Methodological Recommendations (For the Mobilization of Work Collectives, Family Members, and Veterans)." The stated goal of the recommendations is "to secure practically 100 percent turnout of workers/employees of enterprises/organizations, the members of their families, and also veterans in the elections on March 18, 2018." The document contains a section called "Principles" that contains six pointers for employers on how to achieve this goal:

- "Soft" motivations to turn out
- The exclusion of any type of threatening administrative coercion
- Multiple communicative "contacts"
- The use of appeals from top management
- The absence of agitation for a specific candidate
- Accountability-work according to the employees lists

Of note is the fact that three of the six principles focus on how appeals should be crafted so as not to upset voters. Of course, fearful that they will be unsuccessful, employers often ignore appeals to soften their approach, but it is noteworthy that officials—at least in Rubtsovsk—prefer a lighter touch.

---

[8] *Karta Narusheniye* ID 39747, February 5, 2018.

180 WORKPLACE POLITICS

Voter Responses to Workplace Coercion in the United States

Now we turn to the very different political context of the United States. Here too we find that voters are inclined to punish politicians who encourage employers to pressure their employees to turn out to vote. In an online survey of eleven hundred respondents in February 2020, we asked respondents to consider an election between two candidates.[9] We randomized the race, gender, and partisanship of each candidate, as well as the mobilization techniques that each candidate employed in the campaign. We then explored how each technique influenced the propensity to vote for a particular candidate.

More specifically, we examined how voters would respond to learning that a politician had put pressure on employers to mobilize workers and even encouraged them to "threaten their employees with unpleasantness" if they did not support the candidate. This aggressive form of political mobilization is more commonly found in the less democratic countries in our study, but US employers have also been known to use threats to turn out the vote. On the campaign trail in 2012, Mitt Romney caught some flak for telling members of the National Federation of Independent Business on a phone call, "I hope you make it very clear to your employees what you believe is in the best interest of your enterprise and therefore their job and their future in the upcoming elections."[10] A month before the 2012 presidential election, real estate mogul David Siegal wrote to his eight thousand employees in bold font: "If any new taxes are levied on me, or my company, as our current President plans, I will have no choice but to reduce the size of the company. Rather than grow this company, I will be forced to cut back. This means fewer jobs, less benefits, and certainly less opportunity for everyone."[11]

[9] The survey was conducted by Lucid, which provides a platform for online surveys. Lucid collects demographic information from respondents and uses quota sampling based on categories from the US Census. One recent study found that "subjects recruited from the Lucid platform constitute a sample that is suitable for evaluating many social scientific theories." See Coppock and McClellan (2019).

[10] Phelan, Jessica, "Mitt Romney Tells Employees to 'Make It Very Clear' to Employees How to Vote," *Global Post*, October 18, 2012. The same story notes that Koch Industries sent a voter information pack telling their US employees that "many of our more than 50,000 US employees and contractors may suffer the consequences, including higher gasoline process, runaway inflation, and other ills" if the wrong candidate were elected. Real estate mogul David Siegal in Florida took a further step. "I had my managers do a survey on every employee [8,000 total]. If they liked Bush, we made them register to vote. But not if they liked Gore."

[11] Nolan, Hamilton, "The CEO Who Built Himself America's Largest House Just Threatened to Fire His Employees If Obama's Elected," *Gawker*, October 9, 2012.

In our online survey from February 2020, one in five employed respondents reported that their employer had ever "mentioned wage cuts, plant closings, or job losses in connection with an election result or a government policy decision." Hertel-Fernandez also finds that 20 percent of workers reported ever having received these kinds of threats in his survey of workers in the United States from 2015 (Hertel-Fernandez, 2018, 92).[12] In our YouGov survey of nine hundred employed respondents in the United States in January 2021, 9 percent said that they were told of wage cuts, plant closings, or job losses in connection with the most recent presidential election.

We asked respondents to choose between a pair of two hypothetical candidates in an upcoming election. As Table 7.3 indicates, the two candidates were randomly assigned fake names and partisan affiliations with mirroring politician positions. In the baseline condition, respondents received no additional information and were asked to choose between them based solely on their name (and the connotations it could carry), partisanship, and platform.

The rest of the equally divided sample was assigned to one of three treatment conditions that added information about the mobilization techniques employed by either of the two candidates. In treatment 1, respondents were told that the Democratic candidate had encouraged private employers to pressure their workers to vote for them—even encouraging them to threaten their employees with unpleasantness at work if they did not support their candidacy. In treatment 2, they were told that the Democratic candidate had encouraged union officials to use a similar tactic. In treatment 3, they were told that the Republican candidate had put pressure on private employers to mobilize their workers and to use threats of unpleasantness. We then asked respondents, "Based on the information above, which of the two candidates would you be more likely to vote for? The Democrat, the Republican, or Neither?"

In Table 7.4, we report the results from a linear probability model of the treatment variables on the likelihood of voting for the Democratic candidate using responses from all respondents in column 1. In row 1, we see that the

---

[12] In addition, Hertel-Fernandez (2018) finds that 28 percent of employed respondents said that employer retaliation for not complying with requests to engage is possible, and 5 to 7 percent of respondents said that they knew of a specific case of political retaliation. Both Hertel-Fernandez's 2015 survey and our 2020 survey find a strong correlation between respondent perceptions of job insecurity and employer threats to cut wages, which suggests that threats to cut wages were credible for some voters.

182   WORKPLACE POLITICS

Table 7.3 Framing Experiment in the United States

	Candidate 1	Candidate 2
Randomized Names	Allison Nelson, Todd Mueller, Jamal Rivers and Latoya Rivers is a...	
Randomized Partisanship	Democrat who favors significantly higher taxes on the wealthy, an increase in the minimum wage, and universal background checks on gun buyers.	Republican who favors significantly lower taxes even for the wealthy, opposes an increase in the minimum wage, and opposes universal background checks on all gun buyers.
Randomized Voter Mobilization Technique	Baseline: No New Information	
	Treatment 1: Let's say that you learned that the Democratic candidate encouraged private employers to get their workers to vote at all costs— even encouraging them to threaten their employees with unpleasantness at work if they did not support their candidacy.	
	Treatment 2: Let's say that you learned that the Democratic candidate had encouraged union officials to get out the vote at all costs—even encouraging them to threaten their members with unpleasantness at work if they did not support their candidacy.	
	Treatment 3: Let's say that you learned that the Republican candidate encouraged private employers to get their workers to vote at all costs— even encouraging them to threaten their employees with unpleasantness at work if they did not support their candidacy.	

average respondent was about 14 percent less likely to support a Democratic candidate who encouraged employers to put pressure on their workers to support their candidacy relative to the baseline condition of respondents who received no additional information. In row 2, we find that the average voter was about 11 percent less likely to support a Democratic candidate who pressured union members to use coercive tactics. In row 3 in column 1, we learn that the average voter is no more likely to vote for the Democratic candidate upon learning that the Republican candidate urged employers to pressure their workers.

Column 2 limits the sample to self-identified Democrats.[13] As rows 1 and 2 in column 2 indicate, Democratic voters sharply reduced their support for a Democratic candidate who either put pressure on firms to get their employees to the polls or encouraged unions to threaten their members with unpleasantness. Just as in Russia, co-partisans in the United States are unlikely to excuse politicians who engage in workplace mobilization.

In columns 3 and 4, we examine how information about a candidate encouraging the use of workplace mobilization influenced the likelihood of voting for a Republican candidate. Row 3 in column 3 shows that the average voter did not punish a Republican candidate who encouraged employers to pressure their workers to vote. In column 4, which limits the sample to only Republicans, however, we find that Republicans reduced their support for a Republican candidate by about 14 percentage points upon learning that this candidate encouraged employers to use coercion. In sum, respondents appear willing to punish co-partisan candidates who use this aggressive mobilizing tactic.

Across diverse political and economic settings, we find that the average voter disapproves of employers engaging in more aggressive forms of workplace mobilization. Voters in Russia and the United States in a hypothetical election report a willingness to reduce their support for candidates who use coercive forms of mobilization in the workplace to get voters to the polls. At the very least, we show that politicians cannot escape electoral blowback for workplace mobilization by relying on polarized supporters to excuse them for their illiberal behavior. Even in a highly polarized setting like the United States, co-partisans are willing to punish their own candidates for engaging in workplace mobilization.

More generally, these findings illustrate the ample reasons that politicians have for concealing workplace mobilization. If workplace mobilization only angered supporters of the opposing party, then it might have limited effects on a candidate's support levels. But we find that in addition to enraging the opposition and turning off some swing voters, workplace mobilization also leads to a loss of support among core supporters. In the next section, we

---

[13] Here we categorize "leaners" as partisans. Lucid uses a 10-point scale for party identification. We include very strong Democrats, not very strong Democrats, and independent Democrats as Democrats, and very strong Republicans, not very strong Republicans, and independent Republicans as Republicans. Others are independents. The results are largely similar if we exclude leaners from their respective parties and focus only on very strong and not very strong partisans. Results are essentially unchanged using weighted data or dropping the covariates. The results are also very similar using a multinomial logit.

184 WORKPLACE POLITICS

begin to explore how the difficulty of concealing workplace mobilization shapes incentives to engage in it.

Press Freedom and Workplace Mobilization

If the average voter is turned off by learning that a candidate has employed workplace mobilization, we might expect politicians to use this tactic less often when voters are likely to learn about it. Anecdotal and survey evidence in Russia indicates that news of workplace mobilization does indeed reach the general public. A particularly illustrative example is a controversy that surrounded the politically motivated firing of dozens of Moscow Metro employees in early 2021. All the fired employees had either personally attended demonstrations or signed a petition on the website *Free.Navalny.com* calling for opposition leader Alexey Navalny to be freed from prison.[14] The website's database was later hacked and released to the public. In informal conversations, Moscow Metro officials explained that the dismissals were a direct result of their employees' oppositionist political

Table 7.4 US Survey Experiment Results

	Voted for Democratic Candidate		Voted for Republican Candidate	
	(1)	(2)	(3)	(4)
Democrat Pressures Firm	−0.144***	−0.274***	0.029	0.089
	(0.042)	(0.049)	(0.040)	(0.059)
Democrat Pressures Union	−0.110**	−0.215***	0.011	0.038
	(0.043)	(0.051)	(0.041)	(0.062)
Republican Pressures Firm	0.031	−0.014	−0.042	−0.144**
	(0.042)	(0.039)	(0.040)	(0.063)
R^2	0.066	0.103	0.054	0.092
Observations	1,069	507	1,069	381
Subset	All	Democrats	All	Republicans
Covariates	✓	✓	✓	✓

***p<0.01, **p<0.05, *p<0.1 This table presents results from the framing experiment on the US survey. The outcome in columns 1 and 2 is whether the respondent voted for the Democratic candidate, while the outcome in columns 3 and 4 is whether the respondent voted for the Republican candidate. We subset to the aligned partians in columns 2 and 4. All models use a linear probability model with demographic covariates (not shown) and robust standard errors.

[14] Open Media, "Moscow Metro Fires Dozens of Employees Who Registered for Navalny Solidarity Protest," *Meduza*, May 14, 2021.

behavior, rather than the official reasons of absenteeism that were given. The fired workers quickly filed lawsuits, citing violations of their constitutional rights that protected political speech. Most interesting for our argument is how widespread the coverage of the incident became. By June 2021, dozens of national and regional media outlets had picked up the story, from independent stalwarts such as RBK and Kommersant, to state-run media such as TASS and RIA Novosti. Kremlin spokesperson Dmitry Peskov even felt compelled to directly address questions about the reasons for the dismissals.[15]

Our surveys of voters in Russia indicate that information on workplace mobilization can spread widely. Indirect exposure via friends and family is one such mechanism. In our 2014 survey of Russian voters, we asked respondents if they had heard "from your family or friends about their employers during the last campaign placing pressure on employees to turn out and vote or vote for a certain candidate or party?" Sixteen percent of all respondents said that this had happened to a friend or family member.

Another common way of finding out about workplace mobilization is via mass media and online social networks. In our 2021 survey, we asked a similar (though slightly different) question of respondents, inquiring whether they had "heard or read stories in the past few years about how an employer put pressure on employees so that they would vote or vote for a specific candidate." Fully 44 percent of respondents said that they had heard of such instances. We asked them further to specify where they had heard or read this. Twenty-four percent said that they had read instances of this on social networks, and 26 percent said that they had read about this in mass media. It is noteworthy that even in the highly restricted media environment that existed in Russia in 2021, almost one in four voters had read about workplace mobilization in the press.

These descriptive results indicate that the impact of workplace mobilization can extend far beyond the specific employees who are targeted by it. The general public in Russia is exposed to stories of workplace mobilization. For this reason, freedom of the press can be an important factor determining when and how politicians use workplace mobilization. If the media broadcast misdeeds, the electoral costs extend beyond the immediate network of the mobilized workers and are thus likely to be far higher for the politician.

---

[15] Batmanova, Anastasiya, Polina Khimshiashvili, and Artem Korenyako, "Kreml' otvetil na dannyye ob uvol'neniyakh v metro iz-za mitinga Naval'nogo," *RBC*, May 18, 2021.

186   WORKPLACE POLITICS

We therefore expect that in settings of greater media freedom, politicians would be less likely to employ workplace mobilization.

We take advantage of the variation in the information environment across Russia's more than eighty regions to test this argument. Media freedom has declined precipitously in all regions across Russia in recent years, but at the time of our surveys (2011 to 2018), it varied dramatically. Workplace mobilization, especially the more extreme varieties, was and is frequently reported on in the Russian press. Russia is an opportune setting to test our arguments.[16]

To explore this hypothesis, we turn again to our postelection surveys of the mass public. We begin by pooling data from four postelection surveys implemented by the Levada Center, including two national polls carried out after parliamentary elections in December 2011 and September 2016, the regionally representative poll in twenty regions in which elections were held in September 2014, and the nationally representative postelection poll carried out in March 2018 after presidential elections. In any one poll, we lack enough respondents to make cross-regional comparisons feasible, but by pooling these surveys, we gain sufficient power to test our hypotheses about the impact of press freedom on workplace mobilization across regions. We placed (nearly) identical questions on workplace mobilization on all of these surveys, which also facilitates pooling.[17] Given our interest in workplace mobilization, we only analyze data from employed respondents.

We employ three main outcome variables that we create from a series of questions that ask respondents about their experience with workplace mobilization: *AnyMobilization* is a binary variable equal to 1 if the respondent experienced any workplace political activity (employers discussing elections, endorsing candidates, distributing materials, providing transportation to the polls, holding rallies, or asking employees to vote);[18] *MoreCoercive* is a binary variable equal to 1 if the respondent reported that their employer had engaged in any of the more subversive forms of workplace mobilization, such as threatening workers with punishment for not voting or asking an employee to vote for a specific candidate. *LessCoercive* is a binary variable that equals 1 when when an employee had experienced any of the less

---

[16] The cross-regional analysis within Russia allows us to hold constant some variables that would be difficult to account for in a cross-national setting.

[17] Standard demographic and employment questions were also (nearly) identical across all surveys.

[18] These are the minimal forms of workplace mobilization that were included across all surveys.

coercive forms of mobilization, such as seeing flyers about the election at work, discussing politics with their superior, or having been asked to vote by their manager.

Our main independent variable is a 4-point scale of press freedom measured at the regional level. This scale, which has been used in many quantitative studies of Russian politics (Reuter and Szakonyi, 2015; Schulze, Sjahrir, and Zakharov, 2016; Beazer et al., 2022; Pyle, 2006), is based on an expert survey of journalists across regions in Russia conducted by the Glasnost Defense Foundation (GDF).[19] Founded in 1991, the GDF is dedicated to protecting press freedom in Russia and began creating an index of press freedom across Russia's regions in 2002.[20] The GDF surveyed regional experts in order to rank each region's press freedom as free, relatively free, relatively unfree, or unfree.[21] We use data from the last such survey in 2010. In this survey, experts considered that none of the regions in Russia had a free press, sixteen had a relatively free press, forty-four had a relatively unfree press, and twenty-two had an unfree press. These measures were little changed from prior rounds of the survey.

This measure has few categories and does not capture change over time, but it is temporally prior to our four surveys, which should reduce concerns of reverse causality.[22] Because it is based on an expert survey, there could be concerns about the subjectivity of the responses. This is true, but almost all measures of press freedom fundamentally entail subjective judgments. The best one can do is use a measure that aggregates responses from multiple experts. Another strength of the index is its comprehensiveness, as it covers eighty-two regions. Moreover, the index does not cluster in easily identifiable ways. Within each of Russia's seven territorial districts, we find regions whose media environments range from relatively free to unfree.

As a robustness check, we also include a media freedom index compiled by two experts on regional politics at the Carnegie Moscow Center, Nikolai Petrov and Alexei Titkov. This measure is a 5-point scale for regional media

---

[19] For more information on the Glasnost Press Freedom Index, see http://www.gdf.ru/map/.

[20] The regional press monitoring project was funded by a grant from the MacArthur Foundation but ended in 2010. The GDF was declared a "foreign agent" in 2015, but continues to collect data on abuses of press freedom in Russia.

[21] Here we treat regional levels of media freedom as exogenous to the likelihood of workplace mobilization and cannot rule out the possibility that regional media freedom might be correlated with unobserved variables that are correlated with workplace mobilization.

[22] To the extent that press freedom in Russia has declined over time, we may find less variance in our measure of press freedom in later elections, which would likely make it more difficult to uncover significant relationships in later elections. See the Appendix of this chapter for a regional representation of this index.

188   WORKPLACE POLITICS

freedom and was created as part of a broader effect to measure the level of democracy across regions in Russia. This measure too has been used in a number of academic studies (Saikkonen, 2017; Lankina and Skovoroda, 2017; Semenov, 2020). Both measures are imperfect, but using them in conjunction gives us additional confidence in the results.

We adopt a conservative estimation strategy that includes multiple control variables. All models build upon insights from previous chapters and include standard demographic controls as well as a control for whether the respondents work in the state sector, one of the strongest predictors of workplace mobilization in Russia.[23] In addition, we include variables related to the respondents' previous voting patterns (turnout in the most recent election and support for Putin), employment status, and geographic location (regional level of economic development, urbanization, population, and vote for United Russia). In order to account for within-region error correlation, all analyses cluster standard errors at the level of the region; results are robust to using random effects models. All models also include dummy variables for each survey wave.

Media freedom is not randomly assigned, and we cannot rule out possible endogeneity bias between media freedom and workplace mobilization. However, these possible biases may be less damaging than they appear. For example, if respondents in regions with less media freedom are more likely to experience workplace mobilization and less likely to report it due to fear of repression, then it should be harder to find differences in the level of reported workplace mobilization in regions with low and high levels of media freedom. Similarly, if governors in regions are both more likely to limit free media and to engage in workplace mobilization, then we should be less likely to find that media freedom inhibits workplace mobilization. Nonetheless, without stronger means of causal identification we note that our evidence is correlational.

The results in Table 7.6 show that *Press Freedom* is negatively correlated with the frequency of workplace mobilization. In regions with more press freedom, respondents are less likely to report being mobilized to vote by their employers. More specifically, in Model 1, we see that the GDF measure of Press Freedom is negatively and significantly correlated with the

---

[23] Our largest sample includes state bureaucrats, but using this measure does not allow us to include a control for firm size or sector. A reduced sample includes only respondents employed outside the state bureaucracy and includes controls for firm size and sector. The results across the two samples are similar.

likelihood of a respondent reporting any form of workplace mobilization. In Model 2, we see that the Carnegie Center measure of *Press Freedom* is negatively associated with a respondent experiencing any form of workplace mobilization, but is imprecisely estimated.

In Models 3 and 4, we explore the relations between media freedom and the more coercive forms of workplace mobilization. As our argument suggests, both measures of press freedom are negatively and significantly correlated with the likelihood that a respondent experienced more coercive forms of workplace mobilization. The coefficients on press freedom are negative and statistically significant, suggesting that employers may be deterred from engaging in the most coercive forms of workplace mobilization when the press is more free. The relationship between *Press Freedom* (as measured by the GDF) and coercive workplace mobilization is also strengthened when we only compare regions with relatively free media (the second-highest category) with regions with relatively unfree and completely unfree media (the bottom two categories). Coercive mobilization appears to become more common immediately as regions start to lose independent media outlets.

In Models 5 and 6, we explore the less coercive forms of workplace mobilization, such as an employer distributing election materials at work, discussing politics with workers around elections, publicly supporting a candidate, asking employees to turn out to vote, or holding a campaign meeting in the workplace. Here we find no relationship between media freedom and these less coercive forms of workplace mobilization across regions in Russia.[24] These less coercive forms may not be considered sufficiently important to merit media attention. In sum, free media is associated with employers reducing their use of more coercive forms of workplace mobilization, but not with their use of less coercive forms.

As a placebo test, we conduct a similar set of regressions that examine how *Press Freedom* affects the likelihood of an employee being mobilized by a party activist. Here we expect variation in press freedom across region to be unrelated to the likelihood that a voter is mobilized in the workplace because voters are unlikely to attach the same normative disapproval to mobilization by party activists as to mobilization by employers.[25] The results conform to

---

[24] Other variables performed as expected. In line with our argument, small cities are an especially likely site for workplace mobilization. We also find that respondents who are more skeptical of Putin are more likely to be mobilized than Putin supporters.

[25] Unfortunately, questions on party mobilization were only included in the 2016 and 2018 surveys, so data are limited to those two surveys.

Table 7.5 Press Freedom and Workplace Mobilization

	Mobilized in Workplace		More Coercive		Less Coercive	
	(1)	(2)	(3)	(4)	(5)	(6)
Male	−0.020	−0.020	−0.004	−0.004	−0.022	−0.023
	(0.018)	(0.017)	(0.008)	(0.008)	(0.024)	(0.024)
Age (log)	0.017	0.018	0.021	0.022	0.025	0.022
	(0.023)	(0.023)	(0.014)	(0.015)	(0.024)	(0.025)
Education	0.014***	0.014***	−0.0001	-8.5×10^{-5}	0.023***	0.023***
	(0.005)	(0.005)	(0.004)	(0.004)	(0.006)	(0.006)
City Size	−0.038***	−0.038***	0.005	0.005	−0.045***	−0.047***
	(0.009)	(0.010)	(0.007)	(0.007)	(0.016)	(0.016)
Public Sector Employee	0.144***	0.143***	0.034**	0.033**	0.093***	0.095***
	(0.024)	(0.024)	(0.013)	(0.013)	(0.027)	(0.026)
Economic Status	0.024**	0.025**	−0.0007	−0.0008	0.002	0.003
	(0.011)	(0.012)	(0.009)	(0.009)	(0.016)	(0.016)
Turned Out in Recent Parliamentary Election	0.070***	0.071***	0.030**	0.030**	0.043	0.044
	(0.016)	(0.016)	(0.013)	(0.013)	(0.027)	(0.027)
Binary Putin Approval	−0.036*	−0.038*	−0.045***	−0.044***	0.010	0.005
	(0.021)	(0.021)	(0.016)	(0.016)	(0.031)	(0.031)
Regional Population (log)	0.044	0.041	0.026	0.042	0.077	0.031
	(0.045)	(0.044)	(0.032)	(0.032)	(0.083)	(0.057)
Regional Unemployment (%)	−0.0005	−0.0006	−0.011***	−0.010***	−0.002	−0.004
	(0.013)	(0.013)	(0.003)	(0.004)	(0.025)	(0.024)

Gross Regional Product (log)	−0.016	−0.005	−0.009	−0.010	−0.024	−0.017
	(0.021)	(0.024)	(0.018)	(0.015)	(0.045)	(0.042)
UR Regional Vote (PR)	−0.104	−0.100	−0.062	−0.110*	−0.137	0.062
	(0.127)	(0.131)	(0.062)	(0.060)	(0.197)	(0.214)
Press Freedom (GDF)	−0.056**		−0.018		−0.019	
	(0.022)		(0.011)		(0.041)	
Press Freedom (Carnegie)		−0.029		−0.021**		0.041
		(0.023)		(0.009)		(0.037)
R^2	0.056	0.054	0.037	0.039	0.100	0.102
Observations	3,453	3,453	1,999	1,999	1,999	1,999
Survey Fixed Effects	✓	✓	✓	✓	✓	✓

***p<0.01, **p<0.05, *p<0.1 This table examines the effect of press freedom on different types of workplace mobilization by pooling the four individual-level Russia surveys. The sample is restricted to only employed respondents in either the public or private sector who work in nonmanagerial positions. The outcome variable in columns 1 and 2 is a binary indicator for whether the respondent experienced any kind of workplace mobilization. In columns 3 and 4, the outcome includes only respondents who were explicitly threatened by their employer to turn out or were explicitly asked to vote for a certain candidate; these types of mobilization are "more coercive" in nature. Columns 5 and 6 use a binary indicator for whether a respondent experienced any of the "less coercive" types of workplace mobilization (they saw flyers, discussed politics with their superior, etc.). The reason for the reduced sample size in columns 3 through 6 is that the specific questions used to define degrees of coercion were only asked in our 2014 and 2018 surveys. All models include survey wave fixed effects and cluster standard errors on region.

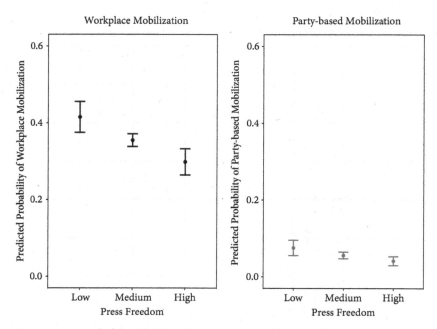

Figure 7.1 Workplace Mobilization at Different Levels of Press Freedom

Note: This figure shows the predicted probabilities of workplace mobilization for the different values of GDF press freedom holding all other variables at their means. The outcome in the left panel is a binary indicator for a respondent being mobilized in the workplace, with the model used for the prediction shown in Table 7.5, column 1. The right panel uses an identical specification, but with an outcome for whether a party activist asked a respondent to vote for a specific candidate. Errors bars show 95 percent confidence intervals.

our intuition. In Figure 7.1, we present the predicted probabilities of experiencing any form of workplace mobilization as estimated above. In the panel on the left, we report the results of the predicted probability that a respondent will be mobilized by an employer at three levels of media freedom as captured by the GDF Index. We find that respondents are significantly more likely to be mobilized by employers when media freedom is low than when it is high.

In the panel on the right, we present the predicted probability of being mobilized by a party activist conditional on the level of media freedom. The probability of a respondent being mobilized by a party activist does not depend on the level of press freedom. Respondents were about as likely to be mobilized by a party activist in regions with low media freedom as they were in regions with high media freedom. The confidence intervals also overlap between the coefficients for regions with higher and lower values of media freedom. Finally, in regression analysis, the coefficients on both measures of media freedom are not statistically significant predictors of party mobilization. In sum, employers appear less likely to engage in workplace mobilization in regions with more media freedom, but the same is not true for party mobilization. This placebo test gives us additional confidence in our results.

One might be concerned that respondents in regions with less press freedom would be less willing to report to a survey researcher that they experienced workplace mobilization. It is difficult to identify the scale of this potential form of respondent bias, but to the extent it is present it would reduce the impact of our results, as we would capture even fewer reports of workplace mobilization in regions with less media freedom. Given the direction of this potential reporting bias, we are likely understating the impact of press freedom on the likelihood of workplace mobilization.

These findings suggest that expectations of electoral backlash by the broader public can influence a politician's choices about whether to mobilize voters via the workplace. They also point to one reason why more coercive forms of workplace mobilization are likely to be less common in more open and democratic settings. As data from Chapter 2 indicated, more coercive forms of workplace mobilization are more common in more autocratic countries. More autocratic Russia and Venezuela experience higher levels of the more coercive forms of workplace mobilization than do more democratic Argentina and Indonesia.[26] In addition, in the US, employers are much more likely to employ less coercive forms of workplace mobilization.

Conclusion

Workplace mobilization turns off voters in a range of political settings. Voters were most strongly opposed to more coercive forms of workplace mobilization, but also objected in large numbers to employers' seemingly innocuous attempts to get their workers to participate in politics. Our survey experiments also demonstrate that voters reported a willingness to punish

---

[26] These results also may have relevance for the US case where employers rarely publicize their more partisan and coercive efforts to get out the vote.

candidates, even co-partisan candidates, in a hypothetical election conditional on learning that they had employed workplace mobilization. Finally, we showed a negative correlation between media freedom and various forms of workplace mobilization across regions in Russia. These findings lead to several broader conclusions.

By looking at how voters in the general public respond to learning about voter mobilization in the workplace, we draw a richer picture of electoral clientelism that goes beyond dyadic relations between politicians and brokers and between brokers and their clients. In addition, we have identified an important trade-off facing politicians. Politicians and employers can use their leverage to compel employees to turn out to vote, but doing so can also lose votes among the broader public that disapproves of this tactic. This trade-off is particularly acute in settings of greater media freedom, where citizens are likely to learn that a candidate or firm has employed an unpopular tactic for mobilizing voters.

More generally, we contribute to broader debates about the benefits of transparency for governance. The fear of public backlash may act as a deterrent to workplace mobilization, particularly to its more coercive forms. Word about workplace mobilization spreads widely and quickly, angering citizens who believe that politics should have no place at work. Recognizing these political risks, politicians and employers prefer to use workplace mobilization where the public is less likely to detect it, which suggests that strengthening the free press can increase the costs to politicians and employers of employing this tactic. The easier it is for the voting public to learn about employers threatening the workforce, the less likely that employees will be mobilized in such a manner.

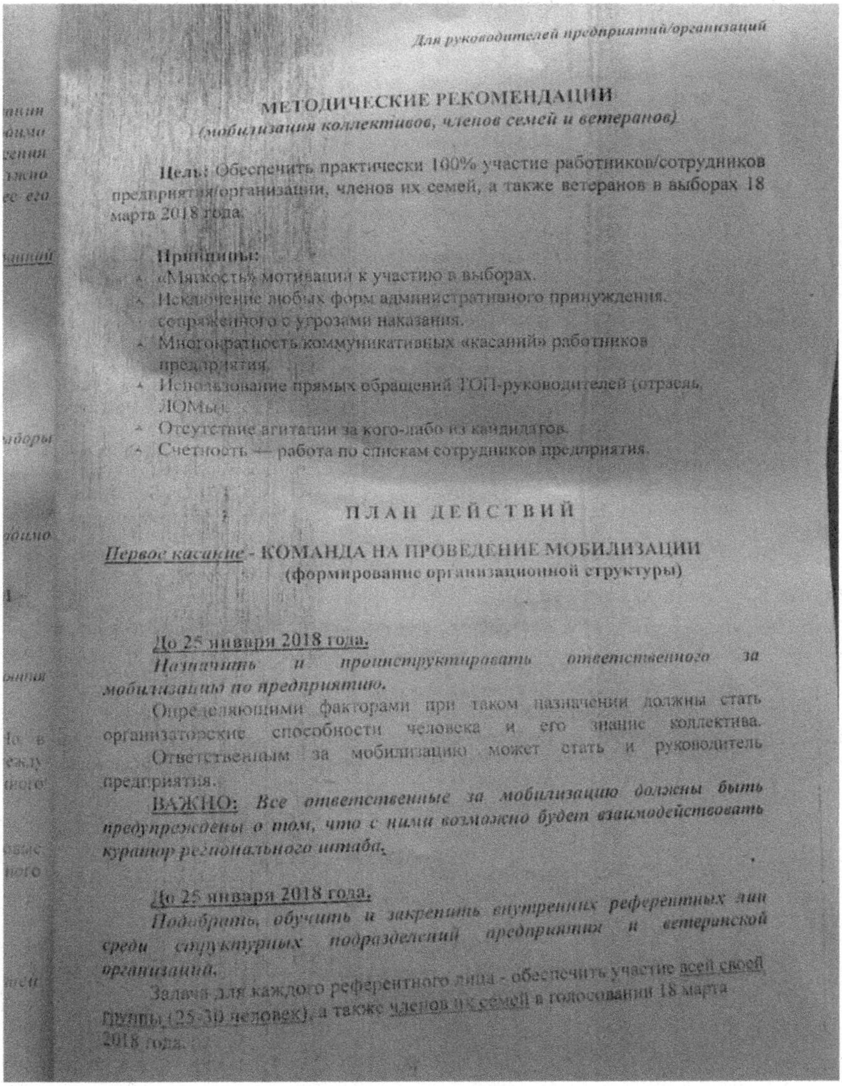

Для руководителей предприятий/организаций

МЕТОДИЧЕСКИЕ РЕКОМЕНДАЦИИ
(мобилизация коллективов, членов семей и ветеранов)

Цель: Обеспечить практически 100% участие работников/сотрудников предприятия/организации, членов их семей, а также ветеранов в выборах 18 марта 2018 года.

Принципы:
- «Мягкость» мотивации к участию в выборах.
- Исключение любых форм административного принуждения, сопряженного с угрозами наказания.
- Многократность коммуникативных «касаний» работников предприятия.
- Использование прямых обращений ТОП-руководителей (отрасль, ЛОМы).
- Отсутствие агитации за кого-либо из кандидатов.
- Счетность — работа по спискам сотрудников предприятия.

ПЛАН ДЕЙСТВИЙ

<u>*Первое касание*</u> - КОМАНДА НА ПРОВЕДЕНИЕ МОБИЛИЗАЦИИ
(формирование организационной структуры)

<u>До 25 января 2018 года.</u>
Назначить и проинструктировать ответственного за мобилизацию по предприятию.
Определяющими факторами при таком назначении должны стать организаторские способности человека и его знание коллектива.
Ответственным за мобилизацию может стать и руководитель предприятия.
<u>ВАЖНО:</u> *Все ответственные за мобилизацию должны быть предупреждены о том, что с ними возможно будет взаимодействовать куратор регионального штаба.*

<u>До 25 января 2018 года.</u>
Подобрать, обучить и закрепить внутренних референтных лиц среди структурных подразделений предприятия и ветеранской организации.
Задача для каждого референтного лица - обеспечить участие <u>всей своей группы (25-30 человек)</u>, а также <u>членов их семей</u> в голосовании 18 марта 2018 года.

Plate 7.1

7.5 Appendix

Figure 7.2 Glasnost Defense Fund Map of Press Openness

Note: This figure depicts the breakdown in press freedom scores across Russia as compiled by the Glasnost Defense Fund.

8

Is Workplace Mobilization Undemocratic?

We have identified a range of tactics that employers use to get their workers to the polls, examined the conditions under which workplace mobilization occurs, and explored how institutional factors like freedom of the press influence the incentives to engage in workplace mobilization. Our findings demonstrate that workplace mobilization is shaped by a layered set of power relations. The power of politicians over employers and the latter's power over their employees influence the incentives of employers to engage in workplace mobilization. Our research shows that these power imbalances often give rise to coercion—both by politicians against employers and by employers against their workers.

This critical role of coercion leads to important questions about the normative implications of workplace mobilization. This chapter takes up these questions.[1] In the pages that follow, we seek to identify the conditions under which workplace mobilization should be seen as acceptable from the perspective of democratic theory. Exploring the normative implications of workplace mobilization puts our theoretical argument and empirical analysis in a broader context. We argue that for workplace mobilization to be defended as enhancing democracy, two conditions should be met:

1. Workplace mobilization should not infringe on voter autonomy.
2. Workplace mobilization should not lead to systematic bias in electoral outcomes.

When workplace mobilization can satisfy these two conditions, it can improve the quality of democracy by providing useful information to voters, increasing turnout, and raising interest in politics more generally. However, as we shall demonstrate, these conditions are difficult to satisfy in practice. That employers often use threats to mobilize workers, that those most vulnerable to economic and political pressure are often the targets of

---

[1] For a lively discussion of the normative implications of employer control over employees inside and outside the workplace, see the essays and comments in Anderson (2019).

Workplace Politics. Timothy Frye, Ora John Reuter, and David Szakonyi, Oxford University Press.
© Oxford University Press (2025). DOI: 10.1093/9780197802045.003.0008

198 WORKPLACE POLITICS

workplace mobilization, and that incumbents are far better positioned to engage in workplace mobilization than challengers all suggest that many forms of workplace mobilization are squarely at odds with democratic practice.

It should therefore come as no surprise that many Western democracies—including Australia, the United Kingdom, Germany, Japan, and Canada—have outlawed discrimination at work based on political activity or beliefs (Hertel-Fernandez and Secunda, 2016). These statutes are typically rooted in national labor law or constitutional provisions on basic political rights that have been backed by court decisions (Hertel-Fernandez and Secunda, 2016; 4–16). Most dramatically, the European Court of Human Rights in *Redfearn versus the United Kingdom* found that the absence of legislation prohibiting political discrimination in the workplace was incompatible with the freedom of association as stated in Article 11 of the European Convention on Human Rights.[2]

One exception to this pattern is the United States, where recent legal changes—in particular, the *Citizens United* decision by the Supreme Court in 2010—have eliminated many barriers to workplace mobilization. The analysis in this chapter draws on our broad sample of cases, but also relies heavily on the experience of the United States—a country that has experienced periods where employers applied the coercive methods frequently cited in past chapters and more recent periods where such techniques have largely been replaced by more sophisticated tactics that require more nuanced normative judgments. Throughout this evolution, judges, politicians, regulators, and election officials have left a valuable record of their attempts to wrestle with the implications of different forms of workplace mobilization, and these records are instructive for our analysis.[3] Recent developments, such as the apparent uptick in workplace mobilization after the *Citizens United* decision, have also provided an impetus for American legal scholars and social scientists to consider the moral implications of the practice.

---

[2] *Redfearn v. United Kingdom*, 2012; European Court of Human Rights, 19876 (2006).

[3] This dilemma of workplace mobilization of state employees is hardly new. Then-president Thomas Jefferson wrote in 1801, "The right of any [state] officer to give his vote at elections as a qualified citizen is not meant to be restrained, nor, however given, shall it have any effect to his prejudice; but it is expected that he will not attempt to influence the votes of others, nor take any part in the business of electioneering, that being deemed inconsistent with the spirit of the Constitution and his duties to it" (Commission, 1941; 148).

Coercion, Free Speech, and Workplace Mobilization

In nineteenth-century America, employers saw nothing wrong with putting pressure on their workers to vote, and corporations could freely provide such services to politicians in ways that would have been familiar to company managers in contemporary Russia and Venezuela. A US Senate report from 1880, "Alleged Fraud in the Late Election," notes many instances of the practice. For example, it recounts how agents of the Douglass Axe Company in Massachusetts "stood at the door of the election house, watched every one of the employees who came in, passed him a copy of the Republican ticket, and told him that it would be in his interest to vote the ticket"(United States Senate Report, 1880; 5, 1–10). In the absence of a secret ballot and with few voter protections, nineteenth-century business owners frequently resorted to bribery, coercion, and intimidation to get their workers to the polls (Barnes, 1947; Bensel, 2004; Keyssar, 2009). The introduction of the secret ballot in most states in the late 1800s drastically reduced the most blatant forms of workplace pressure (Cox and Kousser, 1981). These types of direct forms of voter intimidation are easy to condemn from a normative point of view.

A trickier issue involves free speech. Democratic theorists have viewed freedom of speech as a critical component of democracy. Given this priority, courts have generally set a high bar for establishing restrictions in this area and have been particularly loathe to restrict political speech. Such a concern for employer free speech on political issues provides one justification for supporting some forms of workplace mobilization that rely less on intimidation than on conveying employer preferences to their workers.

Indeed, beyond the free speech rights of employers, there may be benefits to granting employers rights to discuss politics with workers because employers are well placed to inform workers about how pending election results might influence the company's bottom line and worker welfare at the company. At the same time, free speech rights are far from absolute, and courts have long recognized that individuals have privacy rights that should allow them to avoid unwanted speech. Courts have shown a key interest in protecting political speech, but they have also recognized that citizens cannot be compelled to listen to political speech.

Trying to resolve this dilemma, over the course of the twentieth century, Congress, the National Labor Relations Board, and the Federal Election Commission created a framework that sought to balance the free speech

200 WORKPLACE POLITICS

rights of businesspeople and the privacy rights of their employees. The National Labor Relations Board made a key intervention in this debate in 1969 by recognizing that

> any balancing of those [employer and employee] rights must take into account the economic dependence of the employees on their employers, and the necessary tendency of the former, because of that relationship, to pick up intended implications of the latter that might be more readily dismissed by a more disinterested ear.... What is basically at stake is the establishment of a non-permanent, limited relationship between the employer, his economically dependent employee and his union agent, not the election of legislators or the enactment of legislation whereby that relationship is ultimately defined and where the independent voter may be freer to listen more objectively and employers as a class freer to talk.[4]

This reasoning recognized the power differences between workers and owners, distinguished between political speech inside and outside the employment relationship, and helped to provide the legal basis for worker protections against unwanted political speech in the workplace.[5]

In line with this ruling, corporations were allowed to communicate with employees regarding policy issues and pending legislation, but were not permitted to "expressly advocate the election or defeat of one or more clearly identified candidate(s) or the candidates of a clearly identified political party" (Harvard Law Review Notes, 2014: 672). In addition, managers could not direct employees to engage in any type of political activity, no matter whether they were compensated for their effort. So-called captive audience meetings, in which employers compelled employees to attend meetings on political topics while at work, were also barred.[6] Moreover, employers were limited in their ability to request political donations from their employees. Employers could only solicit political contributions from employees twice each year, and then only in a format in which they could not tell whether an employee had contributed—for example, with only aggregate contributions

---

[4] *National Labor Relations Board v.Gissel Inc.*, 395 US 575, 1969.
[5] *Mariani v. United States*, 80 F. Supp. 2d 352 (M.D. Pa. 1999). Employers face greater restrictions their interactions with their employees in elections to create unions within a plant than in elections for political office. Ackerman, Bruce, and Ian Ayres, "How to Stop Employers from Telling Workers Whom to Vote For," *Slate*, November 2, 2012.
[6] Employers have greater rights to hold captive audience meetings during union drives and are allowed to discuss the formation of unions during mandatory meetings held in the workplace during the workday.

from a company being disclosed (Harvard Law Review Notes, 2014: 672). Detailed regulations ensured that political solicitations from employers to their employees would be "infrequent, at arms-length, and ensure dissenters' anonymity" (Harvard Law Review Notes, 2014: 672). These broad injunctions provided workers significant protection from political coercion by their employers.

In 2010, however, the Supreme Court undercut the legal basis for these protections. On one level, the court sought to determine whether the non-profit corporation Citizens United could air the film *Hillary: The Movie*, which expressed opinions about Hillary Clinton's fitness for the presidency. But the larger issue at stake was whether First Amendment protections extended to corporations. By a 5-4 margin, the court ruled in favor of Citizens United on the grounds that corporate funding of independent political broadcasts in candidate elections cannot be limited. Such restrictions violated the free speech rights of employers.[7] Writing for the majority, Justice Kennedy noted, "If the First Amendment has any force, it prohibits Congress from fining or jailing citizens, or associations of citizens, for simply engaging in political speech." The court ruled that political speech is central to democracy, even when conducted by corporations. Supporters hailed the decision as a victory for free speech and noted that the requirements to name the sources of funding to political candidates would allow voters sufficient information to judge the merits of arguments for themselves.[8]

In the rare cases where US state law does not prohibit these actions, employers can now make appeals to their workers to vote for particular candidates and parties, compel workers to attend meetings in support of candidates, and potentially retaliate against workers for their political views.[9] Federal law bars explicit or implicit threats against anyone for political activity like voting, but employers can compel their workers to attend meetings

---

[7] Prior to the *Citizens United* decision, corporations could use separate segregated funds (SSFs) to participate in politics, but these SSFs were heavily regulated and included many protections from political coercion against employees. The *Citizens United* decision made SSFs obsolete because corporations could use political action committees to donate to politicians and parties and ended the legal protections for employees embedded in these provisions.

[8] Will, George F., "Campaign Finance: A 'Reform' Wisely Struck Down," *Washington Post*, January 28, 2010.

[9] New Jersey, Oregon, and Wisconsin bar captive-audience meetings, while Washington, DC, has made political affiliation a protected category under antidiscrimination law. California, Louisiana, and Nebraska have expanded protections against dismissals based on independent political activity. Burke, Lindsay B., and Robert D. Lenhard, "Politics in the Workplace: A Primer for 2016," March 18, 2016.

202 WORKPLACE POLITICS

on political topics in the workplace during the workday and, in many cases, fire them for disobeying.

A good example of the changed legal landscape occurred on August 13, 2019, when President Donald Trump visited a Shell petrochemicals plant under construction in Monaca, Pennsylvania. Before an assembled crowd of workers and against the background of a large American flag with red, white, and blue bunting, Trump took aim at Democrats and argued, "If my opponent won... you would have stopped construction before you started too much. Without us, you would never have been able to do this." (Shell actually announced plans to build the plant in 2012 midway through President Obama's term.)[10] Shell executives praised Trump for protecting the interests of the energy sector.[11]

Shell management also made clear that employees who did not attend the event would have to use paid time off or not receive pay for that day.[12] A memo noted that "attendance was not mandatory," but also reminded workers that only those who scanned their work cards before 7 a.m. and were prepared to stand through lunch (but without being fed) would be paid.[13] These are precisely the kinds of captive audience meetings that were barred prior to the *Citizens United* decision in 2010.

A related issue involves employers influencing the political activity of their employees during the workday. Concerned about the impact that a second Trump term might have on immigration policies, some Silicon Valley companies paid workers to attend anti-Trump rallies during the workday.[14] Facebook announced a policy not to penalize workers who attended a May 2020 pro-immigration rally rather than come to work.[15] Prior to 2010, employers could not take such actions, but they are now legal. These efforts were explicitly voluntary but, again, involved appeals from management to take part in political action. How employees perceived these actions is unclear.

[10] Colvin, Jill, "Trump Claims Credit for Shell Plant Announced under Obama," *Associated Press*, August 13, 2019.

[11] President Trump's remarks are available at "Remarks by President Trump during Tour of the Shell Pennsylvania Petrochemicals Complex, Monaca, PA," White House Archives, August 13, 2019.

[12] Westwood, Sarah, and Yon Pomrenze, "Workers Had 3 Options: Attend Trump's Speech, Use Paid Time Off or Receive No Pay," *CNN*, August 17, 2019.

[13] Vendel, Christine, "Union Workers Had to Attend Trump Event in Western PA to Get Paid: Report," *Pennlive*, August 17, 2019.

[14] AOL Staff, "These Companies Will Give You Paid Time Off to Protest President Trump," *AOL*, April 19, 2017.

[15] Bhattarai, Abha, "The Newest Silicon Valley Perk? Paid Time Off to Protest Trump." *Washington Post*, October 23, 2021.

The *Citizens United* decision significantly increased employers' ability to engage in politics at work, but in the absence of new legislation, it also raised questions about what specific types of political activity are allowed. For example, the law is clear that employers cannot compel employees to make financial contributions to campaigns, but is less clear about other forms of support. The Federal Election Commission has done little to clarify the issue, often due to partisan gridlock on its six-member panel. For example, in 2012 the Murray Corporation in Ohio forced workers to attend an appearance by presidential candidate Mitt Romney at the plant during work hours. Employees were given anti-Obama signs to wave, and photos of the event were used in the Romney campaign. The FEC voted 3-3 along partisan lines not to declare the Murray Corporation in violation of the law.[16]

Indeed, without further legislation clarifying the rights of employers and employees in the workplace, employers and employees are operating in a gray area. Employers may be tempted to push the envelope. One analyst noted, "When you have ... the compliance people and the outside lawyers saying, 'Look, be careful here, stay well within the line,' and then they see a case like the Murray case," Noble says, "they'll be like, 'Why are we being so conservative about this? Why don't we get more aggressive?'" Other legal experts echo this sentiment.[17] With companies engaging in increasingly creative ways of engaging their workers politically, we should expect more rulings down the line from election officials determining what is and is not allowed under the current legal framework.

US state laws provide a patchwork of protections for workers, but also are not based on a legal or normative consensus. In general, state laws prohibit employers from punishing employees for political activity outside of work, but do far less to protect employees from being compelled to engage in political activity during work hours. And again, there is considerable variation from one jurisdiction to another, with some such as Montana, Washington, DC, and California banning political discrimination in the workplace (Hertel-Fernandez and Secunda, 2016).[18]

---

[16] First General Counsel's Report, Federal Election Commission, MUR 6651, April 23, 2013.

[17] Employment lawyers from Covington and Burling noted, "For corporate counsel, the price of the freedom corporations have won with *Citizens United* and similar legal rulings is an increasingly complex world of regulation, and perhaps a mistaken mood among many companies that this freedom means that no rules exist. The truth, unfortunately, is far more complicated." Burke and Lenhard, "Politics in the Workplace."

[18] For more detail, see Burke and Lenhard, "Politics in the Workplace."

204 WORKPLACE POLITICS

Given the murkiness of the legal and regulatory landscape, it is helpful to take a step back and consider workplace mobilization in terms of democratic theory. Here we focus on how various forms of workplace mobilization should be judged in light of voter autonomy and political bias—two concerns that have long been central to democratic thought. We explore the normative implications of employers seeking to encourage voter turnout rather than influence their vote choice because arguments about the former generally apply to the latter with even greater force.[19]

Condition 1. Voter Autonomy: The Concept

Voter autonomy is a key component of democracy. Autonomous individuals choosing to support a candidate without expectation of reprisal lies at the heart of democratic theory. The US Supreme Court has held that "the right to vote freely for the candidate of one's choice is the essence of a democratic society and any restrictions on that right strike at the heart of representative government."[20] These rights extend beyond simply casting a ballot, as voters also rely on freedom of expression and rights of free speech to inform their choices.

Voter autonomy also includes the right not to participate in elections. Nonvoting need not represent political apathy. It can be considered an expression of either satisfaction with or opposition to the choices on offer. In a democracy, voters should retain their right to voice their objections by not voting or by spoiling their ballot. Writing about the United States, legal scholar Jeffrey Blomberg maintains that the "right to abstain from politics without penalty logically follows from the right to vote" and argues that this right should receive all the protections associated with voting (Blomberg, 1995; 20).[21]

Abstention gains greater importance in nondemocratic settings where leaders use turnout as an indicator of their legitimacy. In such settings, those who abstain from voting may be closer to expressing their sincere preferences than are those who take part in the ritual of voting in elections without choice. Thus, we should recognize that the act of voting is not necessarily an

---

[19] For a good discussion of employees' speech rights in the United States, see Garden (2022).
[20] Cited in Blomberg, 1995. *Reynolds v. Sims*, 377 U.S. 533, 555 (1964).
[21] Frequent purging of electoral rolls of nonvoters erodes this right of nonvoting by removing from voters the power to protest by not voting.

unalloyed expression of democracy, and that making normative judgments about voting depends on the political context.

To be sure, recognizing voter autonomy does not mean one believes that voters make their decisions in a vacuum. Coworkers, co-religionists, friends, family members, parties, and unions can and do try to sway voters with positive and negative sanctions. A long line of research finds that people often vote under real or perceived pressures from various sets of peers and social organizations (Berelson, Lazarsfeld, and McPhee, 1954; Mutz and Mondak, 2006; Gerber and Rogers, 2009; Funk, 2010). As noted in Chapter 2, however, the rewards and sanctions held by social peers and social organizations are often less consequential than the carrots and sticks that employers use. In addition, what makes workplace mobilization particularly fraught from a normative perspective is the hierarchical nature of the relationship between workers and employers. The power differentials between employers and employees are often far greater than they are between social peers or within social organizations. The hierarchy of the workplace and the size of the rewards and benefits that employers offer present especially salient threats to voter autonomy.

At the same time, high turnout is generally seen as good for democracy, and workplace mobilization may contribute to this good. With high voter turnout, it is much more likely that those who cast a ballot are closer to a representative sample of the electorate. This makes political outcomes reflect the preference of a broader range of voices. Indeed, in settings like the United States—where voters tend be wealthier, better educated, and whiter than nonvoters—low voter turnout may be especially problematic.[22] Getting more voters to the polls is especially important in local and off-cycle elections that are prone to low turnout. That just 23 percent of New Yorkers cast a ballot in the mayoral elections of 2021 may indicate overwhelming support for the political status quo or, more likely, raise concerns about the health of democracy in the country's largest city.[23]

---

[22] Brennan Center, "Large Racial Turnout Gap Persisted in 2020 Election," *Brennan Center for Justice*, February 23, 2023. But see Kasara and Suryanarayan (2020) for comparative data on the topic.

[23] Bergin, Brigid, "New York City Voter Turnout Hits Record Low for a Mayoral Election," *Gothamist*, December 1, 2021.

Coercive Appeals

Employers' appeals to explicit or implicit coercion raise clear concerns for democratic theory by violating voter autonomy.[24] In a broad range of countries, we have provided numerous examples of employers threatening workers with job loss, pay cuts, or increases in workload; monitoring voter behavior with the goal of influencing it; and simply ordering workers to vote with an implied, but unstated, threat of negative consequences should they disobey. In settings where employers wield considerable leverage, employees may fear implicit pressure to choose the "correct" candidate, even if there has been no explicit suggestion or threat levied. Moreover, these threats are well understood as such by their employees. In addition, we have provided instances where politicians reward and punish employers for their political activities in the workplace, which are equally problematic from the view of democratic theory.[25]

Forms of workplace mobilization that target the most vulnerable merit particular scrutiny. As prior chapters have demonstrated, employers in a variety of settings often seek to mobilize workers with less job security and those who work in slack labor markets and therefore have less power to defend their interests. This is even true in the United States where workers who express less job security are more likely to be mobilized (Hertel-Fernandez, 2018).[26]

Even if workplace mobilization is coercive, one might argue that the costs of coercion in terms of lost voter autonomy are offset by increases in political participation from those who might otherwise stay at home. This consequentialist defense of workplace mobilization may justify mild forms of coercion in the name of increased turnout. Given that some believe that voting is "habit-forming," the costs of coercion may not need to be applied repeatedly (Gerber, Green, and Shachar, 2003). However, this argument includes strong assumptions that the costs of coercion are small and that

---

[24] In line with Mansbridge et al., we see coercive power as "A's preferences or interests causing B to do (or changing the probability that B will do) what B would not otherwise would have done through the threat of sanctions or the use of force" (Mansbridge et al., 2010). Our arguments reflect long-standing debates on the faces of power; see Dahl (1957); Bachrach and Baratz (1962); Lukes (2021); and Gaventa (1982).

[25] Employers may be required to expend significant resources mobilizing in their workplace for political causes that they personally do not support.

[26] More recent data from our two online surveys in the United States confirm this finding.

other, noncoercive means of increasing voter turnout are less effective than more coercive forms. This argument would also only apply to instances where mildly coercive forms of workplace mobilization turn out voters who would otherwise have not voted. And, of course, it would be unlikely to apply to the most explicit forms of coercion around vote choice. As we shall see, these costs of coercion may be borne differently by employers and employees.

Aspects of workplace mobilization may also appeal to those who support compulsory voting as a means of increasing political participation and strengthening democracy. Currently, about one in four countries have some requirements for voting, with various types of punishments imposed for staying home on election day (Birch, 2016). Most famously, Lijphart (1997) used his American Political Science Association Presidential Address to make the case for compulsory voting on the grounds that it was the best remedy against unequal political influence induced by unequal turnout. There is some empirical support for this view. Carey and Horiuchi (2017) find that the elimination of compulsory voting in Venezuela in 1993 starkly reduced voting rates, particularly among the poor, and led to greater income inequality.

However, compulsory voting and workplace mobilization differ in important ways. Both involve a degree of coercion against citizens, but the former is universal and the latter applies only to a subset of those in the working population. Compulsory voting importantly balances coercion against the significant benefit of ensuring that all voices are heard at the ballot box. Workplace mobilization, on the other hand, boosts the voices of those who are employed in sectors where workplace mobilization is easier to conduct, and therefore increases disparities in voting rates between those who are and are not mobilized. Moreover, employer punishments for not voting are often far greater than the small penalties levied by states that enforce compulsory voting.[27] Finally, compulsory voting entails absolutely no implicit (or explicit) coercion over vote choice. This is often not the case with workplace mobilization, even if those requests are not made explicit.

---

[27] Another significant difference between compulsory voting and workplace mobilization lies in the identity of the enforcer. With compulsory voting the state holds the threat of coercion, while with workplace mobilization an employer does.

208 WORKPLACE POLITICS

Conditionality

Mobilization efforts that make a reward or benefit conditional on political behavior also raise concerns for democratic theory. Stokes, Dunning, and Nazareno (2013) argue that targeting specific groups with positive or negative inducements in exchange for their votes robs vote sellers of their influence on policy and skews public policy away from their interests. The same is true for forms of workplace mobilization that make rewards or punishments dependent on political behavior. In essence, conditionality silences the policy preferences of those managers or workers who are rewarded or punished for their political activity.

Even attempts to reward managers or workers for voting are problematic.[28] Because these benefits accrue only to those employers or employees who do a politician's bidding, they raise concerns about equal treatment of citizens regardless of their political behavior. These concerns are far from hypothetical. Chapter 4 reported that firms in Russia that mobilized their workers were significantly more likely to receive government contracts than those that did not. While employers are generally more likely to use negative than positive inducements, we do find examples of worker benefits (such as bonuses, paid leave, etc.) being made conditional on their voting activity. Many forms of workplace mobilization run a high risk of compromising voter autonomy via conditionality. Highly visible activities—such as compelling workers to make political donations, attend rallies, and sign petitions—can be problematic because they more easily allow employers to selectively reward and punish employees on whether they comply.

The secret ballot is designed to bolster voter autonomy by ensuring that one's vote is counted, but remains known only to the voter and is kept secret from prying eyes. This makes it hard for politicians or managers to condition political behavior on voting for a particular candidate or party. Empirical

---

[28] Negative inducements like coercion are easy to condemn from the perspective of democratic theory, but positive inducements are somewhat more complicated. While most observers critique the practice, especially in the form of vote buying or turnout buying, Mansbridge et al. (2010) note, "Inducements pose a problem as yet unresolved in the theory of power," in part because it may involve greater freedom to choose. With a positive inducement, one can choose to improve their lot, but with a negative inducement one is forced to make themselves worse off." The distinction between positive and negative inducements makes little sense from an economic perspective, but asymmetries in the domain of gain and loss has a strong basis in psychology. See Mansbridge et al. (2010). Nonetheless, the conditionality of even positive inducements is problematic in that it robs the voters of their agency and introduces inequalities among voters. See Stokes, Dunning, and Nazareno (2013).

studies from the United States find that the introduction of the secret ballot resulted in lower turnout by reducing vote-buying and voter intimidation (Cox and Kousser, 1981; Keyssar, 2009). In practice, however, the secret ballot does not fully eliminate this problem, especially in the contemporary world where smartphones are ubiquitous. Even in the United States where formal violations of the secret ballot are extraordinarily rare, many Americans perceive that their vote choices are not secret. Gerber et al. (2013) find that one in four Americans believe that their votes are not secret, while roughly one in three believe that it would "not be difficult" or only "somewhat difficult" for politicians, union leaders, or the people who you work with to find out how they voted.[29] These figures are often higher (although not by much) in less democratic settings. For example, in a somewhat differently worded question, in our survey in Russia in 2016 we found that 24 percent believed that it would be relatively easy for employers or state officials to learn how they voted if they so desired. Employers have many tools at their disposal to enforce conditionality and deprive voters of their ability to exercise their political views autonomously.

Noncoercive, Nonconditional Forms of Workplace Mobilization

Forms of workplace mobilization that do not involve coercion or conditionality are much more defensible on normative grounds. Run-of-the-mill, nonpartisan get-out-the-vote (GOTV) campaigns at work, provided workers do not feel any sort of pressure to turn out and do not receive benefits conditional on participation should be encouraged, particularly in democracies where voter turnout is usually low. Indeed, nonintrusive, nonpartisan GOTV campaigns in the workplace appear to be increasingly common in democracies such as the United States and India, and this is to be welcomed. Systematic data over time are hard to come by, but our empirical results find that even in the wake of the *Citizens United* decision in 2010, workplace mobilization in the United States generally relies on persuasion and gently getting out the vote rather than employing various means of coercion.[30] In our 2021 survey of nine hundred employed respondents, we found that

---

[29] Researchers asked, "As far as you know, when you go to a polling place and vote, are your choices about which candidate you voted for kept secret unless you tell someone, or are your choices not kept secret?" Twenty-five percent of respondents chose the latter (Gerber et al., 2013).

[30] Data on workplace mobilization are rare prior to 2010, when employers were far more limited in their ability to mobilize their workers.

210   WORKPLACE POLITICS

about half of US workers were exposed to at least one of six common forms of workplace mobilization.[31]

At the same time, much of this activity was at least nominally nonpartisan. Almost three times as many workers were encouraged to turn out to vote (27 percent) than to vote for a particular candidate (9 percent).[32] We have little evidence in the United States of the more egregious forms of workplace mobilization that we found in other settings. Instances of forced voting, explicit threats against specific employees, and extensive monitoring of voting and vote choice that we have documented in other settings occur far less frequently in the United States. While common in the United States, workplace mobilization is much less likely to take the most coercive forms that we have seen in the other countries in our study.

Perhaps as a result, US workers whose employers asked them to vote reported less opposition to this tactic than in other cases in our study. We asked respondents who reported exposure to a range of different forms of workplace mobilization whether these interactions made them feel uncomfortable, indifferent, or comfortable. Even among the 20 percent of respondents in our March 2020 survey who reported that their employer mentioned wage cuts, plant closings, or job losses in connection with an election result or a policy decision, less than a quarter reported that these interactions made them uncomfortable. Respondents were also not overly dismayed about employer requests to vote for a particular party; about 30 percent of mobilized workers were made uncomfortable by such requests. This suggests that employers in the United States use a lighter touch when mobilizing their workers or that employers are targeting their message to workers who share their political preferences and may therefore find their overtures less objectionable. Either case implies that employers in the United States rely more heavily on persuasion than on coercion.[33]

---

[31] In our 2021 survey of nine hundred employed respondents, one in two were contacted by a political party outside of work and one in five were contacted by a union.

[32] The most coercive forms of workplace mobilization were also less common in the United States than in other countries in our sample. For example, in the 2021 survey only 9 percent of respondents reported management invoking threats of wage cuts, plant closings, or job loss in connection with an election result or government policy decision. The figures are higher in the 2020 survey, but still lower than in other countries in our sample. Moreover, we lack the kinds of qualitative anecdotal evidence of the more egregious forms of workplace mobilization that we found in other settings.

[33] Mutz and Mondak (2006) find that political conversations among workers are especially important to democracy. Based on five surveys of employees in the United States conducted between

IS WORKPLACE MOBILIZATION UNDEMOCRATIC? 211

Employers in the United States have touted their nonpartisan GOTV campaigns at work as a form of corporate social responsibility. In 2018, 135 corporations, including Walmart and The Gap, took part in the Time to Vote campaign, which gave employees time off to vote on election day.[34] That same year more than 250 companies signed a pledge with Election-Day.Org that included calls to support voting rights and provide paid leave for employees to vote on election day. Blue Cross Blue Shield of Minnesota ran a yearlong civic participation project that included a voter registration drive and provided to their employees nonpartisan political information about candidates and issues. Patagonia has been a leading corporate voice in support of voter rights, along with Tumblr, Ben and Jerry's, and the National Hockey League.[35] Low turnout in the United States suggests that these efforts may be particularly justified. We also observe similar dynamics taking shape in India, where companies such as Coca-Cola, HSBC, and Infotech have conducted meetings encouraging employees to vote, and even allowed them to work from home on election day in order to find time to make it to the precinct.[36]

Some employee mobilization efforts that are expressly nonpartisan and resemble standard GOTV campaigns, however, shade into advocacy by emphasizing how changes in policy might affect the company. For example, whether a company claiming that an Obama victory might lead to job losses is advocacy or education is difficult to determine. Here there is a need to balance the speech rights of employers and the information provided by these campaigns against possible violations of voter autonomy.

Moreover, to the extent that there is an "inherent power" differential between employers and employees, even nonpartisan GOTV campaigns can be seen as coercive by employees depending on the specific language used. Interpreting the impact of nominally nonpartisan appeals is complicated in part because what constitutes a "partisan appeal" is in the eye of the

---

1984 and 2000, the researchers find that the workplace is one of the few venues where workers regularly encounter diverse political views. Workplace mobilization by employers that silences these kinds of conversations by trying to create a party line at work would undercut the positive role of worker-to-worker conversations in promoting democracy.

[34] McGregor, Jena, "How Employers Are Trying to Drive Election Day Turnout," *Washington Post.* October 22, 2018.

[35] Byars, Tessa, "Patagonia Joins Other Businesses, Voting Rights Groups in Calling for Senate Approval of the For the People Act," *Patagonia Works,* June 24, 2021.

[36] "Go Out and Vote, Cool Companies Tell Their Employees," *Hindustan Times,* December 2, 2013.

212 WORKPLACE POLITICS

beholder.[37] Senior counsel at the Brennan Center for Justice Adam Skaggs (2010) notes that "an official email from the boss saying something like 'your job depends on who wins the race' could be interpreted as coercion or intimidation."[38] In the Russian case, focus group participants cited in Chapter 2 frequently noted that appeals to vote for particular parties or candidates were not needed, because everyone understood who the employer backed. The need for explicitly partisan appeals could also be obviated in democratic settings if the political stances of the employer are well known. In addition, nonpartisan appeals that do not explicitly mention a party may still be partisan in practice if employers target them to employees whose political preferences align with their own.

Employees are generally attuned to the difference between mobilizing turnout and making appeals to vote for specific politicians. As noted in Chapter 7, we find greater normative support for nonpartisan GOTV campaigns than for other forms of mobilization across a range of countries. This is true in the United States as well. For example, whereas only 20 percent of respondents in our online survey from February 2021 opposed employers appealing to their workers to vote, 82 percent and 85 percent, respectively, opposed employers' appeals to vote for specific parties or candidates. While disapproving of more partisan and coercive forms of workplace mobilization, US workers appear to have a higher tolerance for more nonpartisan GOTV campaigns, perhaps because they enjoy more robust legal protections than workers in the other countries we surveyed. More generally, our survey evidence in Chapter 7 indicates that employees around the world prefer to keep politics out of the workplace. Recent work also finds this to be the case in the United States.[39]

It is also not hard to find specific examples in which employees perceive that their employers may retaliate against them for political views. For example, in the summer of 2020 the CATO Institute asked Americans whether they were worried that they would miss out on job opportunities if

[37] Ashley Spillane and Sofia, "Gross are the authors and How Companies Invest in Get-o Out-the-Vote Efforts," *Harvard Business Review*, August 6, 2019

[38] Adam Skaggs from the Brennan Center quoted in Lee S. Fang, "Is Your Boss Going to Mine Your Vote?," *The Nation* (blog), October 19, 2012.

[39] One survey of three thousand working Americans conducted in October 2020 found that 53 percent believed that discussing politics at work could negatively affect their career opportunities, and 57 percent believed that political discussions in the workplace should be discouraged. This study also found that one in two employees reported that their supervisor openly talked about supporting a particular candidate in the 2020 election (Wells, 2020).

their political opinions became known. Almost one in three said that they were either "very worried" or a "little worried" that expressing their political views would have negative impacts on their career.[40]

In sum, workplace mobilization that does not infringe on voter autonomy and can thereby enhance democracy is possible and should be encouraged. However, given the inherent asymmetries in the employer-employee relationship, democracy-enhancing forms of workplace mobilization are rare in practice. It is difficult to find many such examples, particularly in countries where politicians are unaccountable to the public and the rule of law is weak. Our evidence from Russia, Venezuela, and Turkey underscores this point. Even in democratic cases with better legal protections for workers— such as the United States—there are good reasons in most circumstances to be skeptical that workplace mobilization respects voter autonomy.

Condition 2. Introducing Bias: Conceptual Discussion

A second cornerstone of democratic theory is that political competition takes place on a relatively level playing field. Democracy is often described as a system of "institutionalized uncertainty" where elections are held with some degree of uncertainty about the outcome (Przeworski, 1991). Where institutional rules or power relations consistently reduce uncertainty and tilt electoral outcomes in favor of a particular group, the underlying premise of democratic competition comes under threat. This view has empirical support in that democracies "are more likely to survive when no single force dominates politics completely and permanently" (Cheibub et al., 1996).

Bias differs from partisanship. As it relates to our project, bias includes systematic advantages that accrue to one side—often incumbents—at the expense of others. Employers' expression of partisan views is less problematic and indeed may bring some benefits when these views provide new information for employees. But bias comes into play when workplace mobilization systematically tilts the playing field in favor of one party or candidate.

---

[40] Ten percent were "very worried" while 21 percent were a "little worried" about negative consequences. This fear may also be due to rising polarization in the country. with more ideological matching observed between workers and workplaces. Cato Institute, "Political Expression at Work," Summer, 2020, 1–8.

214 WORKPLACE POLITICS

We explore how workplace mobilization often generates two forms of bias. First, it exacerbates advantages for political incumbents at the expense of political challengers. Second, it disproportionately affects workers in settings where workplace mobilization is easier to conduct. We call the former *incumbent bias* and the latter *structural bias*.

Incumbent Bias

Workplace mobilization may provide systemic advantages to political incumbents because their privileged access to state resources makes it easier to both coerce and incentivize managers and employers to engage their workers politically. This form of bias takes a variety of forms. For one, incumbents have leverage over state sector workers, which gives them an advantage over rivals. Previous chapters have shown that the state bureaucracy is a key site of workplace mobilization in many countries.

In addition to being able to put pressure on state employees, incumbents have greater access to state resources that can be used to induce private sector firms to get their workers to the polls—through either negative or positive sanctions. Heightened access to state resources tilts the playing field against challengers. As we found in Chapter 4, firms in Russia that mobilized their workers were more likely to receive state contracts than those that did not, which again points to the benefits of access to state resources.

Indeed, in Russia the vast majority of workplace mobilization favors United Russia. Press reports overwhelmingly associate workplace mobilization with the Putin regime. We asked all our focus group and interview respondents who their managers favored. Only one reported that she had witnessed workplace agitation in favor of an opposition party or candidate. The response from our Zlatoust focus group was telling. When the moderator asked whether workplace agitation was carried out in favor of just one party or several, the group responded with laughter. "Mostly from one," clarified one participant. Our survey data confirm these impressions. In the 2016 Russian Electoral Study, 20 percent of employed respondents said that their manager endorsed a party, and of those respondents, 92 percent said that the director endorsed United Russia.

In Nigeria, we asked respondents the following question: "During the recent election campaign, did your manager/supervisor make it clear to you which candidate or party he/she supported?" As in Russia, most supervisors endorsed the then-incumbent party, the PDP, but a large share of respondents (40 percent) said that their employer endorsed an opposition party or candidate. In Turkey, we asked respondents which party was referenced when their employer suggested that they vote for a specific candidate or attend a rally. Sixty-three percent of respondents said that the incumbent AKP was invoked, with another 8 percent hearing appeals to vote for the MHP, an ally of the AKP. In contrast, just 29 percent said that managers advocated for an opposition party.[41] Greater access to state resources and administrative levers allows incumbents to exercise more influence over employers than the opposition can, further skewing the playing field.

However, an important qualification to this pattern is that incumbent bias is likely to be reduced in settings where strong institutions—for example, the rule of law, and free and fair elections—limit the ability of incumbents to abuse state resources. Here again the case of the United States is instructive. With greater political competition, media freedom, and stronger rule of law, it is more difficult for incumbent politicians to leverage their access to state resources to their advantage. As a result, we see that workplace mobilization is more bipartisan. In the immediate wake of *Citizens United*, managers backing Republican candidates were more active, even though they were the opposition party at the time. Hertel-Fernandez (2017) found that employees were more likely to report that employer messages were conservative rather than liberal.

Our own survey data indicate that both parties in the United States now use this tool. Of the workers who were mobilized by their employers in our 2020 survey, 35 percent were mobilized on behalf of Democratic candidates, 26 percent on behalf of Republican candidates, and 40 percent in a nonpartisan fashion. Among those mobilized by their employers in our 2021 survey, 21 percent were mobilized in support of Democrats and 19 percent in favor of Republicans, and 60 percent were mobilized without explicit mention of a party. In comparison to prior work, we find that employees report receiving appeals by Democrats and Republicans at about the same rates.[42]

---

[41] We also examined this question in our Nigeria, Turkey, and Venezuela surveys by analyzing variation in workplace mobilization across provinces. In all three countries, workplace mobilization is much more common in regime-controlled regions.

[42] More work is needed to confirm the bipartisan nature of workplace mobilization in the United States, but to the extent that workplace mobilization becomes normalized and loses its negative stigma among the public, it will be more difficult to reduce it by changes in policy. That employers appear to conduct workplace mobilization on behalf of both parties in the United States may reduce bias, but it also has the potential to reduce voter autonomy because more workers may then be

216 WORKPLACE POLITICS

In sum, incumbents have advantages that are difficult to eradicate completely. Their privileged access to state resources gives them more leverage over employers, and workplace mobilization that involves the use of state resources tilts the playing field still further in favor of incumbents. However, institutions that prevent incumbents from abusing office in these ways can help prevent the systematic bias stemming from workplace mobilization.

Structural Biases

In addition to providing a systematic advantage to incumbents, workplace mobilization also tilts the playing field because it makes democratic voice depend on one's place of employment. Turnout in elections becomes biased in favor of firms with features more conducive to workplace mobilization. In democracies, the extent of this bias depends on the nature of the mobilization. In the rare cases where workplace mobilization is noncoercive, workers in large firms, in sectors with low asset-specificity, or in the state bureaucracy are likely to be especially advantaged relative to those who are not so easily mobilized.

Moreover, these sectors are often already privileged due to their structural features. In the more likely case where mobilization strategies are coercive, these same types of voters will be especially disadvantaged because their sincere preferences are less likely to be expressed than their peers working in sectors where workplace mobilization is more difficult to conduct. In such cases, outcomes are also likely to be biased toward the preferences of the managers of these firms. In this way, workplace mobilization constitutes an additional pathway by which policy can be skewed away from the preferences of the median voter and toward the preferences of economic elites (Gilens and Page, 2014; Bartels, 2016).

Thus, workplace mobilization tends to induce political bias in favor of employers and those in occupations that are vulnerable to mobilization. This raises troubling normative implications for democracy. When political voice depends on one's occupation, democracy is undermined.

---

exposed to the practice. Thus, bipartisan workplace mobilization comes with a trade-off of reducing voter autonomy.

Policy Suggestions

Ensuring that workplace mobilization respects voter autonomy and avoids political bias is challenging because the practice is driven in large part by power relations. As past chapters have shown, politicians are well placed to pressure employers who depend on them for sales, financing, and good treatment. In turn, employers are well placed to pressure employees who have few other options for work, and these power relations are especially effective at promoting workplace mobilization when the media are unfree. Over the longer haul, reducing workplace mobilization of voters requires changing power relations, which is not easy.

Institutional efforts to reduce workplace mobilization can focus on the relationships both between politicians and employers and between employers and workers. For the former, the most important thing is to make it harder for politicians to abuse state resources in service of workplace mobilization. This can take different forms, including enforcing laws on corruption, which would reduce the ability of incumbent politicians to reward and punish firms for their political activity. It might also entail administrative reforms, which would reduce the role of patronage in the public sector. Unfortunately, these are reforms and choices that have distributional consequences, and incumbents usually have little reason to bind their hands in this way (Geddes, 1994).

It is perhaps not surprising that efforts in the United States to limit the ability of incumbents to use state employees for political advocacy were often passed following scandals that weakened the incumbent government. The Pendleton Act of 1883—which for the first time protected 10 percent of federal bureaucrats from some forms of political pressure by elected officials—passed following the assassination of President Garfield by a deranged bill collector who felt he had been passed over for a patronage job. The public uproar over the assassination sparked efforts to reform the spoils system. Moreover, this legislation passed in a lame-duck session of Congress in which an outgoing Republican majority sought to tie the hands of the incoming Democratic Party. Subsequent efforts in the United States follow a similar pattern. Consider the Hatch Act of 1939, prohibits state employees from taking part in many political activities on the job or in their official capacity, while also allowing most employees to take part in political activity outside of work.[43] This act passed in the wake of a

---

[43] "The Hatch Act: A Primer—Federation of American Scientists," *Congressional Research Service*, April 20, 2020.

218   WORKPLACE POLITICS

scandal in which newspaper reports revealed that federal officials of President Franklin Delano Roosevelt's Works Progress Administration (WPA) engaged in patronage appointments, the sale of public offices, and the use of WPA jobs for political advantage. Republican members of Congress and dissident Democrats coalesced against Roosevelt on this issue in a temporary alliance (Smith, 2006). Shifts in power that weakened incumbents were crucial in the passage of both pieces of legislation.

These measures were passed in response to cases of politicians pressuring federal employees to work on electoral campaigns. In other settings, we find that politicians and state managers frequently mobilize state employees during elections, but this is now far less likely in the United States. Indeed, regression analyses from our 2020 survey indicate that state employees in the United States are significantly less likely to experience workplace mobilization than their private sector counterparts, controlling for a respondent's demographic characteristics, political partisanship, size of workplace, and perceived job security. In the United States most workplace mobilization occurs in the private, not the state sector, and is a far less useful tactic for incumbents than in other settings.

One possible source of leverage for reducing the worst abuses is the public's normative distaste for workplace mobilization. The countries in our study span much of the globe, with different legal and political traditions and diverse economic systems, but citizens almost across the board view workplace mobilization, especially its more partisan and coercive forms, as problematic. From Russia to Turkey to Argentina and the United States more than 80 percent of respondents thought it inappropriate for employers to ask their employees to vote for a particular candidate. In many cases, majorities even oppose employers simply asking employees to turn out to vote. In the cases where we have comparable data, citizens see workplace mobilization as more problematic even than vote buying. In Russia, employers themselves felt the practice was unseemly and rated workplace mobilization's "inappropriateness" as the most common reason for not engaging in the practice.

Public sentiment can deter politicians and employers from some forms of workplace mobilization. Results from Chapter 7 found that even in the far-from-friendly environment of Russia, free media helped to curtail the most abusive forms of workplace mobilization. This suggests that one path to strengthening voter autonomy and reducing political bias induced by workplace mobilization lies in strengthening worker voice and bolstering the public norm against the practice. This might occur via media reporting, but one could also imagine that employee education campaigns that focus on political rights, the creation of phone hotlines or internet portals to spread the word, and other types of information campaigns might help reduce the most odious forms of workplace mobilization, while also respecting the free speech rights of employers.

A more general solution that would address the structural inequities that drive workplace mobilization would be to increase labor mobility. Doing so would reduce the capacity of managers to pressure workers into political activity. Where workers face low costs of exit, and employers have to compete furiously for workers, many of the dilemmas discussed here evaporate.[44] The Russian case is especially helpful here. Our research from Russia finds that the more coercive forms of workplace mobilization thrive where single-company town provide few easy exit options for workers. Even in the United States, which has a much different political and legal environment, job insecurity is associated with greater frequency of workplace mobilization.

Another option to balance the power of employers would be to bolster unions. Labor organizing would give employees the power to resist workplace mobilization. In most cases in our sample, unions have limited reach. In the United States, roughly one in ten workers belong to a union, and only 6 percent of workers in the private sector belong to unions. In Russia, Nigeria, Indonesia, and Ukraine, they play only minor roles in the labor market. Of course, unions are far from a panacea, as they can also politicize the workplace and infringe on voter autonomy when workers are pressured to vote for union-backed candidates. But no other organization is as well placed to blunt political pressure from employers.

Legal remedies to limit more coercive forms of workplace mobilization are another potential solution, but need to be put in place by the same actors who benefit from the practice. Moreover, where the rule of law is weak, purely legal solutions will have limited effectiveness. Changes in the legal code may raise the costs of violating worker autonomy at the margin, but will do little to address the core issue.

In cases where the rule of law is relatively strong, like the United States, the prospects might be somewhat better. One proposed solution might be

---

[44] Indeed, one reason autocrats might be reluctant to liberalize labor markets is that they would be less able to direct firms' political activity.

to provide greater legal protections to workers. For example, one possibility would be to treat political affiliation or activity as a protected class so that workers cannot be fired on such basis (Hertel-Fernandez and Secunda, 2016). Similar guarantees are in place for religion, disability, race, age, gender identity, and sexual orientation. Several states have passed legislation that grants workers greater protection from employer efforts to engage in politics at work.

The European Union, Germany, Japan, Austria, and others have protections against dismissal based on political views or activities. Workers in the state sector in the United States have greater protections against being fired for their political views than do private sector workers. These reforms suggest that it is possible to reduce some of the more problematic forms of workplace mobilization, but our research suggests that the path to doing so is fraught with challenges.

9

Implications and Next Steps

As noted earlier, we began this project in 2011 studying a topic that didn't yet have a name. Some previous work on electoral subversion in historical settings had shown that coercion of workers can happen when bosses have leverage over their employees (Ziblatt, 2009; Mares, 2015; Baland and Robinson, 2008). This seemed to fit with our impressions of the practice in Russia, but our survey data immediately showed that the picture was more complicated. Relations between managers and the state were also a key part of the story, and as we would soon discover, so was the broader voting public. Empirically, our initial surveys in Russia led us to wonder more about the details and scope of the practice in other countries. With the help of a few research grants, we embarked on a broader study using more detailed surveys in Russia and surveys in a diverse set of countries around the world, finding that workplace mobilization of voters is more widespread than is commonly realized.

We quickly realized that employers are especially interesting because they differ in theoretically important ways from more frequently studied vote brokers, such as party activists. They often possess greater leverage over their clients, have a more diverse menu of tactics, and boast more autonomy than many other brokers. They also interact with politicians in far different ways. Some employers are dependent on the state for their livelihood and are therefore more likely to mobilize their workers, while other employers do so only in exchange for financial benefits from the state. Moreover, employers' primary tactic for mobilizing voters is far less normatively acceptable than the techniques that other vote brokers more commonly use. The broader public views voter mobilization by party activists as business as usual, but views with disdain voter mobilization by employers. This public aversion to workplace mobilization influences the decision of managers to bring politics into the workplace.

Looking back on our efforts over the last decade, we believe that our research helps inform broader debates in comparative politics. Most fundamentally, our work shows that employers shape the way people vote in a

Workplace Politics. Timothy Frye, Ora John Reuter, and David Szakonyi, Oxford University Press.
© Oxford University Press (2025). DOI: 10.1093/9780197802045.003.0009

222   WORKPLACE POLITICS

variety of settings. This should make employers of interest to scholars in a number of research areas. For one, our research contributes to debates on clientelism (Scott, 1972; Stokes, Dunning, and Nazareno, 2013). This literature has focused on an array of brokers, including party activists, chiefs, strongmen, bosses, and local intermediaries. Employers, by contrast, have received far less attention. Our work shows that they are important clientelist brokers in a range of contemporary settings. Indeed, workplace mobilization is a form of clientelist exchange that can (and does) occur even in settings where grassroots party organization is weak (Stokes, 2005).

Shifting the study of clientelism to the workplace generates a more contemporary look at an age-old practice. While scholars have noted that vote-buying and traditional clientelism decline as societies grow richer, workplace mobilization may persist even in the industrialized world. As old hierarchies crumble in modernizing societies, new ones emerge in the workplace, especially where fiscal dependence on the state is high, assets are specific, and labor markets are slack.

We also place clientelism in a richer political context by examining how the broader electorate views the practice (Weitz-Shapiro, 2014; Mares and Young, 2019). Opposition to workplace mobilization among the public is an important constraint on those who would consider pressuring their workers to vote. Looking beyond dyadic relations between brokers and voters to consider how public opinion shapes workplace mobilization reveals insights that may be overlooked in more traditional studies of clientelism that tend to focus only on brokers and voters.

Finally, we put the broker-voter relationship in an institutional context by examining how variations in media freedom influence incentives to engage in workplace mobilization. The public depends on free media to learn about instances of workplace mobilization and reduce the incentives of politicians and employers to use this tactic. This finding is in line with a large literature on the benefits of free press for governance (Besley and Burgess, 2002; Ferraz and Finan, 2008). Looking forward, scholars could explore in more detail precisely how voters not directly exposed to workplace mobilization learn about and understand this tactic.

Our work also adds to recent studies of electoral fraud by examining how politicians and employers can use coercion in the workplace to subvert elections. In addition to ballot stuffing, vote buying, and media manipulation, we suggest that scholars include workplace mobilization in their studies of electoral subversion (Simpser, 2013; Rundlett and Svolik, 2016). Indeed, as attention to highly visible forms of electoral fraud has increased, less visible techniques like workplace mobilization have become more attractive (Szakonyi, 2022). We contribute to the growing literature that explores how economic and political elites have undermined elections in a variety of historical and geographic settings. Future research might focus on whether workplace mobilization serves as a substitute or complement to other forms of electoral subversion.

In turn, these new insights about workplace mobilization also have broader implications for the study of political regimes. Our work suggests an additional reason why economic and political liberalization so often go hand in hand (Przeworski, 1991; Frye, 2010; Hellman, 1998). Economic liberalization increases the autonomy of company managers from the state and makes it harder for politicians to subvert elections by inducing employers to engage in workplace mobilization. Indeed, politicians may oppose economic liberalization not just to receive economic rents but for political reasons as well.

Our research contributes to the literature on elections under autocracy. Some scholars emphasize that elections heighten instability in autocracies given the unintended consequences of an election campaign, while others argue that elections can buttress autocratic rule by dividing the opposition, generating information, and increasing opportunities for coopting potential rivals (Gandhi and Lust-Okar, 2009; Blaydes, 2010). Our research suggests that workplace mobilization may buttress autocratic rule in the short run by allowing incumbents to get out the vote, but it also risks alienating voters who disapprove of this tactic and may reduce support for the regime over time.

Finally, our findings also generate new insights into economic theories of democratization. Like Boix (2003) and Acemoglu and Robinson (2006), we find that holders of specific assets like natural resources or land may seek to block the expansion of democratic rights, but we suggest an alternative mechanism linking asset specificity with autocracy. Whereas standard accounts trace opposition to democratization among holders of specific assets to the median voter's fear of high rates of taxation, we suggest that asset specificity may also undermine democracy because the holders of such assets are particularly vulnerable to pressures from politicians to mobilize their workers. This insight also differs from traditional treatments documenting how labor repression undermines democracy (Gerschenkron, 1962; Moore, 1993). In these accounts, landlords and industrialists repress

224 WORKPLACE POLITICS

labor to support their economic interests, while our work recognizes that employers with specific assets may mobilize their workers at the behest of politicians for political reasons.

Next Steps

We have explored workplace mobilization in great detail in Russia and to a more limited extent in seven other cases and have learned a good deal about the practice. One insight from our research is that workplace mobilization—whether in its more coercive forms in autocratic regimes or less coercive forms in democracies—is not going away. Even as the practice declines in some advanced industrial democracies with strong legal protections for workers, the expansion of formal employment in other developing countries is creating new opportunities for workplace mobilization.

We have seen employers getting their workers to the polls in a wide range of political and economic settings. Much effort remains before we can understand how these different contexts influence workplace mobilization. For example, our research suggests that future studies might consider how features of democracy influence workplace mobilization. Democracies typically have greater media freedom and stronger legal institutions that might reduce incentives to engage in coercive workplace mobilization. Fearing blowback from popular opinion, politicians and employers may think twice before pressuring employers to mobilize their workers. At the same time, democracies have more political competition, which may motivate employers to get their workers to the polls in tight races. Fearing that one's political rival might engage in workplace mobilization to push the marginal voter to the polls, a candidate may be tempted to do the same. In this case, the heightened political competition inherent in democracies might increase workplace mobilization, especially in its less coercive forms. Identifying the conditions under which either of these two trends is likely to predominate would be an important contribution to our understanding of workplace mobilization.

It would also be helpful to know more about the role of the informal sector in workplace mobilization. Many workers in industrializing countries are not formally registered with the state, or they receive salary and benefits that are designed to evade taxes. On one hand, these informal sector workers have fewer legal protections and are therefore more vulnerable to workplace mobilization. However, workers in the informal sector also tend to work in small firms with mobile assets that do not depend on the state for revenue. These factors would tend to raise the costs of mobilizing informal workers and might deter employers from trying to get them to the polls. Again, future research might help us learn the conditions under which either of these tendencies is likely to prevail.

Finally, looking ahead, the field would benefit by learning more about how technological developments are likely to shape workplace mobilization. New technologies that allow managers to better monitor the political activity of their workers may encourage workplace mobilization.[1] For example, technologies that improve the ability of managers to recognize employees in political protests, track the online political behavior of their employees, and monitor the voting habits of their workers will likely make workplace mobilization more attractive for employers. Similarly, technologies that increase the capacity of politicians to monitor employers' efforts to mobilize their workers may have a similar effect.

However, over the longer run, technological advances may make it harder to mobilize workers—at least in the more coercive forms we see in many autocracies. As countries move from an industrial to an information economy, the leverage of managers is likely to decrease. To the extent that the industrializing economies induce workers to develop skills specific to a company and the information economy does not, workers should have greater mobility and be less vulnerable to pressure from their bosses in modern information-intensive economies. Similarly, information economies tend to have less asset specificity than industrialized economies as companies are far less tethered to specific geographic locations. The lower levels of asset specificity of firms in an information economy relative to an industrial economy may weaken the ability of politicians to pressure managers. Politicians contemplating putting political pressure on employers may be deterred by the threat of businesses moving to another location or line of production. Indeed, we may see a version of a Kuznets curve in workplace mobilization where it is minimal in preindustrial economies, but increases with industrialization, and falls again with the movement to an information economy (Kuznets, 1955). The longer-run determinants of workplace mobilization are an especially interesting topic for future research.

---

[1] Of course, protesters can also use video and social media to identify and shame their persecutors. Mozur, Paul, "In Hong Kong Protests Faces Become Weapons," *New York Times*, July 26, 2019.

226 WORKPLACE POLITICS

Reassessment of Voting Rights and Electoral Subversion

To conclude, our efforts to understand the dynamics of voter mobilization and electoral subversion in the workplace are part of a broader reassessment of voting rights in recent years. Inspired in part by instances of democratic erosion and the rise of hybrid regimes that mix democratic and autocratic features, scholars have come to treat voting rights less as a static feature rooted in institutional guarantees than as a dynamic process that is shaped by power relations and political strategies (Keyssar, 2009). Scholars have documented how even in some otherwise robust democracies, voting rights have long been and remain an arena of contention, with powerful groups seeking to exclude those who are less likely to vote for them in a variety of subtle and not-so-subtle ways (Horwitz, 1992). Politicians may shape voting rights by changing formal institutions that make it harder to register or to vote, or by using informal means, such as intimidation and social pressure to limit access to the ballot. Regardless of method, these efforts are an ongoing struggle in democracies of varying quality from the United States to Brazil to Nigeria.[2]

In recent years, scholars of autocracy have also changed their views on the role of voting and elections. Rather than viewing elections as mere façades, social scientists have documented how voting rights and elections shape the quality of property rights, the rate of economic growth, and the tenure of autocratic rule in nondemocratic settings (Wright, 2008; Geddes et al., 2018; Knutsen, Nygård, and Wig, 2017). At the individual level, they have shown how, under autocracy, violations of voting rights can undermine support for the government even among core supporters (Reuter and Szakonyi, 2021). More recent scholarship does not argue for an equivalence between voting in democracy and autocracies, but it is fair to say that this body of research has provided a much more nuanced and historically informed view of voting rights in democracies and autocracies that challenges long-held views.

We hope that we have contributed to this reassessment by focusing on one crucial and understudied dimension of voting rights. Twelve years ago, we began studying a topic that did not even have a proper name. We have

---

[2] Ionova, Ana, André Spigariol, Laís Martins, and Jack Nicas, "Brazil's Election Officials Demand Answers for Police Stops of Buses Carrying Voters," *New York Times*, October 30, 2022; "Nigeria: Impunity, Insecurity Threaten Elections," *Human Rights Watch*, February 6, 2023.

come a long way and still have much to learn. Together with other scholars, we have tried to spark a discussion about the drivers and normative status of workplace mobilization so that researchers will help us all better understand this important topic. If our efforts accomplish anything, it should be to encourage others to explore the dynamics of workplace mobilization in a broader comparative perspective as well as to dig deeper into specific cases.

Bibliography

Acemoglu, Daron, and James A. Robinson. 2006. *Economic Origins of Dictatorship and Democracy*. Cambridge: Cambridge University Press.

Acemoglu, Daron, James A. Robinson, and Rafael J. Santos. 2013. "The Monopoly of Violence: Evidence from Colombia." *Journal of the European Economic Association* 11 (suppl_1): 5–44.

Acemoglu, Daron, and Alexander Wolitzky. 2011. "The Economics of Labor Coercion." *Econometrica* 79 (2): 555–600.

Albertus, Michael. 2015. "The Role of Subnational Politicians in Distributive Politics: Political Bias in Venezuela's Land Reform under Chávez." *Comparative Political Studies* 48 (13): 1667–1710.

Aldrich, John H. 1995. *Why Parties? The Origin and Transformation of Political Parties in America*. Chicago: University of Chicago Press.

Alexander, Robert M. 2002. *Rolling the Dice with State Initiatives: Interest Group Involvement in Ballot Campaigns*. Westport, CT: Praeger.

Allina-Pisano, Jessica. 2010. "Social Contracts and Authoritarian Projects in Post-Soviet Space: The Use of Administrative Resource." *Communist and Post-Communist Studies* 43 (4): 373–382.

Anderson, David M. 2002. "Vigilantes, Violence and the Politics of Public Order in Kenya." *African Affairs* 101 (405): 531–555.

Anderson, Elizabeth. 2019. *Private Government: How Employers Rule Our Lives (and Why We Don't Talk about It)*. Princeton, NJ: Princeton University Press.

Argersinger, Peter H. 1985. "New Perspectives on Election Fraud in the Gilded Age." *Political Science Quarterly* 100 (4): 669–687.

Aschhoff, Birgit, and Wolfgang Sofka. 2009. "Innovation on Demand: Can Public Procurement Drive Market Success of Innovations?" *Research Policy* 38 (8): 1235–1247.

Austin, Erica Weintraub, Rebecca Van de Vord, Bruce E. Pinkleton, and Evan Epstein. 2008. "Celebrity Endorsements and Their Potential to Motivate Young Voters." *Mass Communication and Society* 11 (4): 420–436.

Bachrach, Peter, and Morton S. Baratz. 1962. "Two Faces of Power." *American Political Science Review* 56 (4): 947–952.

Baland, Jean-Marie, and James A. Robinson. 2008. "Land and Power: Theory and Evidence from Chile." *American Economic Review* 98 (5): 1737–1765.

Baland, Jean-Marie, and Jim Robinson. 2007. "How Does Vote Buying Shape the Economy?" In *Elections for Sale: The Causes and Consequences of Vote Buying*, ed. Frederic Charles Schaffer, Boulder, CO: Lynne Rienner 123–142.

Barnes, James A. 1947. "Myths of the Bryan Campaign." *The Mississippi Valley Historical Review* 34 (3): 367–404.

230 BIBLIOGRAPHY

Bartels, Larry M. 2016. *Unequal Democracy.* Princeton, NJ: Princeton University Press.

Bates, Robert H. 2014. *Markets and States in Tropical Africa: The Political Basis of Agricultural Policies.* Los Angeles: University of California Press.

Beazer, Quintin H., Charles D. Crabtree, Christopher J. Fariss, and Holger L. Kern. 2022. "When Do Private Actors Engage inCcensorship? Evidence from a Correspondence Experiment with Russian Private Media Firms." *British Journal of Political Science* 52 (4): 1790–1809.

Beccerra, Manuel, and Anil K. Gupta. 1999. "Trust within the Organization: Integrating the Trust Literature with Agency Theory and Transaction Costs Economics." *Public Administration Quarterly* 23 (2): 177–203.

Bensel, Richard Franklin. 2004. *The American Ballot Box in the Mid-nineteenth Century.* Cambridge: Cambridge University Press.

Berelson, Bernard R., Paul F. Lazarsfeld, and William N. McPhee. 1954. *Voting: A Study of Opinion Formation during a Presidential Campaign.* Chicago: University of Chicago Press.

Besley, Timothy, and Robin Burgess. 2002. "The Political Economy of Government Responsiveness: Theory and Evidence from India." *The Quarterly Journal of Economics* 117 (4): 1415–1451.

Best, Michael Carlos, Jonas Hjort, and David Szakonyi. 2023. "Individuals and Organizations as Sources of State Effectiveness." *American Economic Review* 113 (8): 2121–2167.

Biezen, Ingrid van, and Thomas Poguntke. 2014. "The Decline of Membership-Based Politics." *Party Politics* 20 (2): 205–216.

Birch, Sarah. 2016. *Full Participation: A Comparative Study of Compulsory Voting.* Manchester: Manchester University Press.

Blaydes, Lisa. 2010. *Elections and Distributive Politics in Mubarak's Egypt.* Cambridge: Cambridge University Press.

Blomberg, Jeffrey A. 1995. "Protecting the Right Not to Vote from Voter Purge Statutes." *Fordham Law Review* 64: 1015–1050.

Boix, Carles. 2003. *Democracy and Redistribution.* Cambridge: Cambridge University Press.

Borges, Marcelo, and Susana Torres. 2012. *Company Towns: Labor, Space, and Power Relations across Time and Continents.* New York: Springer.

Brady, Henry E., Kay L. Schlozman, and Sidney Verba. 1995. "Prospecting for Participants: A Rational Expectations Approach to Mobilizing Activists." Presented at the Annual Meeting of the American Political Science Association. Chicago, IL, August 31-September 4.

Brierley, Sarah, and Noah L. Nathan. 2022. "Motivating the Machine: Which Brokers Do Parties Pay?" *The Journal of Politics* 84 (3): 1539–1555.

Calvo, Ernesto, and Maria Victoria Murillo. 2013. "When Parties Meet Voters: Assessing Political Linkages through Partisan Networks and Distributive Expectations in Argentina and Chile." *Comparative Political Studies* 46 (7): 851–882.

Camp, Edwin. 2017. "Cultivating Effective Brokers: A Party Leader's Dilemma." *British Journal of Political Science* 47 (3): 521–543.

Caravella, Serenella, and Francesco Crespi. 2021. "The Role of Public Procurement as Innovation Lever: Evidence from Italian Manufacturing Firms." *Economics of Innovation and New Technology* 30 (7): 663–684.

Carey, John, Katherine Clayton, Gretchen Helmke, Brendan Nyhan, Mitchell Sanders, and Susan Stokes. 2022. "Who Will Defend Democracy? Evaluating Tradeoffs in Candidate Support among Partisan Donors and Voters?" *Journal of Elections, Public Opinion and Parties* 32 (1): 230–245.

Carey, John M., and Yusaku Horiuchi. 2017. "Compulsory Voting and Income Inequality: Evidence for Lijphart's Proposition from Venezuela." *Latin American Politics and Society* 59 (2): 122–144.

Chebankova, Elena. 2013. *Civil Society in Putin's Russia*. Abingdon: Routledge.

Cheibub, Jose Antonio, Adam Przeworski, Fernando Papaterra Limongi Neto, and Michael M. Alvarez. 1996. "What Makes Democracies Endure?" *Journal of democracy* 7 (1): 39–55.

Chwe, Michael Suk-Young. 1990. "Why Were Workers Whipped? Pain in a Principal-Agent Model." *The Economic Journal* 100 (403): 1109–1121.

Collier, Paul, and Pedro C. Vicente. 2012. "Violence, Bribery, and Fraud: The Political EconomyoOf Elections in Sub-Saharan Africa." *Public Choice* 153 (1–2): 117–147.

Coppock, Alexander, and Oliver A. McClellan. 2019. "Validating the Demographic, Political, Psychological, and Experimental Result Obtained from a New Source of Online Survey Respondents." *Research & Politics* 6 (1): 2053168018822174.

Corstange, Daniel. 2018. "Clientelism in Competitive and Uncompetitive Elections." *Comparative Political Studies* 51 (1): 76–104.

Cox, Gary W. 2009. "Swing Voters, Core Voters, and Distributive Politics." *Political Representation* ed. Ian Shapiro, Susan C. Stokes, Elizabeth Jean Wood, and Alexander S. Kirshner, 342–357. Cambridge University Press.

Cox, Gary W., and J. Morgan Kousser. 1981. "Turnout and Rural Corruption: New York as a Test Case." *American Journal of Political Science* 25 (4): 646–663.

Crowley, Stephen. 2015. "Monotowns and the Political Economy of Industrial Restructuring in Russia." *Post-Soviet Affairs* 32 (5): 397–422.

Cruz, Cesi. 2019. "Social Networks and the Targeting of Vote Buying." *Comparative Political Studies* 52 (3): 382–411.

Cruz, Cesi, Philip Keefer, and Julien Labonne. 2016. *Incumbent Advantage, Voter Information and Vote Buying*. Technical Report IDB-WP-711, IDB Working Paper Series, Washington, DC.

Cruz, Cesi, Julien Labonne, and Pablo Querubin. 2017. "Politician Family Networks and Electoral Outcomes: Evidence from the Philippines." *American Economic Review* 107 (10): 3006–3037.

Dahl, Robert A. 1957. "The Concept of Power." *Behavioral Science* 2 (3): 201–215.

Dahl, Robert A. 1998. *Democracy and Its Critics*. New Haven, CT: Yale University Press.

Darden, Keith. 2008. "The Integrity of Corrupt States: Graft as an Informal State Institution." *Politics & Society* 36 (1): 35–59.

232 BIBLIOGRAPHY

Dean, Adam. 2022. *Opening Up by Cracking Down: Labor Repression and Trade Liberalization in Democratic Developing Countries.* Cambridge: Cambridge University Press.

De Kadt, and Horacio A. Larreguy. 2018. "Agents of the Regime? Traditional Leaders and Electoral Politics in South Africa." *The Journal of Politics* 80 (2): 382–399.

Dyer, Jeffrey H., and Wujin Chu. 2003. "The Role of Trustworthiness in Reducing Transaction Costs and Improving Performance: Empirical Evidence from the United States, Japan, and Korea." *Organization Science* 14 (1): 57–68.

Ennser-Jedenastik, Laurenz. 2014. "Political Control and Managerial Survival in State-Owned Enterprises." *Governance* 27 (1): 135–161.

Ferraz, Claudio, and Frederico Finan. 2008. "Exposing Corrupt Politicians: The Effects of Brazil's Publicly Released Audits On Electoral Outcomes." *The Quarterly Journal of Economics* 123 (2): 703–745.

Ferree, Karen E., and James D. Long. 2016. "Gifts, Threats, and Perceptions of Ballot Secrecy in African Elections." *African Affairs* 115 (461): 621–645.

Finan, Frederico, and Laura Schechter. 2012. "Vote-Buying and Reciprocity." *Econometrica* 80 (2): 863–881.

Forrat, Natalia. 2018. "Shock-Resistant Authoritarianism: Schoolteachers and Infrastructural State Capacity in Putin's Russia." *Comparative Politics* 50 (3): 417–449.

Friebel, Guido, and Sergei Guriev. 2005. "Attaching Workers through In-Kind Payments: Theory and Evidence from Russia." *The World Bank Economic Review* 19 (2): 175–202.

Frieden, Jeffry A. 1991. *Debt, Development, and Democracy: Modern Political Economy and Latin America, 1965–1985.* Princeton, NJ: Princeton University Press.

Friedgut, Theodore H. 1979. *Political Participation in the USSR.* Princeton, NJ: Princeton University Press.

Frye, Timothy. 2010. *Building States and Markets after Communism: The Perils of Polarized Democracy.* Cambridge: Cambridge University Press.

Frye, Timothy. 2019. "Economic Sanctions and Public Opinion: Survey Experiments from Russia." *Comparative Political Studies* 52 (7): 967–994.

Frye, Timothy, Ora John Reuter, and David Szakonyi. 2014. "Political Machines at Work: Voter Mobilization and Electoral Subversion in the Workplace." *World Politics* 66 (2): 195–228.

Frye, Timothy, Ora John Reuter, and David Szakonyi. 2018. "Hitting Them with Carrots: Voter Intimidation and Vote Buying in Russia." *British Journal of Political Science* 49 (3): 857–881.

Frye, Timothy, Ora John Reuter, and David Szakonyi. 2019. "Vote Brokers, Clientelist Appeals, and Voter Turnout: Evidence from Russia and Venezuela." *World Politics* 71 (4): 710–746.

Frye, Timothy, Scott Gehlbach, Kyle L. Marquardt, and Ora John Reuter. 2017. "Is Putin's Popularity Real?" *Post-Soviet Affairs* 33 (1): 1–15.

Funk, Patricia. 2010. "Social Incentives and Voter Turnout: Evidence from the Swiss Mail Ballot System." *Journal of the European Economic Association* 8 (5): 1077–1103.

Gailmard, Sean, and John W. Patty. 2012. "Formal Models of Bureaucracy." *Annual Review of Political Science* 15: 353–377.

Gandhi, Jennifer, and Ellen Lust-Okar. 2009. "Elections under Authoritarianism." *Annual Review of Political Science* 12: 403–422.

Gans-Morse, Jordan, Sebastián Mazzuca, and Simeon Nichter. 2014. "Varieties of Clientelism: Machine Politics during Elections." *American Journal of Political Science* 58 (2): 415–432.

Garden, Charlotte. 2022. *Was It Something I Said? Legal Protections for Employee Speech.* Technical report. Economic Policy Institute.

Gaventa, John. 1982. *Power and Powerlessness: Quiescence and Rebellion in an Appalachian Valley.* Champaign: University of Illinois Press.

Geddes, Barbara. 1994. *Politician's Dilemma: Building State Capacity in Latin America.* Los Angeles: University of California Press.

Geddes, Barbara, Joseph George Wright, Joseph Wright, and Erica Frantz. 2018. *How Dictatorships Work: Power, Personalization, and Collapse.* Cambridge: Cambridge University Press.

Gerber, Alan S., Donald P. Green, and Ron Shachar. 2003. "Voting May Be Habit-Forming: Evidence from a Randomized Field Experiment." *American Journal of Political Science* 47 (3): 540–550.

Gerber, Alan S., Gregory A. Huber, David Doherty, and Conor M. Dowling. 2013. "Is There a Secret Ballot? Ballot Secrecy Perceptions and Their Implications for Voting Behaviour." *British Journal of Political Science* 43 (1): 77–102.

Gerber, Alan S., and Todd Rogers. 2009. "Descriptive Social Norms and Motivation to Vote: Everybody's Voting and So Should You." *The Journal of Politics* 71 (1): 178–191.

Gerschenkron, Alexander. 1962. *Economic Backwardness in Historical Perspective: A Book of Essays.* Cambridge, MA: Belknap Press of Harvard University Press.

Gervasoni, Carlos. 2018. *Hybrid Regimes within Democracies: Fiscal Federalism and Subnational Rentier States.* Cambridge: Cambridge University Press.

Gilens, Martin, and Benjamin I. Page. 2014. "Testing Theories of American Politics: Elites, Interest Groups, and Average Citizens." *Perspectives on Politics* 12 (3): 564–581.

Gimpelson, Vladimir, and Anna Lukiyanova. 2009. Are Public Sector Workers Underpaid in Russia? Estimating the Public-Private Wage Gap. Technical Report No. 3941. IZA discussion paper.

Gingerich, Daniel W., and Luis Fernando Medina. 2013. "The Endurance and Eclipse of the Controlled Vote: A Formal Model of Vote Brokerage under the Secret Ballot." *Economics & Politics* 25 (3): 453–480.

Gonzalez-Ocantos, Ezequiel, Chad Kiewiet de Jonge, Carlos Meléndez, David Nickerson, and Javier Osorio. 2020. "Carrots and Sticks: Experimental Evidence of Vote-Buying and Voter Intimidation in Guatemala." *Journal of Peace Research* 57 (1): 46–61.

Gonzalez Ocantos, Ezequiel, Chad Kiewiet Jonge, and David W. Nickerson. 2014. "The Conditionality of Vote-Buying Norms: Experimental Evidence from Latin America." *American Journal of Political Science* 58 (1): 197–211.

Gorodnichenko, Yuriy, and Klara Sabirianova Peter. 2007. "Public Sector Pay and Corruption: Measuring Bribery from Micro Data." *Journal of Public Economics* 91 (5–6): 963–991.

234 BIBLIOGRAPHY

Graham, Matthew H., and Milan W. Svolik. 2020. "Democracy in America? Partisanship, Polarization, and the Robustness of Support for Democracy in the United States." *American Political Science Review* 114 (2): 392–409.

Green, Donald P., and Alan S. Gerber. 2015. *Get Out the Vote: How to Increase Voter Turnout*. Washington, DC: Brookings Institution Press.

Grossman, Gene M., and Elhanan Helpman. 2001. *Special Interest Politics*. Cambridge, MA: MIT Press.

Guardado, Jenny, and Leonard Wantchékon. 2018. "Do Electoral Handouts Affect Voting Behavior?" *Electoral Studies* 53: 139–149.

Guriev, Sergei, and Daniel Treisman. 2022. *Spin Dictators: The Changing Face of Tyranny in the 21st Century*. Princeton, NJ: Princeton University Press.

Gutiérrez-Romero, Roxana, and Adrienne LeBas. 2020. "Does Electoral Violence Affect Vote Choice and Willingness to Vote? Conjoint Analysis of a Vignette Experiment." *Journal of Peace Research* 57 (1): 77–92.

Hale, Henry. 2005. *Why Not Parties in Russia? Democracy, Federalism, and the State*. Cambridge: Cambridge University Press.

Hale, Henry E. 2018. "How Crimea Pays: Media, Rallying 'round the Flag, and Authoritarian Support." *Comparative Politics* 50 (3): 369–391.

Handlin, Samuel. 2016. "Mass Organization and the Durability of Competitive Authoritarian Regimes: Evidence from Venezuela." *Comparative Political Studies* 49 (9): 1238–1269.

Hartley, Roger C. 2010. "Freedom Not to Listen: A Constitutional Analysis of Compulsory Indoctrination through Workplace Captive Audience Meetings." *Berkeley Journal of Employment and Labor Law* 31 (1): 65–125.

Hellman, Joel S. 1998. "Winners Take All: The Politics of Partial Reform in Postcommunist Transitions." *World Politics* 50 (2): 203–234.

Hertel-Fernandez, Alexander. 2016. "How Employers Recruit Their Workers into Politics—And Why Political Scientists Should Care." *Perspectives on Politics* 14 (2): 410–421.

Hertel-Fernandez, Alexander. 2017. "American Employers as Political Machines." *The Journal of Politics* 79 (1): 105–117.

Hertel-Fernandez, Alexander. 2018. *Politics at Work: How Companies Turn Their Workers into Lobbyists*. Oxford: Oxford University Press.

Hertel-Fernandez, Alexander, and Paul Secunda. 2016. "Citizens Coerced: A Legislative Fix for Workplace Political Intimidation Post–Citizens United." *UCLA Law Review Discourse* 64: 1–16.

Hicken, Allen. 2009. *Building Party Systems in Developing Democracies*. Cambridge: Cambridge University Press.

Hicken, Allen. 2011. "Clientelism." *Annual Review of Political Science* 14 (1): 289–310.

Hicken, Allen, and Noah L. Nathan. 2020. "Clientelism's Red Herrings: Dead Ends and New Directions in the Study of Nonprogrammatic Politics." *Annual Review of Political Science* 23: 277–294.

Hillman, Amy J., Gerald D. Keim, and Douglas Schuler. 2004. "Corporate Political Activity: A Review and Research Agenda." *Journal of Management* 30 (6): 837–857.

BIBLIOGRAPHY 235

Holland, Alisha C., and Brian Palmer-Rubin. 2015. "Beyond the Machine: Clientelist Brokers and Interest Organizations in Latin America." *Comparative Political Studies* 48 (9): 1186–1223.

Horwitz, Morton J. 1992. *The Transformation of American Law, 1870–1960: The Crisis of Legal Orthodoxy.* Oxford: Oxford University Press.

Hsieh, Chang-Tai, Edward Miguel, Daniel Ortega, and Francisco Rodriguez. 2011. "The Price of Political Opposition: Evidence from Venezuela's Maisanta." *American Economic Journal: Applied Economics* 3 (2): 196–214.

Jensen, Michael C., and William H. Meckling. 1976. "Theory of the Firm: Managerial Behavior, Agency Costs and Ownership Structure." *Journal of Financial Economics* 3 (4): 305–360.

Kasara, Kimuli, and Pavithra Suryanarayan. 2020. "Bureaucratic Capacity and Class Voting: Evidence from across the World and the United States." *The Journal of Politics* 82 (3): 1097–1112.

Keefer, Philip, and Razvan Vlaicu. 2008. "Credibility, Clientelism and Democracy." *Journal of Law, Economics and Organization* 24 (2): 1–36.

Keyssar, Alexander. 2009. *The Right to Vote: The Contested History of Democracy in the United States.* New York: Basic Books.

Kim, Joon Ho. 2018. "Asset Specificity and Firm Value: Evidence from Mergers." *Journal of Corporate Finance* 48: 375–412.

Kitschelt, Herbert. 2000. "Linkages between Citizens and Politicians in Democratic Polities." *Comparative Political Studies* 33 (6–7): 845–879.

Kitschelt, Herbert, and Steven I. Wilkinson. 2007. *Patrons, Clients and Policies: Patterns of Democratic Accountability and Political Competition.* Cambridge: Cambridge University Press.

Knutsen, Carl Henrik, Håvard Mokleiv Nygård, and Tore Wig. 2017. "Autocratic Elections: Stabilizing Tool or Force for Change?" *World Politics* 69 (1): 98–143.

Koter, Dominika. 2013. "King Makers: Local Leaders and Ethnic Politics in Africa." *World Politics* 65 (2): 187–232.

Koter, Dominika. 2022. "Religion and Electoral Competition in Senegal." In *The Oxford Handbook of Politics in Muslim Societies,* ed. Melani Cammett, and Pauline Jones. Oxford: Oxford University Press pp. 295–311.

Kramon, Eric. 2016. "Electoral Handouts as Information: Explaining Unmonitored Vote Buying." *World Politics* 68 (3): 454–498.

Kramon, Eric. 2017. *Money for Votes: The Causes and Consequences of Electoral Clientelism in Africa.* Cambridge: Cambridge University Press.

Kreps, David M. 1990. "Corporate Culture and Economic Theory." *Perspectives on Positive Political Economy, ed. James Alt and Kenneth Shepsle,* 90 (90–142.) Cambridge University Press 1990.

Kuenzi, Michelle, and Gina Lambright. 2001. "Party System Institutionalization in 30 African Countries." *Party Politics* 7 (4): 437–468.

Kuznets, Simon. 1955. "Economic Growth and Income Inequality." *The American Economic Review* 45 (1): 1–28.

236 BIBLIOGRAPHY

Lankina, Tomila, and Rodion Skovoroda. 2017. "Regional Protest and Electoral Fraud: Evidence from Analysis of New Data on Russian Protest." *East European Politics* 33 (2): 253–274.

Larreguy, Horacio, John Marshall, and Pablo Querubin. 2016. "Parties, Brokers, and Voter Mobilization: How Turnout Buying Depends upon the Party's Capacity to Monitor Brokers." *American Political Science Review* 110 (1): 160–179.

Lawson, Chappell, and Kenneth F. Greene. 2014. "Making Clientelism Work: How Norms of Reciprocity Increase Voter Compliance." *Comparative Politics* 47 (1): 61–85.

Lehoucq, Fabrice. 2003. "Electoral Fraud: Causes, Types, and Consequences." *Annual Review of Political Science* 6 (1): 233–256.

Lemarchand, René. 1972. "Political Clientelism and Ethnicity in Tropical Africa: Competing Solidarities in Nation-Building." *American Political Science Review* 66 (1): 68–90.

Levitsky, Steven, James Loxton, Brandon Van Dyck, and Jorge I. Domínguez. 2016. *Challenges of Party-Building in Latin America.* Cambridge: Cambridge University Press.

Levitsky, Steven, and Lucan A. Way. 2010. *Competitive Authoritarianism: Hybrid Regimes after the Cold War.* Cambridge: Cambridge University Press.

Lijphart, Arend. 1997. "Unequal Participation: Democracy's Unresolved Dilemma," presidential address, American Political Science Association, 1996. *American Political Science Review* 91 (1): 1–14.

Linz, Juan José. 2000. *Totalitarian and Authoritarian Regimes.* Boulder, CO: Lynne Rienner Publishers.

Lukes, Steven. 2021. *Power: A Radical View.* London: Bloomsbury Publishing.

Magaloni, Beatriz. 2006. *Voting for Autocracy: Hegemonic Party Survival and Its Demise in Mexico.* Cambridge: Cambridge University Press.

Mainwaring, Scott. 1999. *Rethinking Party Systems in the Third Wave of Democratization: The Case of Brazil.* Palo Alto, CA: Stanford University Press.

Mainwaring, Scott, and Timothy Scully. 1995. *Building Democratic Institutions: Party Systems in Latin America.* Palo Alto, CA: Stanford University Press.

Mansbridge, Jane, James Bohman, Simone Chambers, David Estlund, Andreas Føllesdal, Archon Fung, Cristina Lafont, Bernard Manin, and José Luis Martí. 2010. "The Place of Self-Interest and the Role of Power in Deliberative Democracy." *Journal of Political Philosophy* 18 (1): 64–100.

Mares, Isabela. 2015. *From Open Secrets to Secret Voting: Democratic Electoral Reforms and Voter Autonomy.* Cambridge: Cambridge University Press.

Mares, Isabela, Aurelian Muntean, and Tsveta Petrova. 2016. "Economic Intimidation in Contemporary Elections: Evidence From Romania and Bulgaria." *Government and Opposition* 53 (3): 486–517.

Mares, Isabela, and Boliang Zhu. 2015. "The Production of Electoral Intimidation: Economic and Political Incentives." *Comparative Politics* 48 (1): 23–43.

Mares, Isabela, and Lauren Young. 2016. "Buying, Expropriating, and Stealing Votes." *Annual Review of Political Science* 19: 267–288.

BIBLIOGRAPHY 237

Mares, Isabela, and Lauren E. Young. 2019. *Conditionality and Coercion: Electoral Clientelism in Eastern Europe.* Oxford: Oxford University Press.

Marx, Karl, and Friedrich Engels. 1967. *The Communist Manifesto.* Trans. Samuel Moore. London: Penguin.

McMann, Kelly M. 2006. *Economic Autonomy and Democracy: Hybrid Regimes in Russia and Kyrgyzstan.* Cambridge: Cambridge University Press.

McPherson, Miller, Lynn Smith-Lovin, and Matthew E. Brashears. 2006. "Social Isolation in America: Changes in Core Discussion Networks over Two Decades." *American Sociological Review* 71 (3): 353–375.

Medina, Luis Fernando, and Susan Stokes. 2007. "Monopoly and Monitoring: An Approach to Political Clientelism." In *Patrons, Clients and Policies: Patterns of Democratic Accountability and Political Competition,* ed. Herbert Kitschelt and Steven I. Wilkinson. Cambridge: Cambridge University Press, pp. 68–83.

Mi, Zhou, and Xiaoming Wang. 2000. "Agency Cost and the Crisis of China's SOE." *China Economic Review* 11 (3): 297–317.

Moore, Barrington. 1993. *Social Origins of Dictatorship and Democracy: Lord and Peasant in the Making of the Modern World.* Boston: Beacon Press.

Mutz, Diana C., and Jeffery J. Mondak. 2006. "The Workplace as a Context for Cross-Cutting Political Discourse." *The Journal of Politics* 68 (1): 140–155.

Nichter, Simeon. 2008. "Vote Buying or Turnout Buying? Machine Politics and the Secret Ballot." *American Political Science Review* 102 (01): 19–31.

Nichter, Simeon, and Brian Palmer-Rubin. 2015. "Clientelism, Declared Support, and Mexico's 2012 Campaign." In *Mexico's Evolving Democracy: A Comparative Study of the 2012 Elections,* ed. Jorge Dominguez, Kenneth Greene, Chappell Lawson, and Alejandro Moreno. Baltimore, MD: Johns Hopkins University Press, pp. 220–26.

Novaes, Lucas M. 2018. "Disloyal Brokers and Weak Parties." *American Journal of Political Science* 62 (1): 84–98.

Oliveros, Virginia. 2016. "Making It Personal: Clientelism, Favors, and the Personalization of Public Administration in Argentina." *Comparative Politics* 48 (3): 373–391.

Oliveros, Virginia. 2021. *Patronage at work: Public jobs and political services in Argentina.* Cambridge: Cambridge University Press.

Pfeifer, Christian. 2011. "Risk Aversion and Sorting into Public Sector Employment." *German Economic Review* 12 (1): 85–99.

Pisano, Jessica. 2022. *Staging Democracy: Political Performance in Ukraine, Russia, and Beyond.* Ithaca NY : Cornell University Press.

Poltoratskaya, Viktoriia. 2024. "The Big Brothers: Measuring Influence of Large Firms on Electoral Mobilization in Russia." forthcoming *Post-Soviet Affairs.*

Przeworski, Adam. 1991. *Democracy and the Market: Political and Economic Reforms in Eastern Europe and Latin America.* Cambridge: Cambridge University Press.

Pyle, William. 2006. "Collective Action and Post-communist Enterprise: The Economic Logic of Russia's Business Associations." *Europe-Asia Studies* 58 (4): 491–521.

Pyle, William, and Laura Solanko. 2013. "The composition and interests of Russia's business lobbies: Testing Olson's hypothesis of the "encompassing organization." *Public Choice* 155: 19–41.

238 BIBLIOGRAPHY

Ravanilla, Nico, Dotan Haim, and Allen Hicken. 2022. "Brokers, Social Networks, Reciprocity, and Clientelism." *American Journal of Political Science* 66 (4): 795–812.

Remington, Thomas F. 1984. *Building Socialism in Bolshevik Russia: Ideology and Industrial Organization, 1917–1921.* Pittsburgh: University of Pittsburgh Press.

Remington, Thomas F., and Israel Marques. "Partnerships for skill development in Russia." Post-Communist Economies 32, no. 1 (2020): 1–23.

US Senate, Report. 1880. "Alleged Frauds of the Late Election." *46th Congress* (46th Congress).

Reuter, Ora John. 2017. *The Origins of Dominant Parties.* Cambridge: Cambridge University Press.

Reuter, Ora John, and David Szakonyi. 2015. "Online Social Media and Political Awareness in Authoritarian Regimes." *British Journal of Political Science* 45 (1): 29–51.

Reuter, Ora John, and David Szakonyi. 2021. "Electoral Manipulation and Regime Support: Survey Evidence from Russia." *World Politics* 73 (2): 275–314.

Robinson, James A., and Ragnar Torvik. 2009. "The Real Swing Voter's Curse." *The American Economic Review* 99 (2): 310–315.

Rosenfeld, Bryn. 2020. *The autocratic middle class: how state dependency reduces the demand for democracy.* Princeton NJ: Princeton University Press.

Rosenfeld, Bryn. 2023. "Survey Research in Russia: In the Shadow of War." *Post-Soviet Affairs* 39 (1–2): 38–48.

Rosenstone, Steven J. and John Mark Hansen. 1993. *Mobilization, Participation, and Democracy in America.* New York: Longman Publishing Group.

Rosenzweig, Steven C. 2021. "Dangerous Disconnect: Voter Backlash, Elite Misperception, and the Costs of Violence as an Electoral Tactic." *Political Behavior* 43 (4): 1731–1754.

Rueda, Miguel R. 2017. "Small Aggregates, Big Manipulation: Vote Buying Enforcement and Collective Monitoring." *American Journal of Political Science* 61 (1): 163–177.

Rundlett, Ashlea, and Milan W. Svolik. 2016. "Deliver the vote! Micromotives and Macrobehavior in Electoral Fraud." *American Political Science Review* 110 (1): 180–197.

Saikkonen, Inga AL. 2017. "Electoral Mobilization and Authoritarian Elections: Evidence from Post-Soviet Russia." *Government and Opposition* 52 (1): 51–74.

Scarrow, Susan E. 2000. "Parties without Members? Party Organization in a Changing Electoral Environment." In *Parties without Partisans: Political Change in Advanced Industrial Democracies*, ed. Russell J. Dalton and Martin P. Wattenberg. Oxford: Oxford University Press, pp. 79–101.

Schaffer, Frederic Charles. 2007. *Elections for Sale: The Causes and Consequences of Vote Buying.* Boulder CO: Lynne Rienner Publishers.

Schuler, Paul. 2021. *United Front: Projecting Solidarity through Deliberation in Vietnam's Single-Party Legislature.* Palo Alto CA: Stanford University Press.

Schulze, Günther G. Bambang Suharnoko Sjahrir, and Nikita Zakharov. 2016. "Corruption in Russia." *The Journal of Law and Economics* 59 (1): 135–171.

Scott, James C. 1972. "Patron-Client Politics and Political Change in Southeast Asia." *American Political Science Review* 66 (1): 91–113.

BIBLIOGRAPHY 239

Secunda, Paul M. 2010. "Addressing Political Captive Audience Workplace Meetings in the Post-Citizens United Environment." *Yale Law Journal Online* 120 https://www.yalelawjournal.org/forum/addressing-political-captive-audience-workplace-meetings-in-the-post-citizens-united-environment.

Semenov, Andrei. 2020. "Electoral Performance and Mobilization of Opposition Parties in Russia." *Russian Politics* 5 (2): 236–254.

Shen, Xiaoxiao, and Rory Truex. 2021. "In Search of Self-censorship." *British Journal of Political Science* 51 (4): 1672–1684.

Shleifer, Andrei, and Robert W. Vishny. 1994. "Politicians and Firms." *The Quarterly Journal of Economics* 109 (4): 995–1025.

Sidel, John Thayer. 1999. *Capital, Coercion, and Crime: Bossism in the Philippines.* Palo Alto CA: Stanford University Press.

Simpser, Alberto. 2013. *Why Governments and Parties Manipulate Elections: Theory, Practice, and Implications.* Cambridge: Cambridge University Press.

Slater, Dan. 2010. *Ordering Power: Contentious Politics and Authoritarian Leviathans in Southeast Asia.* Cambridge: Cambridge University Press.

Smith, Jason Scott. 2006. *Building New Deal Liberalism: The Political Economy of Public works, 1933–1956.* Cambridge: Cambridge University Press.

Smyth, Regina. 2006. *Candidate Strategies and Electoral Competition in the Russian Federation: Democracy without Foundation.* Cambridge: Cambridge University Press.

Stokes, Susan C. 2005. "Perverse Accountability: A Formal Model of Machine Politics with Evidence from Argentina." *American Political Science Review* 99 (03): 315–325.

Stokes, Susan C. 2011. "Political Clientelism." In *The Oxford Handbook of Political Science*, ed. Robert E. Goodin. Oxford: Oxford University Press, pp. 648–672.

Stokes, Susan, Thad Dunning, and Marcelo Nazareno. 2013. *Brokers, Voters, and Clientelism: The Puzzle of Distributive Politics.* Cambridge: Cambridge University Press.

Szakonyi, David. 2020. *Politics for Profit: Business, Elections, and Policymaking in Russia.* Cambridge: Cambridge University Press.

Szakonyi, David. 2021. "Private Sector Policy Making: Business Background and Politicians' Behavior in Office." *The Journal of Politics* 83 (1): 260–276.

Szakonyi, David. 2022. "Candidate Filtering: The Strategic Use of Electoral Manipulations in Russia." *British Journal of Political Science* 52 (2): 649–670.

Szarzec, Katarzyna, Bartosz Totleben, and Dawid Piątek. 2022. "How do Politicians Capture a State? Evidence from State-Owned Enterprises." *East European Politics and Societies* 36 (1): 141–172.

Usmanova, Svetlana. 2008. "Influence of Pre-election Campaigning on Voter Choice." *Monitoring of Public Opinion: Economic and Social Changes* 1 (85): 37–47.

Van de Walle, Nicolas. 2007. "Meet The New Boss, Same as the Old Boss? The Evolution of Political Clientelism in Africa." In *Patrons, Clients and Policies: Patterns of Democratic Accountability and Political Competition*, ed. Herbert Kitschelt, and Steven I. Wilkinson. Cambridge: Cambridge University Press pp. 50–67.

BIBLIOGRAPHY

Vicente, Pedro C. 2014. "Is Vote Buying Effective? Evidence from a Field Experiment in West Africa." *The Economic Journal* 124 (574). 356–387.

Wang, Zhengxu, and Long Sun. 2017. "Social Class and Voter Turnout in China: Local Congress Elections and Citizen-Regime Relations." *Political Research Quarterly* 70 (2): 243–256.

Weitz-Shapiro, Rebecca. 2014. *Curbing Clientelism in Argentina: Politics, Poverty, and Social Policy.* Cambridge: Cambridge University Press.

Wells, Brett. 2020. Politics in the Workplace. Technical report Perceptyx https://blog. perceptyx.com/politics-in-the-workplace-new-report-from-perceptyx-finds-politics-has-lasting-impact-on-workplaces-company-support-for-voting-significant-to-voter-turnout.

Whiteley, Paul F. 2011. "Is the Party Over? The Decline of Party Activism and Membership across the Democratic World." *Party Politics* 17 (1): 21–44.

Williamson, Oliver E. 1983. "Credible Commitments: Using Hostages to Support Exchange." *The American Economic Review* 73 (4): 519–540.

Wright, Joseph. 2008. "Do Authoritarian Institutions Constrain? How Legislatures Affect Economic Growth and Investment." *American Journal of Political Science* 52 (2): 322–343.

Yakovlev, Andrei, and Andrei Govorun. 2011. "Business Associations as a Business-Government Liaison: An Empirical Analysis." *Journal of the New Economic Association* (9): 98–127.

Ziblatt, Daniel. 2009. "Shaping Democratic Practice and the Causes of Electoral Fraud: The Case of Nineteenth-Century Germany." *American Political Science Review* 103 (1): 1–21.

Index

Page references in *italics* indicate a figure; page references in **bold** indicate a table.

absentee ballots, 43, 48–52, 64, 68n33
Acemoglu, Daron, 16, 142, 144, 223
AKP (Justice and Development Party, Turkey), 41, 75, 215
"Alleged Fraud in the Late Election" (US Senate report), 199
Allina-Pisano, Jessica, 23
Amuragrocenter (soybean processing plant), 1–2, 171
Amur.Info website, 1
Anderson, Elizabeth, 7, 197n
Anderson, Jennifer, 171
Ankara Municipality Water and Sewage (ASKI), 165
Argentina: non-employed population, 38–39
perceptions of workplace mobilization in, *74*
prevalence of various brokers in, **38**
protests in, 158
public opinion survey, 28, 29, 33, **34**, 35
vote buying, 173
workplace mobilization in, 2, 7, 10, 23, 37, 73, *164*
asset specificity, 135, 142, 144, 216, 223, 225
authoritarian regimes: mass-based parties, 6
political apathy, 6, 204
self-censorship, 77
voter turnout, 16

Baland, Jean-Marie, 23
bias: definition of, 213
incumbent, 214–16
vs. partisanship, 213
structural, 216
Blomberg, Jeffrey, 204
Boix, Carles, 16, 144, 223
Brazil: presidential elections of 2022, 171
voting rights in, 226
brokered mobilization, 10, 53, 89
brokers: cross-national comparison of effectiveness of, 93–94, *94*
differences in means between, *95*

impact on voter compliance, 81
leverage over clients, 81–82
in local communities, 5
norms of reciprocity, 66, 68
politicians and, 6
relative effectiveness of, 10, 11, 93, 97, 98
selection of, 79
socially embedded, 83
studies of, 221
tactics of, 4–5, 8
types of, 5, 7, 81, 86, **88**, 92n17
use of clientelism, 80
use of inducements, 80
voter mobilization, 80, 96, 222
business associations, 132–33, 137
Business Industry Political Action Committee (BIPAC), 24

"captive audience" meetings, 41
Carey, John, 207
Chelyabinsk, Russia, 31
Chile: introduction of secret ballot, 23
workplace mobilization in, 7
China: mass party organization in, 6n3
Citizens United decision, 198, 201, 202, 203, 209
clientelism: brokers and, 11, 81
definitions of, 21n2, 81
effectiveness of, 82
forms of, 173
hierarchies, 4, 81
inducements, 18–19
monitoring of, 82–83
practices of, 8, 14
root of, 17
studies of, 10, 18, 19, 173, 222
theories of, 80
turnout-based, 82
workplace mobilization as, 2, 18, 20
Clinton, Hillary, 44
coercion: compulsory voting and, 207

242   INDEX

coercion (*Continued*)
  cost of, 206, 207
  definition of, 206n24
  in labor practices, 81
  legal efforts to limit, 219
  mild forms of, 206
  power imbalances and, 197
  against welfare recipients, 128n2
collective threats, 92
Communist systems: voter turnout, 22
  workplace mobilization in, 22
compulsory voting, 207
construction firms: mobilization of, 135n7
coworkers, 83, 205
Cox, Gary W., 132

Darden, Keith, 23
democracy: economic relations, 16, 223
  freedom to vote, 15
  labor repression, 223
  party systems, 6
  political mobilization in, 180, 197, 224
  as system of "institutionalized uncertainty,"
    213
  voter turnout, 205
Douglass Axe Company, 199
Dunning, Thad, 208

economic liberalization, 223
election day: practice of making it working day,
  43–44
elections: under autocracy, 223
  manipulation of, 15, 64, 109, 176, 222
electoral clientelism. *See* clientelism
electoral subversion: factors facilitating, 16
  institutional context of, 173
  reassessment of, 226
  studies of, 4, 73n40, 76, 222–23
  types of, 15, 174
  workplace-based, 144, 153
employees: as "captive audience" for
  politicians, 40
  compliance with turnout mobilization,
    36–37
  contract renewals, 68
  difficulty in replacement of, 149–50
  dismissal of, 59, 184–85
  employers' leverage over, 81, 83–84, 99, 139,
    149, 150, 151, 197, 202, 221
  fears of job loss, 148–49, 155, 156
  government authorities and, 107–8, 109–10
  inducements of, 47, 49–50, 52, 111

  intimidation of, 59–63
  legal protection to, 203, 220
  managers and, 126
  partisan appeals to, 212
  perception of workplace mobilization, 75,
    105, 106, 147
  political discussions at work, 210n33,
    212n39
  political pressure on, 148, 149
  punishment for non-compliance, 69–70,
    127, 181n12
  reduction in wages or benefits, 59–61, 148
  restrictions on political donations from, 200
  rewards, 103–4
  salaries of, 148
  with second job, 156
  in state-dependent sectors, 16
  state pressure on, 113
  surveys of, 30, 104, **110**, 134, 181
  threatening tactics against, 108, 130
  vulnerability of, 149, 151, 158
employer-based mobilization: costs of, **104**,
    136, 146
  direct appeals in, 43
  effectiveness of, 79
  firm-level variation, 134–35
  forms of, 151
  gains from, 172
  limitations of, 38
  negative effect of, 71
  vs. party mobilization, 7–9
  tactics and tools, 84n3, 125, 221
  by type of employer, **162**
employer-employee relationships, 13, 22, 63,
    82, 93, 166, 211, 213
employers: clientelist exchange, 17, 82, *94*, 96
  coercive appeals, 206
  dependence on state, 12
  distribution of absentee ballots to
    employees, 43, 48–52
  ideological preferences, 11n11
  leverage over employees, 8–9, 81, 83–84, 99,
    139, 150, 151, 197, 202, 221–22
  monitoring schemes, 64
  vs. political parties, 8–9, **10**
  primary objective of, 9
  relations between managers and, 143
  relations between politicians and, 5, 11–12,
    13–14, 41, 102, 143, 221
  restrictions on interactions with employees
    in elections, 200n5

INDEX

rights to discuss politics with workers, 199, 201–2, 203
scholarly studies of, 222
scope of, 9
surveys of, 134–35, 138, **139, 140**
use of inducements, 21, 23, 49, 63, 208
as vote brokers, 7, 127, 172–73
Europe: workplace mobilization in, 7
European Court of Human Rights, 198

Federal Election Commission, 203
First Amendment, 201
focus groups, 30–31, 85
Forrat, Natalia, 158
freedom of speech, 199–200
Free. Navalny website, 184
Frye, Timothy, 77, 18, 70, 77, 134, 223

Gans-Morse, Jordan, 8, 36n, 84
Garfield, James A.: assassination of, 217
Gaventa, John, 7, 23, 151, 206n
Georgia Pacific, 106
Gerber, Alan S., 209
Germany: workplace mobilization in, 7
get-out-the-vote (GOTV) campaigns, 2, 14, 20, 209, 211–12
Ghana: doubts in secret ballots, 69
gifts, preelectoral, 98
Gimpelson, Vladimir, 159
Glasnost Defense Foundation (GDF), 187
Golos (election monitoring group), 31
Gonzalez-Ocantos, Ezequiel, 173
government officials: coercive methods of, 23, 81
effectiveness of, 92, *94*, 96, 98
political activities of, 8, 217–18
pressure on employers, 106, 107, 108, 129, 137, 179
governor campaigning framing experiment, 177, 177–78
grassroots party organizations, 6, 17, 37, 83
Guatemala: punishment of candidates in, 173
Guriev, Sergei, 6, 130
Gutiérrez-Romero, Roxana, 173

Hatch Act of 1939, 217
health care employees: vulnerability of, 161
Hertel-Fernandez, Alexander, 7, 10–12, 23, 25, 75n41, 75n43, 86, 127, 181, 215
Hicken, Allen, 69, 83
Hillary: The Movie (film), 201
Hong Kong: Beijing relations with, 145

corporate enterprises, 145
internal security measures, 145
Legislative Council elections, 145, 146
workplace mobilization in, 145–46
Horiuchi, Yusaku, 207
Hungary: workplace mobilization in, 7

Imperial Germany: workplace mobilization in, 22
incumbents: access to state resources, 214, 216
India: get-out-the-vote campaigns, 209
workplace mobilization, 106, 211
individual threats, 92, 97
Indonesia: public opinion survey, 28, **30, 34**
unions in, 219
workplace mobilization in, 2, 10, 164
inducements: cost of, 128
differences in means between, *95*
measurement of, 96
negative and positive, 8–9, **10**, 18, 21, 98
provision of, 102
relative effectiveness of, 93
type of broker and, 18–19
informal sector, 224–25
information transmission, 128n2
institution-building, 17
intermediaries. *See* brokers

Jefferson, Thomas, 198n3
job insecurity, 155–56

Kabanov, Yuri A.: letter of, 101, 123–24
karusels (ballot-stuffing or multiple-voting scheme), 43, 68n33
Kennedy, Anthony, Justice, 201
KN (Karta Narusheniy) dataset, 31, 53, 57, 63, 102
Koch Industries, 106, 180n10
Kommersant (newspaper), 185
Komsomolskaya Pravda (newspaper), 171
Kramon, Eric, 128n2
Kyrgyzstan: economic coercion in, 23

labor market conditions: workplace mobilization and, 147–48, 150, **157, 168**
labor repression, 16
landlords: leverage over tenants, 22, 81
LeBas, Adrienne, 173
Levada Center, 27, 28, 186
leverage: measurement of, 126
sources of, 130
types of, 146

244   INDEX

Lijphart, Arend, 207
Linz, Juan José, 6

Malaysia: mass party organization in, 6n3
managers: ability to overcome obstacles, 131
  agreements between workers and, 126
  benefits from the state, 128
  elected officials and, 129
  knowledge of firm operations, 133–34
  leverage over employees, 41, 126, 130, 143
  members of business organizations, 132
  partisan ties of, 142
  as political candidates, 40–41
  relations between employers and, 143
  relations between politicians and, 141, 143
  relative autonomy of, 158
  reluctance to mobilize workers, 127
  surveys of, 133, 134
  use of inducements, 131
Mansbridge, Jane, 208n28
Mares, Isabela, 22, 23, 127, 128n2
McMann, Kelly M., 23
media freedom: coercive mobilization and, 189
  decline of, 186
  index of, 187
  map of, 196
  measurement of, 187, 188–89
  party-based mobilization and, 189, 192, 192
  regional variances, 187
  regression analysis, 193
  subjective judgments about, 187
  survey of, 188–89, 193
  workplace mobilization and, 174–75,
    184–93, 190–91, 222
Merkushkin, Nikolai, 109
"Methodological Recommendations (For the
  Mobilization of Work Collectives, Family
  Members, and Veterans), 179, 195
Miass, Russia, 31
Mondak, Jeffrey J., 210n33
monitoring of voter compliance: challenges of,
    63–64
  employee perception of, 68–69
  schemes of, 64, 69
  in small communities, 131
  in social networks, 64
monogoroda. See single-company towns
Montenegro: workplace mobilization, 53
Moscow Metro employees: firing of, 184–85
MosGaz (Moscow's municipal gas provider), 43
Muntean, Aurelian, 23
Murray Corporation, 203

Mutz, Diana C., 210n33

Nathan, Noah L., 69
National Labor Relations Board, 199, 200
Navalny, Alexey, 26
Nazareno, Marcelo, 208
negative inducements, 47, 49, 52, 53, 92–93,
    208n28
negative partisanship, 175n6
neighborhood leaders: effectiveness of, 94
  voter mobilization by, 99
Nichter, Simeon, 132
Nigeria: incumbent party, 214–15
  perceptions of workplace mobilization in, 74
  public opinion survey, 28, 30, 33, 34
  state sector mobilization, 164
  unions in, 219
  voter turnout, 86, 87
  voting rights in, 226
  workplace mobilization in, 2, 10, 41, 73, 86,
    87
nonemployed individuals, 151
nonwage benefits, 136–37, 138–39

Obama, Barack, 106
Oliveros, Virginia, 23, 158, 161
organizational threats, 97, 98
Orlovskaya, Svetlana, 107

Panama: ruling party, 53
Partido Socialista Unido de Venezuela (PSUV),
    92
partisanship in vote mobilization, 132, 178–79,
    212
party activists: appeal to voters, 8
  clientelism, 99
  effectiveness of, 94, 96
  electoral subversion by, 73n40
  leverage over clients, 82, 98
  scope of, 9
  tactics of, 8
  use of inducements, 53, 81–82
  voter mobilization by, 71, 221
patronage (turnout buying), 98
Pendleton Act of 1883, 217
Peskov, Dmitry, 185
Petrov, Nikolai, 187
Petrova, Tsveta, 23
Philippines: doubts in secret ballots, 69
Pisano, Jessica, 23
political councils (politsovety), 142

INDEX

political discrimination in the workplace, 198, 203
political mobilization in the workplace. *See* workplace mobilization
political parties: as agents of mass mobilization, 5–6
vs. employers, 8–9, **10**
as voter brokers, 5, 7–8
political solicitations, 200–201
politicians: ability to overcome obstacles, 131
cost of mobilization for, 129–30
electoral backlash against, 173–74, 178, 193, 194
incentive for workplace mobilization, 127
leverage over managers, 125, 126, 127, 128, 129, 131–32, 158
relations between employers and, 11–12, 13–14, 102, 129, 133, 143, 197
tracking of turnout, 130–31
use of inducements, 128, 131
use of intermediaries, 4–5, 6
voting mobilization, 3, 4, 194
Poltoratskaya, Viktoriia, 75
positive inducements, 92, 208n28
privacy rights of employees, 199–200
procurement system: access to, 115, 122
data collection on, 115–16
seasonality of, 116
total volume of, 114
types of, 114, 115, 116, 118
protest votes, 75
Przeworski, Adam, 213, 223
public opinion surveys, 28–30
public school teachers: electoral work of, 158
public sector workers: benefits, 159, 161
mobilization of, 161–62
political patronage of, 161
protections of, 160
Putin, Vladimir, 19, 26, 77, 134

RBK (media group), 185
reciprocity: norms of, 66, 68
Redfearn versus the United Kingdom, 198
report to management after vote: practice of, 64–65, 66, 67, 68, **69**, 70
Reuter, 6, 7, 18, 21, 70, 173, 178, 187, 236
RIA Novosti (Russian state-run media), 185
right not to participate in elections, 204
right to abstain from politics, 204
Robinson, James A., 16, 23, 144, 223
Romania: workplace mobilization in, 7
Romney, Mitt, 40, 180, 203

Roosevelt, Franklin Delano, 218
Rosenzweig, Steven, 173
Russia: brokered electoral violations in, 53, 54–55
"captive audience" meetings, 41–43
clientelism in, 2, 17, 18, 20, 93, *94*
coercion in, 23
collective appeal to voters, 130
comparison to Venezuela, 89–90
depoliticization of the public sphere, 85n4
directives to firm managers, 158, 159–60
economic development, 13, 90
elections, 26, 31, 35, 39, 43, **54**
employment statistics, 99
focus groups, 30–31
framing experiment, 89, 183
incumbent party in, 214–15
job insecurity, 13
level of democracy, 188
local government officials, 92
media freedom, 186, 187–88, 187n22
negative inducements, use of, 53
party activists, 92, 96
predicted probabilities by broker treatment, *97*
press monitoring project, 187
pressure on employees, 185
procurement system, 114
public opinion polls, 14, 27–28, **28**, **34**, 186
secret ballots, doubts in, 69
self-censorship, 77
social norms against employers involved in politics, 105
state-employer relations, 109–10
state-run media, 185
survey of employers in, 25–27, **27**, **35**, 36
surveys of voters, 27–28, 90, **91**, 185, 186–87
unions in, 219
vote brokers in, 86, **88**, 91
vote buying, 57, 178
voter intimidation practice, 56–57, **58**, 59, 153
voter turnout, 10–11, 85n4
Russian Agency for Strategic Initiatives, 26
Russian Election Study, 28
Russian firms: access to procurement, 122
in business associations, 132–33
customer base, 129
data collection on, 113–15
dependence on the state, 114, 135
federal procurement, 114, 116, *117*
linear probability models of analysis, 137–38

246 INDEX

Russian firms (*Continued*)
  location-specific assets, 129
  municipal procurement, 114, 116, *117*
  political activities of, 113–14
  politicians' leverage over, 114, 129
  regional procurement, 114, 116, *117*
  survey of, 141n12–13
Russia's workplace mobilization: at the behest
    of politicians, 102
  coercive forms of, 14, 19–20, 193
  employers' directives on, 106–7
  in large firms, 1–2
  perceptions of, 1, 12, 73, *74*, 105, 218
  public procurement and, 113–22
  share of employed voters, 37
  techniques, 92
  voter turnout and, 10, 86, **87**, 89
Ryazan Electrical Instrument Factory, 171

Sanders, Bernie, 44
Sarapkin, Alexander, 1
Satka, Russia, 31, 63
secret ballot: doubts in, 69, 84
  introduction of, 23, 199, 209
  monitoring of voter turnout, 36, 64
  public perception of, 209
  purpose of, 208
  violations of, 209
Secunda, Paul, 40
self-censorship, 77
separate segregated funds (SSFs), 201n7
service sector firms, 138
Shell petrochemicals, 202
Shleifer, Andrei, 18
Siegal, David, 106, 180
Silicon Valley companies, 202
"Simple Ask" treatment, 93, *94*, 95, 96
single-company towns: active monitoring in,
    70–71
  cross-country comparison, 150
  definition of, 150
  economic opportunities in, 149
  inducements in, **154**
  job insecurity in, 13
  survey of, 150
  voter intimidation in, 153–54
  workplace mobilization in, 28, **152**, 152–53,
    167
Sivinskii Municipal Rayon in Permskii Krai,
    101
Skaggs, Adam, 212

slack labor markets: workplace mobilization
    and, 140, 146, 148
Smolevo, Valerii, 108
standard principal-agent logic, 128
State Duma elections, 38
state-owned enterprises (SOEs): level of
    procurement, 122
  leverage over managers of, 128–29
  mobilization in, 162
  survey of, 115
state sector mobilization, 146, 159, 218
  cross-country comparison, *164*, 164–65, *166*
  variations in, 162, **163**, **169**
Stokes, Susan, 5, 8, 10, 11, 19, 64, 79, 83, 127,
    173, 208, 222
Svolik, Milan, 173, 175, 222
subbotniks, 71
Szakonyi, David, 7, 18, 40, 70, 114, 116, 173,
    179, 187

TASS (Russian state-run media), 185
Time to Vote campaign, 211
Titkov, Alexei, 187
Treisman, Daniel, 6, 130
Trump, Donald, 202
Turkey: incumbent party in, 2, 215
  parliamentary elections in 2015, 165
  prevalence of various brokers in, **38**
  public opinion survey, 28, **30**, 33, **34**, 35
  vote buying, 57
  voter intimidation, 56–57, **58**
Turkey's workplace mobilization: by civic
    association leaders, 39
  discomfort of, 72, *73*
  by employers, 38
  perceptions of, 73, *74*
  by political party, 41–42
  by religious leaders, 38, 39
  share of employed voters, 37
  in state sector, 164, 165
  study of, 10
  voter turnout and, 86, **87**
turnout propensity, 93, 96

Ukraine: public opinion survey, 28, **30**, **34**, 35
  state sector mobilization, 164
  unions in, 219
  voter turnout, 86, **87**
  workplace mobilization, 2, 7, 10, 23, 86, **87**
United Russia (UR) party: absence of ideology,
    142
  electoral results, 26

INDEX   247

employers' endorsement of, 41, 44–47, 141
hierarchical nature of, 142
level of support for, 178–79
membership in, 141
regional leaders, 132
use of workplace mobilization, 1, 19–20, 132, 214
United Socialist Party of Venezuela (PSUV), 42
United States: coercion and bribery in, 180, 199
employer intimidation, 23
framing experiment, 181, **182**, 183, **184**
get-out-the-vote campaigns, 209, 211
ideological preferences of employers, 11n11
introduction of secret ballot, 199
job insecurity in, 219
partisan appeals to voters, 212
practice of making election day a working day, 44
public opinion surveys, 14, 28, 29
punishment of candidates in, 183
rule of law in, 219
secret ballot, 69, 209
survey of workers in, 181–82
unions in, 219
violations of democratic norms, 173, 209
voter turnout, 211
voting rights in, 226
United States' workplace mobilization:
bipartisan nature of, 215
democratic implications of, 14–15
fear of a popular backlash, 171–72
forms of, 23–24, 40, 199, 209–10
GOTV campaigns, 211
opposition to, 75, 75n43
practice of, 7
in private sector, 218
in state sector, 165
study of, 2, 75n41
voluntary, 106
US Supreme Court: *Citizens United* decision, 198, 201, 202, 203, 209
on voter autonomy, 204
Uzbekistan: public opinion survey, 29

Venezuela: 1X10 Campaign, 43
2015 parliamentary elections, 42–43
Bolivarian Movement, 92
brokers in, 38, 86, **88**, 91, *94*, *97*
clientelism in, 93
coercive forms of mobilization in, 193
comparison to Russia, 89–90
economic structure, 90

elimination of compulsory voting in, 207
employee survey, 28, 29, **30**, 33, **34**, 90, **91**, 130
employment statistics, 99
grassroots organizations, 89
mass party organization in, 6n3
party activists, 92, 96–97
state sector mobilization, 164
use of inducements, 52
voter intimidation, 56–57, **58**
voter turnout, 10–11, 86, **87**, 89
workplace mobilization, 2, 10, 37–38, 42–43, 74, 86, **87**, 89, 99
vote brokers. *See* brokers
vote buying: decline of, 222
effectiveness of, 80
as electoral tactics, 5, 8–9
forms of, 49
party-based, 178
punishment for, 178
in Russian elections, 19, **55**, 56, 57
in single-company towns, 153
studies of, 173
vote choice monitoring, 66, 84
voter mobilization, 4, 99, 130, 132
voters: autonomy of, 15, 174, 204, 208, 218
charisma of candidates and, 175
clientelism and, 173
coercive tactics against, 47, 49, 82, 173
compliance of, 63–64, 85
individualized and collective appeals to, 130
inducements of, 92
intimidation of, 14, 53, **54**, 56–57, 59–62, 153
partisan preferences, 175
power dynamics between employers and, 9
punishment of politicians by, 173–74, 177–78, 193–94
response to workplace mobilization, 9, 16, 171–72, 174, **176**
social networks of, 83
transportation to the polls, 130
voter turnout: in democracy, 205
means to increasing, 207
measurement of, 93, 96
monitoring of, 82–83, 84, 130–31
pressure for, 36
self-reported, 91
workplace mobilization and, 10–11, 84
voting rights, 226–27
VTSIOM polling organization, 26

Weitz-Shapiro, Rebecca, 14

248 INDEX

Wolitzky, Alexander, 142
workers. *See* employees
workplace: discussion networks on, 83
political activity in, 2
workplace mobilization: abuse of state
resources, 217
backlash against, 171–72, 179, *195*
at the behest of politicians, 102
benefits of, 125
benign forms of, 174
bias generated by, 213–16, 218
characteristics of, 32–33
as clientelist exchange, 18, 79
coercive forms of, 14, 20, 39, 45–46, 47, 57,
78, 193, 206–7, 210
commitment problems, 126
in comparative perspective, 22–24, 32–37
vs. compulsory voting, 207
conditional and unconditional forms of,
46–47, 208
context specific, 37–39, 47, 224
costs of, 3, 11, 12, 13, 100, 102, 103, 113, 122,
125, 133, 137, 141, 144, 178
cover-up of, 171
cross-national statistics, 37
data collection and validity, 25–26, 29,
31–32, 76–77, **78**
definition of, 21
democracy and, 197, 213
difference-in-differences model of effect of,
115, 118
by different types of brokers, 37
directives on, 106–7
economic development and, 17, 143–44
effectiveness of, 2–3, 10, 11, 85, 99, 185
electoral implications of, 15, 174–79
employers' directives on, 106–7
enforcement problem, 63–64
at firm that sell to the state, 138
framing experiment, 111–13, **112**
heavy-handed tactics in, 108–9
hypotheses about, 129, 131, 132, 133, 135,
138
incentive problems, 126–27
in industrializing and information
economies, 225
in informal sector, 133, 224–25
institutional efforts to reduce, 217
labor market conditions and, 136, 140,
147–48, 150, 156, **157**, 219
in larger firms, 102, 107, 131, 141, 143
leverage as determinant of, 13, 131

means and methods of, 39–47, 224
media freedom and, 172, 174–75, *192*,
192–93, 218–19
membership in business organizations and,
137
methods of study of, 24–25, 64n30, 142–43
moral implications, 3, 13–14
in nineteenth-century America, 199
noncoercive forms of, 20, 21, 209–10
normative implications of, 14–15, 29, 197
opposition to, 2–3, 75
vs. other mobilizational strategies, 76
partisanship and, 132, 178–79, 181, 183,
183n13, 215
perceptions of, 9, 71, 72, 73, *74*, 175
political implications of, 17–18
political regime and, 16, 26, 153, 223, 224
power relations and, 3–4, 125, 131–32, 146,
197
practice of, 1–2, 7–8
predictors of, 135–37
preparatory work for, 102–3
press reports on, 133, 184–93
in private sector, 218
procurement outcomes and, 113–17, 118–22
public opposition to, 14, 218, 221, 222
regional variations of, 194
risks of, 3, 9
root of, 3
scholarship on, 21, 24, 84–89, 102, 127–28,
133–34
by sector, 135, *136*
in single-company towns, **152**, **167**
in smaller towns and rural areas, 152–53
in state sector, 147, 158, 161–65, **163**
surveys of, 32–33, 34, 76–78
targets of, 136
technological developments and, 225
theoretical framework, 12, 80, 127–33, 204
as transaction, 106–10
unions and, 219
variations in, 2, 12–13
voter autonomy and, 213
voter turnout and, 10–11, 84–85, 86, 87, 89
Works Progress Administration (WPA), 218

YouGov survey, 181
Young, Lauren E., 23, 128n2

Zhu, Boliang, 127
Ziblatt, Daniel, 22
Zlatoust (single-company town), 148